AWESOME
SUPER NINTENDO™
SECRETS 3

J. Douglas Arnold & Zach Meston

Awesome Super Nintendo Secrets 3 is published by Sandwich Islands Publishing, an independent publishing company. This book is not published, authorized by, or associated in any way with Nintendo of America Inc. This book is not related and should not be confused with any publication that is printed or distributed by Nintendo of America Inc. NINTENDO® is a registered trademark of Nintendo of America Inc.

The following are trademarks owned by Nintendo of America Inc.: Super Mario All Stars™, Super Nintendo Entertainment System®, and Super NES®.

Gaming Mastery Series Editors: J. Douglas Arnold & Zach Meston
Publisher: Sandwich Islands Publishing

ORIGINAL COVER ILLUSTRATION BY RICHARD FIELDS.

All products mentioned in this book are trademarks of their respective companies.

Library of Congress Cataloging-in-Publication Data

Arnold, J. Douglas, 1966-
    Awesome Super Nintendo secrets 3 / J. Douglas
Arnold, Zach Meston.
       p. cm. -- (Gaming mastery series ; 3)
       Includes index.
       ISBN 0-9624676-8-5

       1. Nintendo video games. I. Meston, Zach. II. Title.
III. Title: Awesome Super Nintendo secrets three. IV. Series

GV1469.3.D68 1994   794.8'15365
                            QBI93-21915

93 94 95 — 10 9 8 7 6 5 4 3 2 1

HOW TO ORDER:

Quantity discounts are available from the publisher, Sandwich Islands Publishing, P.O. Box 10669, Lahaina, HI 96761; telephone (808) 661-5844. On your letterhead, include information concerning the intended use of the books and the number of books you wish to purchase.

    U.S. Bookstores and Libraries: Please submit all orders to Sandwich Islands Publishing.

    Printed in the United States of America.

AWESOME SUPER NINTENDO™ SECRETS 3

J. Douglas Arnold & Zach Meston

SANDWICH ISLANDS PUBLISHING CO., LTD

P.O. BOX 10669, LAHAINA, HI 96761

ACKNOWLEDGEMENTS

From both of us:

Thanks to the gaming experts that helped master the strategies and find the secrets that fill the pages of this book: **Brock Balinbin**, **Manny Ravida**, **Paul Schones**, **Scott Schones**, **Paz Derham**, **Tony Dickison**, and **Adam Tornatore**.

Thanks to Richard Fields for the awesome covers!

Thanks to all the people who helped us make this book current and complete, including: Phylene Riggs (Acclaim), Grady Hunt (Atlus), Sheila Boughten (Bullet-Proof Software), Laurie Thornton and Erin Shiba (Capcom), Dany Brooks (Electronic Arts), Brian Colin (Game Refuge, Inc.), Patti Hanley (Hot•B), Joe Sislow (Jaleco), Kelly Akers (JVC), Ellen Fuog (Kaneko), Cherrie McKinnon and Marlyse Cohen (Konami), Camela Boswell (LucasArts), Mark Tsai and Jerry Wolosenko (Psygnosis), June Brown (Readysoft), Allan Becker (Sony Imagesoft), Leslie Simmons (Spectrum Holobyte), David Siller (Sunsoft), Larry Stalmah (Taito), Kinya Tago (Takara), George Sinfield (T•HQ), Mary Lynn Slattery (UBI Soft), Robb Alvey (Virgin Games), Yvonne Martins (Viveros and Associates), and Victor Ireland (Working Designs).

From J. Douglas Arnold:

Special thanks to my mother, Joan, for her guidance, encouragement, support, love, friendship, direction and insight.

Thanks to Joe Harabin for his essential help with distribution.

Greetings to Gavin Campbell, Larry Antonio, Adam Dotson, Steve "Smike" Henke, Ewok, Angelo, Danny Han, Mr. Li, Scott at JR's Music; Chris & Jamie & Matthew Arnold; Jack, Val, Tera & Kyle Kidd, Damon & Yvonne, Paul Babel, Mike Boland, Gary Clisby, Ruth Ko, Barbara & Stan, Fran & Don, Helen & Rob, Dan & Naomi Malone, Mark & Judy Ellman, and Linda & Bill Pierce. Thanks for everything!

Howdy to the folks in Missouri: Granny, Grandpa and The Henke Family.

From Zach Meston:

Thanks to Mom for raising me right; Chris Bieniek and Mike Davila at VideoGames for the added income (heh) and the chance to write lots of silly things in a nationally distributed magazine; Brian Colin for the awesome T-shirt and the great tips on General Chaos; and everyone at Game Informer and GamePro for the nice plugs they ran for our last books.

Greetings to Denny Atkin, Andy Eddy, Danny Han, Kay Kusumoto, Scott May, Shari Mitchell, Hillary New, Peter Olafson, John "Frisco?" Prisco, Andy Saito, Scorpia, Lori Sears, and the sickeningly nice Kelly at Readysoft.

CONTENTS

More Than Complete Secrets For...

Just the Essentials...

Aerobiz • Batman Returns • Battleclash • Best of the Best
Brawl Brothers • Cal Ripken Jr. Baseball • The Combatribes
Cool World • Cybernator • Death Valley Rally • F-1 ROC 2
Final Fight 2 • Firepower 2000 • Gods • The Lost Vikings
Mario is Missing • Mechwarrior • Nigel Mansell's World
Championship Racing • Pocky and Rocky • Robocop 3
SimEarth • Sonic Blast Man • Spindizzy Worlds • Star Fox
Street Combat • Super Conflict • Super Strike Eagle
Super Turrican • Super Valis IV • Tecmo Super NBA Basketball
Tiny Toon Adventures • Wayne's World • Wing Commander
WWF Royal Rumble • Yoshi's Cookie

(2S) = 2 player simultaneous option / (4S) = up to 4 players simultaneous with adapter)

INTRODUCTION

Many people thought Nintendo of America was falling behind in the video game race when they delayed releasing their 16-bit machine in the United States, giving their competitors an entire year to build up a huge library of games for potential buyers. Nintendo finally unleashed the Super NES in late 1991, and since then, Nintendo and its dozens of third-party licensees have been releasing a steady flow of incredible titles.

A few of the earliest titles showed *slowdown,* which occured when too many objects were on the screen at once, but programmers soon overcame that problem and now slowdown is extremely rare. Titles that many thought couldn't make the translation from arcade to home have shown the power of the Super Nintendo, with games like Street Fighter 2 Turbo and Mortal Kombat almost exactly the same as the arcade originals. Titles developed specifically for the Super NES have been just as spectacular, in some cases with graphics and sound even *better* than average arcade machines.

The future holds even more promise for the Super NES. The Super FX chip that Nintendo introduced to the world in Star Fox will be appearing in many more games in the future, including Nintendo's own driving game FX Trax. Dolby Surround Sound Stereo is being used in several Super NES games, including Super Turrican and Jurassic Park. And the elusive Super NES CD-ROM has now evolved into a *64-bit* game machine that Nintendo plans to release in late 1995. No word whether it will be compatible with the Super NES, but there's plenty of life left in Nintendo's 16-bit machine, so don't worry. Just start saving your money now!

This book, like all the other books in the Gaming Mastery Series, provides you with the strategies and tips you need to defeat the toughest bosses and overcome seemingly impossible obstacles. Check out the Awesome Strategies if you want to be taken through the game step by step. Refer to the Awesome Secrets if you want cheat codes, passwords, and other game-busting tips. Our future books will include strategies for the newest games as they are made available.

And now for an apology: In our last book, Awesome Super Nintendo Secrets 2, we ran a chapter on Equinox, an adventure from Sony Imagesoft. We were told that Equinox was going to be released at about the same time as our book, but later found out that the game had been delayed for several months (!) due to technical problems. We'll update our Equinox chapter in a future book, depending on how much the game has been changed.

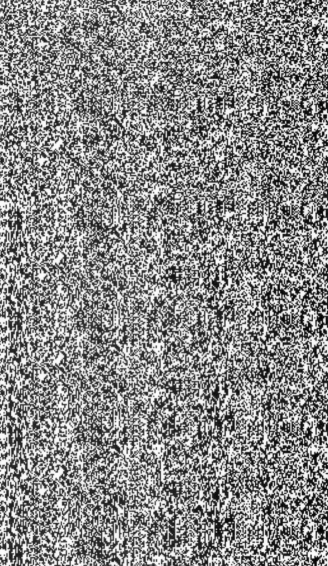

See page 298 for viewing instructions.

AERO THE ACRO-BAT

BY SUNSOFT

Introduction

Sunsoft is known for making the toughest games available, and this is no exception! Aero is one of the toughest games you can play, and it's also one of the most enjoyable. Unless you're a very patient expert player, don't expect to see the end anytime soon. *Aero the Acro-Bat* features over 20 stages in four scenarios, including The Circus, The Funpark, and The

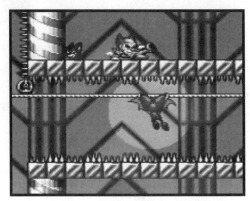

It's Sonic with wings, much more challenging gameplay, and bungee jumping!

Woods. It features several hip events, like bungee jumping and a ride down the rapids. The final stage has Aero searching through a Museum of Horrors, where he'll eventually encounter Edgar Ektor for the final battle.

Awesome Strategies

★ It's fun and easy to play around with the first few acts. After a couple of plays they'll seem simple, and your first goal should be to attempt a perfect round by finding every object before time runs out. For this you'll be rewarded with a free extra life. It's nearly impossible to do past the third act.

★ **Controls:** The most crucial skill to master is the **Spin Attack**. Press B to jump, then press B again to spin in the air. Aero can spin through his enemies to defeat them. If you collect a **Lightning Bolt**, you can spin twice during a single jump. The A button throws Stars, which are limited

With the Lightning Bolt you can do two spin attacks in a row, and reach higher ledges.

Aero The Acro-Bat

and found throughout each stage. Use the C button to flap your wings while in the air (a good way to give yourself an extra second to react), or hang from the tightrope. If you hold the C button and press the control pad left or right, you'll scroll the screen in that direction.

Flap your wings to give yourself an extra moment to react to obstacles below.

★ The bad news: When you lose all of your lives, you can **continue** (up to three times), but you continue at the beginning of the *world* you're on, not the stage within that world. You'll also only have five lives, which may make survival to the end of that world impossible. There are, however, plenty of lives to be gathered or earned along the way.

★ There are three ways to **earn extra lives.** The easiest is to find one of the many Aero Heads, which are usually hidden through a fake wall or along the ceiling. The second way is to earn 20,000 points, which just sort of happens eventually. The third way is to finish a "Perfect Round", which means you've collected all food items, stars, bonus icons and health bar icons before the time has run out. This is fairly easy on the first two acts, then becomes increasingly impossible. Therefore, we'll do our best to point out all of the free Aero Heads along the way.

WORLD 1: CIRCUS WORLD

ACT 1: JUMP ON 7 STAR PLATFORMS

★ You have to jump on the **star platforms** until they disappear completely. The first platform you'll see has two stars, and therefore must be jumped on two times to make it disappear. The one above it has three stars. As you're climbing the ladder to these two platforms you'll notice an Aero A to the right, next to a clock. They are tough to get to as a beginner, but as you master the controls you'll want to grab them in an attempt to make a perfect round (and earn a bonus Aero life).

★ After you hit the **first checkpoint** (pole with a spinning ball), jump and spin into the clown above, then fly down through the large gold rings for bonus points. You can go through the wall at the bottom of the ladder (to the left) to grab the two items mentioned above. Go right and jump on the **trampolines** to reach the **second checkpoint**.

Aero The Acro-Bat

★ Push the human (or bat, in this case) **cannon** to the right halfway between the barriers, then climb into it and press the jump button. Press the jump button again when the cannon power bar reaches its highest point, then hold left to reach a platform. Jump up and spin into the clown to the left, then land on the platform to the left and enter the star ring.

Shoot up from the cannon and hold left to find this star ring to a bonus area with an extra life.

★ You'll be in a **bonus area** where you can collect an **extra life**, three Aero A's (energy items), and some food. There's also a vicious clown in this area that is very talented at blocking your attacks. For now try to avoid him, but later on you'll want to practice spinning into him while he's walking away from you. Go back and jump through the ring to go back to the cannon, then use the cannon to reach the platforms on the left again. Jump on the platforms to make them disappear, then use the cannon to reach the platform to the upper-right.

★ From this platform, jump and spin into the clown to reach the platform to the right with the **wings.** Fly straight up to find eight throwing stars, careful to avoid the deadly spikes. Go back down to the cannon, then shoot back up to the platforms and make them disappear.

★ Go to the right until you reach the **flaming ring.** You can jump to it by making a valiant leap from the platform, but if you're a bit nervous you can always flap your wings (press C) to give yourself an extra second to guide Aero through the ring. Go left, past the ladder, and find the last star platform to jump on. Return to the right to find a spinning ring of stars, signalling the end. If it's not there, you must have missed a star platform.

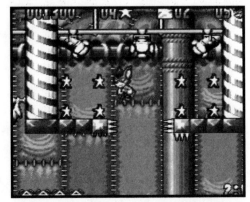

Go right from the cannon and grab wings, then fly straight up to find eight throwing stars.

Aero The Acro-Bat

ACT 2: FIND THE KEY AND RESCUE AERIEL

★ You're safe from enemy harm while riding the unicycle. Above the first trampoline is a charging creature flying back and forth. Use the trampoline to get up to him, then flap your wings to hover while waiting for the perfect opportunity for a spin attack. By grabbing the **B icon** on the platform you'll be able to enter the Bonus Round.

★ The **first checkpoint** pole is up next, and you'll be faced with a choice of two directions to go. Take the ladder going up, and climb down through the maze collecting winged A's along the way. You can only have a maximum of five A's, so leave any extras for your next trip through here. At the bottom of the maze, go left through the wall and walk

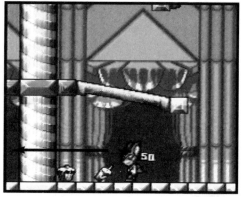

Go down through the maze and jump through this wall to save some time, and find the key.

through the one way doors (the arrows point the way). Hit the checkpoint, then spin attack the two clowns to climb up. Go down the ladder and watch out for a sliding clown ("Buttons") as you sprint to the left. Move the **cannon** to the center of its barriers, then shoot up at about 80% power to find **the key** and an **Aero life** (spikes are above, so don't shoot up too hard). Go back to the right and climb up to find the first checkpoint again. Go back down the maze, collecting any remaining A's.

★ On the next trampoline you can reach a platform to the top left by using your spin attack at the highest point of your bounce. The **Lightning Bolt** allows you to perform two spin attacks per jump now, which is how you collect the stars to the right (from the platform where you found the Lightning Bolt). There's also an Aero Head (life).

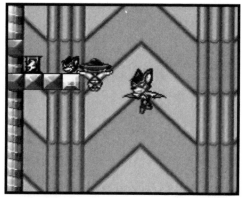

Use the trampoline to reach this Lightning Bolt and extra life, then grab the stars to the right.

Aero The Acro-Bat

★ The **third checkpoint** is ahead, followed by tricky **balloons**. Use the spin attack to get to each of the balloons, or drop to the right of the first balloon to find wings and use them to get to the right ledge. Ride the third balloon from the left all the way up, then go left to a **hidden area** with **two extra lives** and a clock.

Ride up on the third balloon to find a hidden area with two extra lives and a clock.

★ Go to the **right of the cannon** and walk across the floor until you drop through, then go left to find food, a clock, and three A's (protected by a Buttons clown).

★ **Push the cannon** all the way to the right, and shoot up through the rings. Repeat three times to destroy the three bubbles that block your path, then hold left as you shoot through the rings to reach the platform. There's a winged A to the left of the cannon, but it's risky (unless you're going for a perfect round).

★ After hitting the **fourth checkpoint,** jump over the unicycle and walk across the tightrope to get above the row of items. Press C to hang from the tightrope, then drop above the items to collect the parachute and items below it. Go right, through the one-way door, and climb back up to the unicycle. Ride it at full speed to the left until it stops. Rescue the babe in the cage, then hit the exit ring of stars.

CIRCUS BONUS: DIVE INTO THE TANK

★ The goal is to dive through all of the rings and land in the pool. A creature will try to blow you away from the rings. This stage plays very similar to the skydiving event in *Pilotwings*. Hit left or right on the control pad to spin, which will keep you moving in a fairly straight line. Push up or down to dive at a ring.

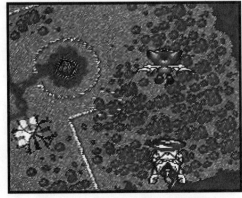

The creature with the fan will likely ruin any chance of a perfect round.

Aero The Acro-Bat

ACT 3: JUMP ON 15 STAR PLATFORMS

★ After grabbing the parachute, guide Aero to grab items to the right, then center, right, left, and right. You only get one chance to grab these items–if you miss you can't get a perfect round. Before going through the second one-way door at the bottom, jump up through the ceiling to grab two winged A's in a **secret room**.

★ Ride the balloon up, then jump to the second balloon to reach an **extra life**. Go back down and jump on the two star platforms, then go right to the cannon.

★ Push the **cannon** to the far right and blast up at full power. Use the spin attack to reach the platform above, then climb and wait for the star ring to appear. Jump in to warp to a **bonus area**. Grab the wings and fly up to the stars, then go back to the cannon.

★ Push the **cannon** under the **flaming rings**. Shoot up through the rings at maximum power, then hold left to hit a checkpoint. Shoot the **trapeze clown** with stars, then grab the trapeze and swing to the right. Jump and fall to the floor, then go left to find an **extra life**. Go up and left to climb the ladder, then ride the **unicycle** across to the next checkpoint.

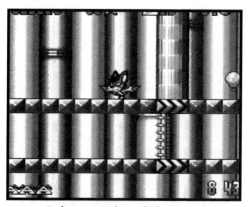

Before going through the second one-way door, jump up through the ceiling.

★ **Dive off** and guide Aero straight down to find items and a tank. If you want to try again, go left through the one-way door and climb back up to the diving board. Go right, jumping over the spinning elephant, and hit the next checkpoint. Go to the far right and climb up to jump on three star platforms. Go back down and climb down the ladder. Shoot the trapeze clown with

After shooting out of the cannon, go left and fall from the trapeze to this extra life.

stars, then fall off the ledge and hold right to get into the **hidden area**. Use the trampoline to get up to the clock and **extra life**.

★ Leave the hidden area and ride the balloon back up to the **trapeze**. Go left across the trapeze to find a **checkpoint**, then ride the **unicycle**. Jump far to the left to find another unicycle, leading to another checkpoint. Climb the ladder and jump on the star platforms. From the top of the ladder use spin attacks to reach platforms to the upper right. Keep going until you find an empty ledge, then wait for the star ring to appear. Jump into it to find a **hidden area** with an invincibility, throwing stars, a clock, an **extra life**, and a winged A (what a score!). Go back to the ladder and go left to find another ladder and a fire ring. Jump through the rings if you want some points, then go left and down again to find a checkpoint. Climb down until you find the **trampoline**, then use it to reach a few winged A's. Go down to the bottom floor and jump through the left wall to find a few items in a **secret room**.

★ To the right is a tough obstacle course. Use spin attacks to clear the spikes and reach the next checkpoint. Jump on the trampolines to reach a **flaming ring**. Jump through for points, then hit the checkpoint. Go left through the one-way door to find an **extra life** and other items. Go back to the checkpoint, then right to the **cannon**. Use your stars to knock out the Buttons clown, or jump over him and attack from behind.

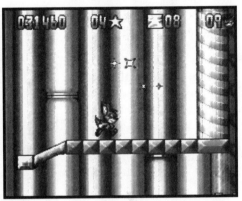

Look for this ledge past the unicycles, then wait to enter a hidden area with an extra life.

★ Push the **cannon** to the far right, under the rings. Shoot up through the rings to destroy the bubbles, then spin attack left to reach several platforms. If you fall you'll have to

Use spin attacks to make long jumps over these life-threatening spikes.

Aero The Acro-Bat

reposition the cannon near the center of the barriers and use the spin attack on your way down to knock out the clowns. There are five platforms to jump on. Above the platforms are tricky balloons to climb across, which lead to a few goodies to the upper-left. It's not worth losing a life over. Use the cannon to shoot back up through the rings and climb up the platforms to find the ring of stars and end this act.

ACT 4: JUMP THROUGH 25 MAGIC HOOPS

★ Climb up two ladders and jump through the first **magic hoop**, then jump up and left to the next ladder and checkpoint. Go right and climb the next ladder, then jump up and left to reach the balloon. Ride up to collect four stars, then go back down to the last ladder and jump off the **diving board**. Go straight down to soar through **five magic hoops** and land in a **pool**.

Go right and climb up, then jump up to the balloon and ride it up. Jump to the next two balloons to reach an **extra life**. Drop down to the right, then go to the bubble machine.

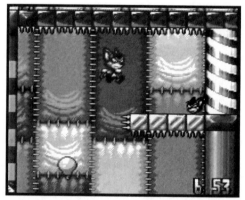

After the dive into the pool, ride the balloons up to find an extra life.

★ Push the **bubble machine** to the right about three blocks (along the floor). Ride the bubbles up to find an invincibility and two winged A's. Ride the balloon up to the left ledge, then use the trampolines to get to the **five magic hoops** to the left. Go right to the next checkpoint, then jump on the seesaw. Use the seesaws to pass through **six more magic hoops.** Hit the checkpoint, then go right and grab the wings. Fly up and left to fly through the ceiling/floor left of the **extra life**. Climb up and go right to get the extra life, then use the seesaw to

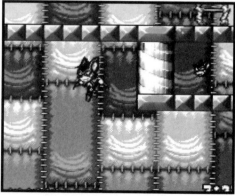

Use the wings to fly up through the floor and easily find an extra life.

reach a clock and two winged A's. Go back down to the checkpoint, then go left to find another seesaw and use it for **two more magic hoops**. That's nineteen hoops so far. Climb up to the next checkpoint. Go left and dive off the diving board, then go straight down to find two magic hoops. Swim left to the next checkpoint. Go up and left to find the last four magic hoops. The exit star ring should appear at the bottom.

ACT 5: TURN ON ALL THE LIGHTS

★ Go right and jump into the rings, but stay near the center because the bottom one is a **fire ring**. Grab the **Lightning Bolt** and hit the checkpoint. Go left and push the **cannon** right to the ring with three bubbles. Keep shooting up until you get through the bubbles, then shoot up at 100% power to reach a ledge with the **first switch** and an **extra life!**

★ Drop back down and go left to the next checkpoint. Go up and ride the bubbles to reach the ledges above. Go up and right to find the next checkpoint. Use the trampoline below to reach an **extra life** and two winged A's to the upper left.

★ Climb across the **balloons**. If you fall off a balloon, flap your wings and look to see if you're near a pair of wings you can grab

Ride the sixth balloon all the way up to find an invincibility, clock, and extra life.

before falling into the spikes below. When you get to the sixth balloon, ride it all the way up to an invincibility, clock and **extra life.** Go back and drop down to the sixth balloon, then continue jumping across to the right. Hit the **second switch** and grab the **extra life**, then grab the parachute and ride down in a zig-zagging pattern to grab items. Go left to exit back to the trampoline. Go to the far left and climb up two ladders to find a trampoline with stars and two winged A's above, then go up and left to find the next checkpoint.

★ To the right are **columns with trampolines** between each. The top of each column has spikes (otherwise it wouldn't be any fun). Use the trampolines to go to the right. Watch the next pit for a trampoline. If there are spikes, use the spin attack to avoid it and go to the next pit. Grab the **Lightning Bolt** and go right to the checkpoint.

Aero The Acro-Bat

★ It's time for more trampolines and spikes, but now the columns are a wider square block. Go right over two spiked squares, then use the trampoline to get to the **wings** above, and the **extra life** above them. Go right and jump down through the magic hoops. Climb up the right ladder to find the **third switch** and an **extra life**. Climb up to a checkpoint, then go right and fall

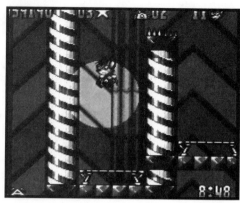

If you can get to the wings, you can fly up to an extra life above them.

through the floor to find a few throwing stars.

★ Go back up and left to find a **trapeze that swings in a full circle.** Ride it around once to collect the stars, then jump off when it's at the top to reach the ledge to the left and an **extra life**. Shoot the trapeze clown with stars, then go left across the trapezes for another **extra life**. Use the next full-circle trapeze to reach the far left wall. Time your jump off the trapeze to avoid the spikes along the ceiling. Climb the ladder to find another checkpoint, then ride the **unicycle** to the wall. Climb off and hang from the tightrope, then climb across to the next unicycle. Ride to the next wall and hang from the tightrope again. You can get the **extra life** above by jumping through the wall on the right, but you'll have to fight or avoid that Buttons clown to get it. Go right to the **final switch**, then jump through the ring of stars.

CIRCUS BOSS: MEET THE STILT BROTHERS

★ You need to move quick to knock these guys down before you take too many hits from their torches. Attack either brother by spin attacking him once or twice, then attack the other brother. As the brothers get shorter, you'll have to use the spin attack on the way down from your jump to hit their feet.

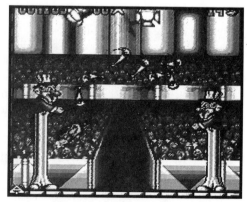

Use high and low spin attacks into the legs of the Stilt Brothers.

Aero The Acro-Bat

Once they're at their shortest height, spin attack their feet three times each. After each attack, they will flash invincible for a few seconds. Attack the other during this time.

World 2: The Funpark

ACT1: JUMP ON 5 STAR PLATFORMS

★ From the **spinning sun platforms**, go up and right, then jump to the balloon and ride to an **extra life**. Hit the star platform, then go right and down.

★ Before riding the **saucer ride**, go up and right to find a star platform (the third). Ride the saucer ride to the top and climb upward.

★ The rest of this act is familiar obstacles and enemies. Just keep climbing upward to find the exit.

Ride the balloons up to find an extra life.

ACT 2: RIDE THE ROLLER COASTER

★ Prepare for frustration. This ride on the roller coaster is anything but fun! Get a friend to yell directions to you while you play.

★ There's a **long jump** near the halfway mark of the first area that may seem impossible to clear. The trick is to keep your speed up as fast as possible. How? By jumping up each hill and jumping over the water pool at the bottom of the first hill. **Spiked walls** are after the water – duck the first, then jump over the second.

★ After going through the **second and third clown**

You must jump up the hills to prevent the roller coaster from slowing down.

Aero The Acro-Bat

mouths you'll be in the second area. Jump while climbing the first hill, and jump at the bottom of the hill to get over the water quickly. Duck under two spiked walls, then another. Jump up the hill, then prepare for a long jump at the bottom of the hill. Duck under a spiked wall, then make a jump and an immediate second jump over a spiked wall. Jump up the hill and duck at the top of the hill under the spiked wall. Enjoy the ride to the end.

ACT 3: KEYS OPEN DOORS

★ You'll see the door right away, but the **key** is a little harder to find. As you climb upward you'll see the key, and getting to it is fairly easy. Go back to the door and search for the next.

★ When searching for the key to the third door, you'll have to blast out of a **cannon** into narrow passages surrounded by spikes. Place the cannon below the far right passage, then use the balloon to the right and ride to an **extra life**. Fall off the side of the balloon before you hit the spikes. Push the cannon over to the next passage (center) to reach the area with the **key** (guarded by a Buttons clown). There's a clock up the left passage, if you care to grab it.

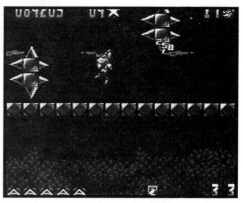

Getting to the fourth key is extremely challenging.

★ When searching for the fourth key, hold right while riding the elevator up and you'll enter a **secret room** with many items, a clock and a winged A. Getting to this key is the toughest. You have to use a few swinging sun platforms to reach the right wall, then climb up and use the spin attack to clear several spiked blocks. One mistake and you're going back to the last checkpoint!

★ There's an **extra life** on the way to the exit star ring in plain view. After walking through the large clown mouth (or climbing over the top), jump on the first balloon and jump right to a small ledge with the extra life.

ACT 4: RIDE THE ROTOR

★ The first rotor ride is easy, just flip over a few times to avoid the poles. There's another **extra life** in plain view near the second rotor. The second rotor is a bit trickier. Watch for two poles in a row after the sixth pole. You'll be able to grab another **extra life** by knocking out an easy floating clown.

★ Before jumping into the third rotor, climb up the left wall to reach the **B icon**, which allows you to play the Bonus Round if you can survive this act. The **third rotor ride** seems totally impossible.

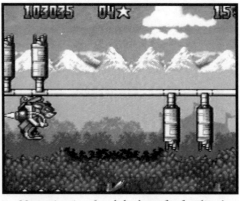

Memorization (and the loss of a few lives) is the key to surviving the Rotor.

Here's the pattern: down, up for two, down, up for three, down for four, up for two, down for two, up for two, down for two, up for two, down for two, up for two, down for two. Try to memorize this pattern before you play, or have a friend yell them to you. Hit Start to pause if you need a rest.

FUNPARK BONUS ROUND: STAY ALIVE

★ It's another roller coaster ride! Jump up the first hill, then jump at the bottom of the hill to clear the water. Duck under spikes, jump over spikes, duck under spikes, jump up hill. Jump over spikes twice. Jump up next hill. Duck under spikes, jump over spikes, jump up hill, then duck under spikes at bottom of hill. That's it! Enjoy the rest of the ride.

The Funpark Bonus Round is another roller coaster ride with tricky obstacles.

ACT 5: JUMP THROUGH 25 MAGIC HOOPS

★ Use the trampoline to reach the second ledge up, and grab the **Lightning Bolt** to the right, then go back down to the lower ledge and

Aero The Acro-Bat

go down to the second ladder. From the top of the ladder, jump off to the right and hold right to find a hole in the wall. From the hole, jump up and do a double spin attack to reach an **extra life**. To the left are the first four magic hoops.

★ You'll hit the 11th-13th hoops while jumping on trampolines over spiked poles. After grabbing the rings, hold right against the wall to enter a **secret room**. Ride the balloon up to grab an **extra life.**

★ When jumping from saucer ride to saucer ride, use your wings to hover for an extra moment and aim for a saucer. If you hold right, you should make it without using your wings.

Stay on the right side of the swinging sun platforms to avoid the spikes.

★ On the **swinging sun platforms**, stay on the right side of each swinging platform to avoid the spikes you swing up to.

★ Near the end you'll jump from a wide platform to a balloon, then two narrow platforms. The exit star ring is to the upper-left, but you can safely grab the items below by falling straight down through them and landing on the balloon below them.

FUNPARK BOSS: MEET MR. BUBBLES

★ The boss rides up and down the right side of the screen. It's a large clown face with a hand in his mouth. The hand reaches out and tries to crush you. Keep moving up and down the platforms, then spin attack into the clown's nose as the hand is retracting. After each hit the clown will cry – avoid the tears by falling to the lower platforms or quickly climbing above the face, then prepare to attack again.

Hit the boss in the nose, then avoid his tears and grasping hand.

Aero The Acro-Bat

World 3: The Woods

ACT 1: FIND THE EXIT

★ It may sound challenging, but this act is fairly easy. From the beginning, you can go left into the rock wall to find a clock guarded by a Buttons clown. Keep going to the right until you reach a tree, then jump into it and go all the way down. Climb out of the left side and keep going left. Just past the tightrope is an **extra life** above a seesaw. Go into the wall to the left of the seesaw to find three winged A's guarded by a Buttons clown. The exit star ring is up to the left.

ACT 2: THE BARREL ROLL

★ This act is similar to the roller coaster and rotor acts. You may need a friend to yell directions. Jump up the hills, like you did for the roller coaster. There are several short hops, then two long jumps over water and a long jump over spikes. At the top of the second hill after the long jumps, be ready for two jumps side-by-side, then two long jumps that look like two short jumps (there's a gap in the middle of the spikes, but you can't land in there). If you see an **extra life**, jump for it! There aren't spikes near any of them.

The Barrel Roll plays similar to the Roller Coaster. Always jump for the extra lives.

ACT 3: DO THE BUNGEE

★ This game might be a little *too* hip. To our knowledge, it's the first to feature bungee jumping – and it's fun! Just stand in the launch pad of the bungee and you'll fall, then guide Aero left or right to avoid the spiked platforms. Always drop straight down the middle for the first fall,

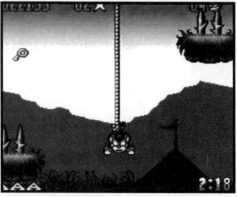

Always dive straight down on the first descent of a bungee jump to watch for obstacles.

Aero The Acro-Bat

then go left or right based on what platforms you see. If you miss the key, step right up and go for another jump. Explore the areas above each bungee jump to find bonus items. After the third bungee jump is the exit star ring.

ACT 4: RIDE THE RAPIDS
★ In this act you slide down logs while avoiding spikes. Once again, a friend yelling directions might come in handy. Without help, try drinking a few Jolt colas so your reflexes will be up to the proper speed. Hit Start if you need a break. You can also slow things down by flapping your wings when jumping, or rapidly jumping up against the current of the rapids. When you see four spikes stacked, duck, and jump when you see only two. On your way down the first area, watch the left side. When you see the first spiked wheel, drop to the log below it and jump up and left to reach an **extra life**.

You can reach a few extra lives by jumping up the logs.

★ You'll see the next **extra life** on your way down in the second rapids area. When you reach the bottom, go left to hit the checkpoint before continuing into the next rapids area.
★ **Third rapids:** After you fall between the two spiked wheels, climb up to the right for an **extra life**. This is the final rapids ride, and there's no boss for this world. Hooray!

World 4: The Museum
ACT 1: EXPLORE THE MUSEUM
★ The title of this act is excellent advice. Try jumping into every wall throughout each of the last acts to search for hidden rooms. There are plenty of **extra lives** to be found, along with all of the other cool items that help you survive. The **bouncing flames** that pop out of the lava will bounce along the platforms – jump over them. You can hit the **white ghosts** while they're jumping in the air. Jump once to fake them out, then jump and spin into them. The **bubbling water** is safe to swim in. Use the spin attack when jumping through **guillotines**.

Aero The Acro-Bat

★ From the first screw elevator, go up and left to find a room with an **extra life.**

★ Use the spin attack to get safely through the blades on the columns between the trampolines. When you reach the right side, go into the upper room to find an **extra life**, then jump against the right wall to enter the lower room and continue toward the exit. Some of

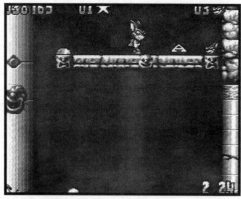

Go up and left from the first screw elevator to find an extra life in a hidden room.

the clowns on the columns in the next area will jump off and attack.

★ The clown in the **red and white striped hat** will spin or jump randomly. If you get hit, quickly run past him while you're still flashing invincible.

ACT 2: RIDE THE CONVEYOR BELTS

★ Ooh! Conveyor belts. What fun! An important note: don't grab the **winged A's** unless you have less than five – you may want to grab the leftovers if you lose a life and have to come back through. Also, **jump rapidly on the conveyor belts** to avoid being dragged by them.

★ From the beginning of this round walk past the first **screw elevator** and go into the wall. After going up the elevator you'll see the first **extra life**. Climb up on the higher belts to reach it, then go left into the wall to find a long **hidden passage** with many extra items (but no extra lives!).

★ At the bottom of the next room of conveyor belts is a hidden room in the

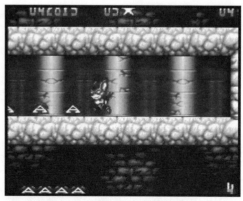

Once you have five winged A's, leave the rest in case you need them later.

right wall with several items. An **extra life** is near the top-right of the conveyor belt room.

Aero The Acro-Bat

ACT 3: THE TOWER

★ If you find the **B icon** on this act you'll get to enter the Bonus Stage where you can collect about 10 extra lives easily. As you're going down the first ramp, watch for an **extra life** below. You have to run and jump to a fire-spitting head to reach it. Go down the ladder below and to the far right, then use the trampoline on the right wall to bounce up to another **extra life**, surrounded by stars. Go down and left to find a **Lightning Bolt**. Use the double spin attack power to climb up from the Bolt and find an **extra life**.

★ **Marvin the Magician** is nearly impossible to kill, but if you spin attack towards him he'll chicken out and disappear.

Use rapid Spin Attacks when walking towards Marvin the Magician to scare him away.

★ There's another **extra life** below the swinging chains of spiked balls. Go down and to the left, then jump on the head and climb up to the extra life.

★ After the Buttons statues that spring to life, hit the trampoline on the left wall to reach an **extra life** surrounded by stars. The exit is two floors down.

ACT 4: EXPLORE THE SECRET PASSAGES

★ If you jump into the walls you can break through some of them. The first wall, to the left of where you start, is a prime example. Go to the right and you'll find another. Watch for **extra lives** – if you can see it you can get it.

★ When you're walking along the **electrical lines**, time your jumps over the blades with the electric bolt flowing through the line.

★ Don't get greedy for the

Most rooms have a couple of walls that can be broken into with a simple spin attack.

Aero The Acro-Bat

extra lives while riding on the logs across the **lava pits.** You can't get across this first lava pit without the log.

ACT 5: THE LABORATORY

★ Sure would be nice to have a password right about now. To get this far, after hours of nonstop playing, and then being forced to start from the very first level – Sunsoft is evil I tell you... evil! This stage is very similar to the last, only the jumps get even trickier (is that possible!?). Use the C button and the control pad to **look around** very often! Jump into every wall to search for hidden rooms with **extra lives**. Go left from the beginning to find a **Lightning Bolt** through the wall.

Don't jump into the exit star ring until you've grabbed this extra life to the left.

★ It's possible to survive the **lava pit** on this act without using the log. Keep scrolling the screen ahead to see where you're going to have to jump next.

★ Grab the **extra life** to the left of the exit star ring before jumping in.

MUSEUM BOSS: EDGAR EKTON'S DOMAIN

★ Okay, it's time to give up. This is one of the toughest final bosses we've ever seen, and we've seen hundreds. Even with 19 lives in reserve we couldn't beat this guy the first time. I know that may not give you a lot of confidence, but keep in mind that we didn't have the benefit of this chapter to help us along. Even with it, this is going to be the ultimate test of your coordination, skill, reflexes, memory and patience. Lotsa luck!

Bust this boss in the jaw five times, then 10 times, then hit him 15 times in the nose. It's not that easy!

Aero The Acro-Bat

To beat the boss you have to climb up through an obstacle course, hit him 5 times, then climb through another tough obstacle course and hit him 10 times, then climb through another obstacle course and hit him 15-17 times (we hit him 16 times the first time and he didn't die, but he gave up after 15 on the second attempt). As if all that wasn't enough, there's an electric beam that will follow you up, and destroy you if you don't climb quickly enough. The instructions that follow are general areas to climb on your way up. It may help to have a friend read it to you while you play, or pause after each section to check what's coming up in the next.

Jump up the left side, then climb the ladder and go right to the trampoline. Go left to the ladder, then climb up to the right. Run to the left and jump up the small steps on the wall, then run to the right and hit the trampolines. Go left to the center and slide down the ladder. Go left and climb up the steps using the spin attack, then go to the right to climb the ladder. Go left and climb the ladder, then climb the steps to the upper-right, go left and jump across the steps to the right, then climb up more steps while avoiding the large spinning chain of spiked balls. Climb up a few more steps and you'll reach the flat floor where you make your first attack.

The boss shoots water from the flowers on each cheek, so beware. When he opens his mouth, quickly spin attack into his jaw to close it. The longer his jaw is open, the more clowns you must fight once you close it. If you hit it quickly enough you may not have to fight any clowns.

After five hits the boss will climb up again. Ugh! Go to the left wall and climb up, then keep climbing up the right side to the pipes. Go to the center to reach the next floor, then continue climbing near the center. Climb the ladder and jump off it near the top to the right to climb the center ladder. Go to the left or right to climb the next area. Hit the trampoline

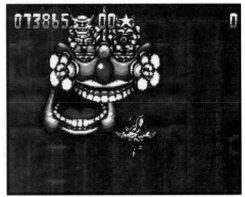

Hit the boss in the jaw as soon as it opens to prevent the clowns from escaping.

on the right wall to bounce back to the center and continue climbing up and left. About two more screens up is the next fighting arena.

The pattern this time is similar. Try to hit the jaw as soon as it opens to stop the clowns from escaping. The flowers will squirt three times between jaw openings. After 10 hits the jaw will drop off and you'll have to make a final climb upward.

Between each series of hits is a long climb up an extremely difficult obstacle course.

Climb up the ladder on the left, then go to the center to the trampoline. Go left to climb, then hit the trampoline to the right. Keep climbing up the left side, then the center. Climb the ladder up the left wall, then run past the laser beam squares. Go left and climb up the center area, then jump over the shocking walls and hit the trampolines on the right wall. Climb down the ladder in the center and hit the trampolines on the left wall. Jump across to the right and climb up, then go left past the flipping spiked balls to reach the final steps to the boss.

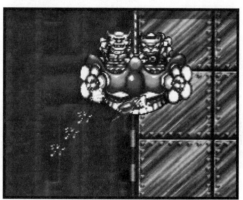

If you can hit the boss 15 more times in the nose, you'll be treated to a cool ending and stats.

If you can get in 15 hits before losing all your lives, you'll win! Now you have to hit the nose on the boss. If you hit the clowns as they are lowering out of the mouth, you can kill them quickly.

After beating the boss you'll get to see a cute ending animation while the credits roll, then you'll get a "Final Statistics" screen with the number of lives remaining (7 for us), lives used (we went through 219!), stars used (212), spins used (4,453), drills used (691), and enemies defeated (455), along with your final score. Wow, that David Siller guy is a genius!

ALIEN 3

BY LJN

Introduction

The weaponry is as fierce as the enemies in this awesome platform battle. The storyline is based loosely on the not-so-hot movie, with enough changes in the plot to make it interesting. You must help Ripley through six stages, each with 6-8 missions. The missions range from simple repairs to intense battles with mother aliens. The graphics and movie-style music are superb, and the gameplay is pure fun.

The mother aliens are Ripley's toughest foes. Approach with caution, then torch her!

Awesome Strategies

★ **CONTROLS:** Use the A button for the pulse rifle, X for the grenade launcher, and Y for the flame thrower. To use the blowtorch, stand in front of the item to be welded, then press and hold the Y button. If you are hit before welding reaches 100%, you'll have to start over again. You can check your ammunition for each weapon by pressing the L or R buttons. To open doors, walk up to them and press Up on the control pad.

★ The **Motion Tracker** can be activated by pressing the Select button. It will shut off automatically after a few seconds, unfortunately, which makes it useless. With or without it, you should always be prepared to defend yourself.

★ Check in at any **terminal** (press up in front of it) at the start of each stage.

Check in at any terminal to select a mission, then return when the mission is completed.

Alien 3

Choose a mission, then examine the blueprints to find the rooms included in your mission. When you complete a mission you'll hear a chime every few seconds until you check into a terminal for your next mission. You must finish every mission in a stage to receive the password for the next stage.

Use the flame thrower when climbing through the ducts to quickly eliminate nearby aliens.

★ Using the Rambo method of **rapid firing** will cause you to run out of ammunition quickly. Stick to the pulse rifle as often as possible, since that ammunition is abundant in all stages. Use short bursts the moment you see an alien appear. On the higher stages all aliens require several hits.

★ The flame thrower is best used when climbing through the **air ducts**. Always duck down when moving horizontally in the air ducts and fire short bursts from the flame thrower as aliens appear. When large aliens attack, hold the button down until you see the alien explode. On the higher stages, aliens will also be climbing vertically in air ducts.

★ Ripley has some *strong* legs! She can survive a fall from any height. Use this to your advantage. Instead of climbing down ladders, which will give the surrounding aliens a chance to approach, hit the jump button and **fall down the ladders**. You'll land safely below, ready for battle.

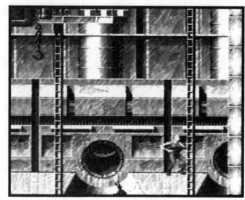

Ripley has strong legs. Jump down the ladders to descend quickly, ready for battle.

★ When **viewing the blueprints** (or our maps), always make yourself familiar with the location of the Medic Bays and Weapons Rooms. As long as you can reach a Medic Bay, you can grab more energy to stay alive. The Weapons Room will need to be visited more often by Rambo-types that waste lots of ammunition. You'll learn quickly that it's better to conserve your firepower. Since the flame

Alien 3

thrower is one of the most useful weapons, it's best to recharge it immediately after viewing your next mission.

★ Each of the various rooms is recognizable once you enter them. The **Cell Blocks** always have prisoners hanging from the walls (until you rescue them). The **Assembly Halls** have dark shadowy characters standing on balconies in the backgrounds. **Alien Hallways** have fog and plenty of eggs. **Medic Bays** have shower curtains and plenty of energy containers (red cross). The **Bugwashes** also have shower curtains, but the energy containers are replaced by a large number of hatching eggs. **Furnace Areas** have a red, glowing background and lava pits along the bottom floor. The **Weapons Room** will have stacked black drums and plenty of weapon power-ups. The **Surface Areas** have a glowing sun on the horizon. Most of the **Mine Areas** look similar to the Cell Blocks, but the Mine Areas have small torches along the bottom floor (which you can safely walk across).

Stage 1

★ There are six missions on this stage. They're all relatively easy to complete, especially with a little practice. Stick to the suggested strategies

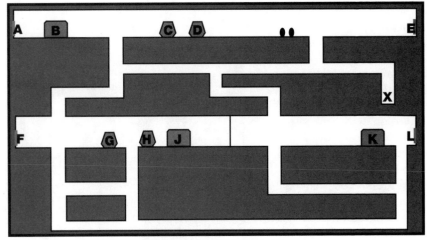

STAGE 1 AIR DUCTS MAP
Terminals are located at positions B, J and K.
DOOR A <> Alien 1 <> Weapon 1
DOOR C <> Assembly Hall 1 <> Cell Block 3
DOOR D <> Bugwash 12 <> Medic Bay 9 <> **DOOR G**
DOOR E <> Waste Area 2
DOOR F <> Mine 22 <> Waste Area 3
DOOR H <> Cell Block 4 <> Medic Bay 8 <> **DOOR L**

Alien 3

above. If you have trouble with a particular mission that causes you to start the stage over, attack that mission first the next time around.

★ There are three items in the ducts at **position X** on the map. The items will appear again after each mission.

★ Any time you're running low on energy, make a run for the **Medic Bay**. You can easily power up to 100% once you get there.

Always know where the Medic Bays are so you can run to them when your energy is low.

★ **HUNT OR BE HUNTED:** This is the first mission on the list, and the easiest to complete. You must rescue prisoners in Cell Blocks #3 and #4. It's easy to get to Cell Block #4 through door H on the map. You can also grab more health in the Medic Bay by entering the other door in Cell Block #4. Getting to Cell Block #3 is a little more complicated. Enter door C and fight your way through the Assembly Hall to find the other door leading to Cell Block #3. In the Assembly Hall, you can run straight to the left to find the door to Cell Block #3. There's an ammo clip on a platform near the center, but it's a bit tricky to reach. You must climb up the right side ladders, climb across the hanging bars, drop to a moving platform, then jump left to the ledge. There is no floor along the girders holding the platforms up, so be sure to leap

across them. In Cell Block #3, destroy the eggs with your flame thrower as you enter and you'll have less aliens to fight on your way back out. There are four prisoners to rescue in this area. In Cell Block #4 there are 4 prisoners to rescue. A flame thrower and first aid are in the upper-left area.

★ **PRESSURE POINT:** There are four pipes to repair in Mine Area #22. Enter door

Save the flame thrower for the eggs and air ducts.

Alien 3

F to get to the Mine Area. The defective pipes have yellow glowing cracks. Stand in front of it and hold the flame thrower on until the meter reaches 100%. If you get hit during a repair, you must destroy the alien and begin the repair from the beginning. If you're standing in front of the crack you won't be able to use the flame thrower to shoot the approaching aliens. Get

Stand in front of broken pipes and use the flame thrower to weld them.

into the habit of shooting them with grenades or bullets.

★ **HEAT IT UP:** Waste Area #3 is filled with 18 alien eggs ready to hatch, and there's another 14 in Alien Corridor #1. Enter door F to get to Mine Area #22, then pass through to the far left to reach the door to Waste Area #3. Alien Corridor #1 is door A at the top left of the ducts. Use the flame thrower on the eggs to torch them quickly and fry any small aliens leaping your way. After passing over the second fire pit in Mine Area #22, you'll see ammo stacked above. Get to the platform above them, then hold down to climb down the chain. Alien Corridor #1 is filled with fog and foreground objects, making aliens tough to spot. Stick to crouching, and blast a quick burst of ammo every few seconds to hit any hidden creatures. When you reach the far end of the corridor, enter the door to stock up on ammo in the Weapons Room. If you run low on energy during any part of this mission, make a run for door G (Medic Bay).

★ **POWER LINK-UP:** Get the ignition unit from Waste Area #2 (door E) and take it to the Generator in Assembly Hall #1 (door C). A flame thrower, ammo, and first aid are conveniently located at location X. The moment after you collect the ignition unit, go right and jump through the

It's tough to see small aliens in the corridors. Use short blasts when your vision is blocked.

wall to reach plenty of first aids and ammo. In Assembly Hall #1 you'll have to climb up the platforms on the right side wall, then climb across the hanging bars and drop to the floating platform. Leap to the ledge at left, and leap across the gap in the girders.

★ **CROSSED WIRES:** Fix the fuse boxes and broken junction box in Waste Area #2 (door E). Don't forget the fake wall hiding the first aids and ammo (see previous mission "Power Link-Up"). If you're doing the missions in order, this area will look quite familiar. After repairing the Junction Box (top center of area), you can leap left through the fake wall next to it.

★ **CLOSED DOORS:** Secure door in Alien Corridor #1 (door A) leading to Weapons Room #11. Crouch and use short bursts of ammo as you pass through this area. When you reach the door, enter and stock up on weapons. Go back out and seal the door with your flame thrower/torch. Easy!

★ **POWER PLUS+:** Repair three fuse boxes in Bugwash #12 (door D) and three in Medic Bay #9 (door H). The right half of Bugwash #12 is only accessible through the door at the bottom right side of Medic Bay #9. Slime is dripping from pipes along the ceiling in the right half of Bugwash #12 – time your steps as they dissolve.

Time your steps across the dripping slime as it dissolves.

★ **TOTAL CONTROL:** Seal off Medic Bay #8 by sealing doors in Corridor #12 (door L) and Cell Block #4 (door H). Go to door L and seal it with the flame thrower/torch, then enter door H and go to the far right to seal the door to Medic Bay #8. You'll have to use the ducts to get from door to door, since a new door blocks your straight path.

Stage 2

★ The Aliens get slightly tougher, requiring one or two extra hits each. Other than that, this stage is more of the same, with a few more detours to get from one location to another. A very important location to know is the duct marked with an X. Here you'll find ammo, grenades, flame thrower fuel, and a first aid. Return here often. You

Alien 3

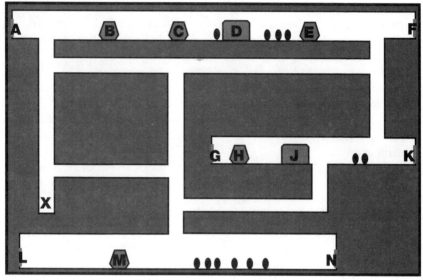

STAGE 2 AIR DUCTS MAP
Terminals are located at positions D and J.
DOOR A <> Medic Bay 3 <> **DOOR M**
DOOR B <> Furnace Area 6 (left side)
DOOR C <> Bugwash 8
DOOR E <> Furnace Area 6 (right side)
DOOR F <> Cell Block 5 <> Furnace Area 7
DOOR G <> Assembly Hall 2 <> Hangar Bay 4 <> **DOOR H**
DOOR K <> Alien Corridor 2 <> **DOOR N**
DOOR L <> Weapons Bay 8

can collect the items at the beginning of a mission, and then often collect them again after the mission (before checking in at the Terminal).

★ **POWER TO THE PEOPLE:** Collect the Power Pack from Hangar Bay #4 (door H) and hook it up to the Generator in Weapons Room #8 (door L). Check the lower platforms in Hangar Bay #4 to find lots of ammo and first aids, but be prepared to shoot a few large aliens. At the far left of the area is a huge chain,

The Power Pack is yellow, and found by climbing a large chain.

Alien 3

which Ripley can climb. Then go right and drop to find the Power Pack (it's yellow). Obviously you'll find plenty of weapons to collect when returning the Power Pack to the Generator, which is up the first ladder in door L.

★ **DEPTHS OF DESPAIR:** Fix three Broken Pipes in Bugwash #8 (door C). Your major obstacles are eggs (use the flame thrower to fry them), and face

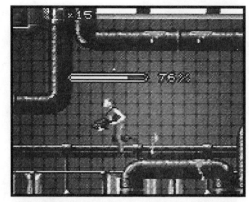

If you get hit by slime you'll flash invincible for a few seconds - run past the slime quickly.

huggers that drop from the ceiling. Clear the bottom floor first, then go back to the right and climb up the pipes. It's nearly impossible to avoid all of the slime to the far left, but if you do get hit you'll be invincible for a few seconds. Use this time to get over and past the slime.

★ **360 DEGREE ACTION:** Torch seven eggs in Corridor #2 (door K) and seal the far right door shut. This mission is very straightforward. Enter door K and seal it behind you, then crouch and use short bursts of ammo to hit any hidden aliens behind foreground objects as you

destroy the eggs with your flame thrower. When you exit at door N you'll have to destroy six more eggs. The Medic Bay is conveniently located at door M, which you'll probably need to visit before checking in at the Terminal.

★ **MERCY MISSION:** There are 4 prisoners to rescue in Furnace #7 (through Cell Block #5, door F). Eight tempting first aids are to the far right of Cell Block #5. Climb the ladder to the

This wall in Cell Block #5 is fake, and hides 8 first aid kits!

left of them, go right and up again, then down at the far right. The wall at the right of the rising platform is fake. Jump through it and collect some ammo and the first aids, then ride the platform up and jump back through the wall. Go into the door at the bottom right to enter Furnace

Alien 3

#7. Prisoners are scattered throughout this area. You'll have to do a lot of climbing, but you can get to all of them with a little searching. When you pass back through Cell Block #5, be sure to collect the ammo and first aid power ups through the hidden wall again. To get out of the Cell Block, you must climb to the top right, climb across the hanging bars, then leap to a moving platform.

★ **ON A SHORT FUSE:** Fix 4 fuses in Medic Bay #3 (door A). Grab the power-ups at position X on the map so you won't run out of flame thrower fuel. There's a huge army of hatching eggs in this area, but there's also plenty of first aids. Don't grab a first aid unless you need it. If you get into trouble later, you can backtrack and grab any you've left.

★ **MISSION IMPOSSIBLE:** Rescue eight prisoners in Furnace Area #6. The trick is there's a solid wall down the center of Furnace Area #6. You can get to the left side by entering door B, and the right side by entering door E.

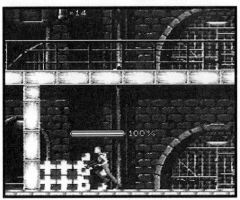

If you don't need a first aid kit, don't grab it. You can always run back to it later if needed.

★ **WATCH YOUR BACK!:** Repair six fuse boxes in Assembly Hall #2. Another solid wall will cause you a lot of extra work. Door G leads to the right side of the Assembly Hall, but to reach the left side you'll have to go through Hangar Bay #4 (door H, right next door to G). Don't forget to search the lower area of Hangar Bay #4 to find plenty of ammo and first aids.

Stage 3

★ A locked door next to terminal C will be your biggest enemy on this stage. There's no way to get through it, so you'll have to go around it. The worst news, of course, is you'll have to return to terminal C after each mission, which is rarely convenient. The only path between terminal C and the other doors is through door B (Cell Block #6). It's tedious and time-consuming, but it's not particularly difficult. At position X in the ducts you'll find ammo, a first aid, and flame thrower fuel. You can return to this spot to collect it every time you return to the ducts from another room. The Medic Bay is in door G.

★ **READY AND WAITING:** Time for your first experience with a mother

Alien 3

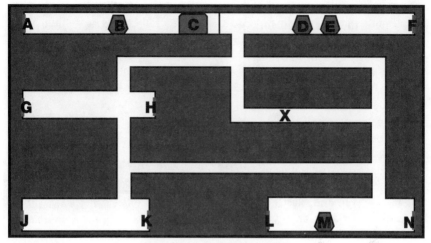

STAGE 3 AIR DUCTS MAP
Terminal is located at position C.
DOOR A <> Surface 6
DOOR B <> Cell Block 6 <> **DOOR E**
DOOR D <> Bugwash 14
DOOR F <> Surface 2 <> Alien 3 <> **DOOR N**
DOOR G <> Medic Bay 5
DOOR H <> Weapons Area 11
DOOR J <> Alien 4 <> Mine 3 <> **DOOR M**
DOOR K <> Assembly Hall 7 <> **DOOR L**

alien. She's very cool looking, so it's worth the trouble to hunt her down. She's located in Surface Area #6 (Door A), which is handy since it's near the terminal. Destroy the eggs with short bursts from your flame thrower, then continue left past the ladder to destroy more eggs. The doberman-sized aliens will slide onto the screen from both sides and above, so be prepared to blast them with a grenade or two. When you reach the next thick wall in the foreground stop (the mother alien is another step forward). Go back and climb the ladder to find more flame thrower fuel. Go

The mother alien looks very cool, but her breath is deadly.

Alien 3

back down and to the left to fight the mother alien. The mother alien leaps from wall to wall, breathing a deadly gas that floats towards you. Stay near the thick wall in the foreground. You'll be safe to the right of the wall. Peek in and watch for the mother alien to get near the right wall or floor, then step in and blast her with the flame thrower (hold it as long as you

Above the first mother alien is a first aid and flame fuel, guarded by two large aliens.

can). Quickly step back out of the area to avoid her breath, then repeat until you've destroyed her. Repair the Junction Box with your torch. If you climb to the top and go to the far left you'll find ammo, a first aid, and flame thrower fuel, guarded by two large aliens.

★ **OPERATION RESCUE:** Rescue four prisoners in Cell Block #6 (door B) and three in Assembly Hall #7 (door L). Try to pay close attention to the patterns of aliens in Cell Block #6, since you'll be passing through this area *very* often to get back to the terminal. Watch out for dripping slime on the platforms along the right side. If you're low on energy, make a run for the Medic Bay (door G) before going to the Assembly Hall. Watch for dripping slime in the Assembly Hall. When you finish with the Assembly Hall, you'll have to go back through Cell Block #6 (door E) and come out at door B to get to the terminal.

★ **SLAUGHTER 'EM HIGH:**
Six more eggs to crack in Surface Area #7 (door F), which are protected by a mother alien you must also crack. Go through door B to come out at door E, right next to F. Make a detour to the Medic Bay (door G) or Weapons Room (door H) if you're low on either. In the Surface Area climb the first ladder, go right and drop to the bottom

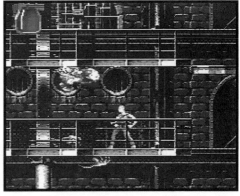

You'll have to pass through Cell Block #6 for nearly every mission.

floor to meet up with the mother alien. Use the same technique as on the first mission, ducking out of the area to avoid her deadly breath. Go back to the moving platforms and climb up and right to find the area with the eggs. Blast them all with the flame thrower, then head back to the terminal.

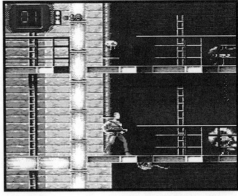

Neptune: When at an item to weld, use your grenade launcher on any nearby aliens first.

★ **OPERATION NEPTUNE:** Go to Mine Area #3 (door M) and repair four pipes. This area has plenty of first aid kits, so energy shouldn't be a problem. Remember if you have 100% energy, don't grab a first aid kit. If you leave it, you can rush back to it if you get into trouble.

★ **SYSTEM FAILURE:** Fix three fuse boxes in Medic Bay #5 (door G), and four more in Bugwash #14 (door D). If you have plenty of energy, save the trip to the Medic Bay for last. Use the grenade launcher to knock out the doberman-sized aliens before beginning to weld a fuse box. The mission description failed to mention a huge mother alien in Bugwash #14 (same size as the last, but a bit tougher to kill). She's to the far right, and guards one of the fuse boxes you need to fix. Also keep an eye out for dripping toxic slime in this area – its red color makes it tough to spot against the background colors. The Medic Bay is a little less challenging, especially with so many first aid kits around.

★ **DOWN TOWN:** Secure Alien Corridors #3 and #4 by welding the doors shut to the far right side of each corridor (leading to Surface Area #7 and Mine Area #3). First go to Alien Corridor #3 (door N) and blast your way through to the far right. Seal the door with the flame thrower, then blast your way back out of this area. My next stop was the Medic Bay (door G), but if you have

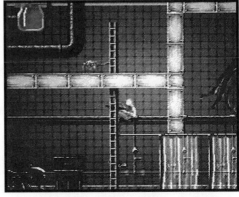

System Failure: The red slime dripping in the Bugwash is tough to see.

Alien 3

enough energy you can proceed directly to Alien Corridor #4 (door J). Blast through all the way to the right again and seal the door, then blast back out.

Stage 4

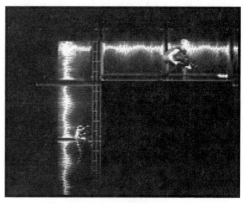

The overly-friendly face huggers now crawl up the ladders!

★ The aliens are tougher and in higher population, but the worse new feature is multiple aliens on each floor (prior stages had one type per floor). You'll be spending more time crawling through the air ducts to get from door to door, and now the face huggers can crawl up and down ladders (up to now they could only crawl horizontally).

★ **MACHINE MANIA:** Fix five fuse boxes in Waste Area #11 (door B). At the bottom right of this area you'll find several eggs to crack. Other than that, it's more of the same stuff you've experienced up to now, but a little tougher. Since you should have full energy when you get here (assuming it's the first mission you tackle), run up the ramp and fix the fuse boxes on the right side of this area, then return to the left

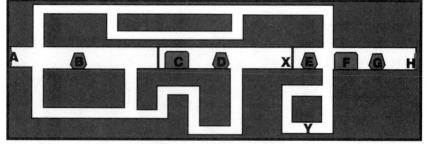

STAGE 4 AIR DUCTS MAP
Terminal is located at position C.
DOOR A <> Mine 18
DOOR B <> Waste 11
DOOR D <> Assembly Room <> Bugwash <> Medic Bay <>
<> Weapons Room <> **DOOR E**
DOOR G <> Cell Block 10
DOOR H <> Alien 5 <> Surface 2

(across the hanging bars on the ceiling) to fix the last fuse box and find two first aid kits.

★ **FREE AND FRY:** Free the prisoners in Cell Block #10 (door G) and destroy any eggs found along the way. The bottom floor is covered with eggs, with plenty of face huggers jumping from the ceilings. Walk low to the ground and blast them with your pulse gun and flame

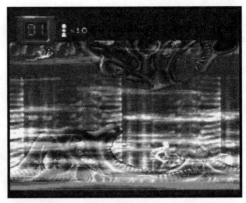

Walk low to the ground and use short blasts to destroy any hidden aliens.

thrower. There are two first aids at the left side of the third floor, which you'll reach about halfway through this battle.

★ **SUPER SEARCH:** Get the Ignition Unit from Mine Area #18 (door A) and take it to the Generator in Weapons Room #14 (door E). The Mine Area is mostly face huggers, with a few eggs to destroy. There are also a few blown fuse boxes. In the weapons room you'll find the Generator just a few steps from the door. If you have energy to spare, collect a few weapon power-ups before heading back to the terminal.

★ **ELECTRIC STORM:** Repair four Junction Boxes in Assembly Hall #4 (door D). This is about the longest trip you'll have to make, through the top air ducts to the far left, then back through the bottom air ducts to the far right. The doberman-sized aliens are your biggest threat in the Assembly Hall, but beware of ladder-climbing face huggers throughout. At the bot-

tom-left corner of this area are three first aid kits, and four ammo units. An **invisible ladder** is on the left wall above the area with the items.

★ **SALVAGE AND SCORCH:** Go to Surface Area #2 (through Alien Corridor #5/door H) and pick up a power pack, then take it to the Generator in Assembly Hall #4 (door D). The trip to Surface

Electric Storm: Climb down this invisible ladder to reach the valuable items below.

Alien 3

Area #2 is a long one, through both sets of air ducts. Stop in the lower duct at the far right to find the items at location Y. When you reach the Surface Area, go to the far left and climb. As you walk up the ramp, jump to the left to reach the next floor up. To the left of this ledge is the power pack and a couple of power ups. Climb to the top floor and go to the far left to find four more first aid kits, if you need them, then head to the Generator, which is located just a few steps inside the Assembly Hall.

★ **FIT TO BURST:** Repair four pipes in Bugwash #19. To get to Bugwash #19 you must go through Assembly Hall #4 (door D). The Bugwash is jam-packed with face huggers. You'll need to use nearly all of your weapons to survive. Also watch for dripping slime. Don't forget the hidden area in the Assembly Hall, mentioned in the last two missions. You can use this to power up on your way to or from the Bugwash.

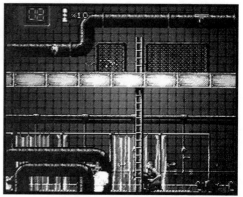

Collect lots of ammo before going into the Bugwash.

★ **HOT TOAST:** Destroy 17 (!) eggs in Medic Bay #1. There are two halves to the Medic Bay, and getting to them is difficult. Go through Assembly Hall #4 (door D) to reach the door to Bugwash #19, then go to the far right to reach the door to the left side of the Medic Bay. In this half you'll find two first aid kits in the top-left area and another four to the right. Go back through the last two areas

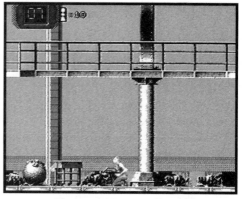

There are 17 eggs to destroy in the "Hot Toast" mission!

to get to the air ducts, then go through Weapons Room #14 (door E) to reach the Medic Bay door at the bottom-right. There isn't much to this half of the Medic Bay, except for those pesky eggs. Make a run back to the terminal and prepare for the next mission!

Alien 3

Stage 5

★ It's a long trip to Waste Area 10, and you'll have to visit it several times during this mission.

★ **MULTI-RESCUE:** Rescue five prisoners in Assembly Hall #5 (door A) and four in Mine Area #2 (deeper through door A). To get to Mine Area #2 you have to go into Door A, then go through to Cell Block #12, then to Mine Area

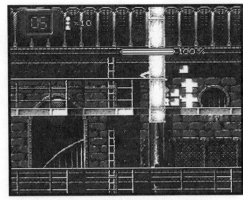

This wall in Cell Block #12 is fake, and hides four first aid kits.

#2. Check the blueprints to make yourself familiar with first aid kit locations. In Cell Block #12 there are four first aid kits located at the top-center of the room, but they're inside the wall. The wall to the left of the kits is fake – just walk through it. Another group of first aid kits (six!) is on the bottom floor below the ramp to the Mine Area door. From the top of the ramp, climb down the nearby ladder and go right through the wall, then climb down the hidden ladder against that wall

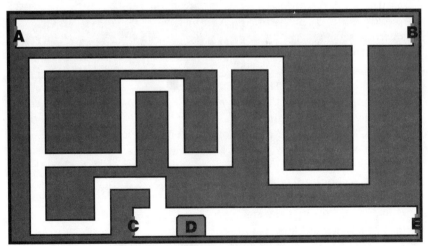

STAGE 5 AIR DUCTS MAP
Terminal is located at position D.
DOOR A <> Assembly Hall 5 <> Cell Block 12 <> Mine 2 <> Waste 10
DOOR B <> Medic Bay 15 <> Bugwash 15 <> Weapons Room 10
DOOR C <> Alien 6 <> Surface 9
DOOR E <> Furnace Area

Alien 3

to reach the first aid kits. The bottom floor of the Mine Area has many eggs, but it's nothing you can't handle by now. Rescue the prisoners (try to keep count), then return to the terminal.

★ **ELECTRO-SHOCK:** Repair six fuse boxes in Furnace Area #8 (door E), and seven in Cell Block #12 (through the Assembly Hall behind door A).

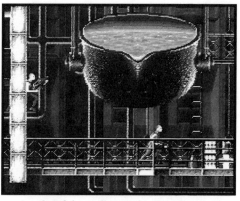

Another fake wall is in the Furnace Area, hiding several valuable items.

The hidden items above the second lava pit in the Furnace Area can be reached by jumping through the wall to the left of the items. While in the Cell Block, don't forget to grab the bountiful supply of first aid kits (see previous mission "Multi-Rescue").

★ **BURNING DESIRE:** Destroy the mother alien in Waste Area #10. The Waste Area is located as deep as you can go into

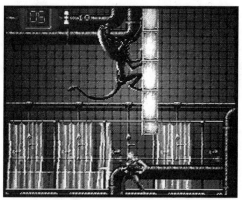

Use the blue flame thrower to quickly torch the mother alien in the Cell Block.

Door A. You'll have to pass through three other areas to reach it, and the same three areas to get back to the air ducts. Remember the first aid kits in the Cell Block (see previous missions). The blue flame thrower will quickly toast the mother alien.

★ **TIP TOE SPECIAL:** Destroy 10 eggs in Bugwash #15. The Bugwash is conveniently located through the Medic Bay (door B), where you'll find seven first aid kits. The bugwash has red slime dripping from the pipes, so watch your step. There are also a few pipes to repair in this area, which will save you some trouble later. To the far left is a large mother alien, which you can toast quickly with the red flame thrower. She guards the door to the Weapons Room, which will probably be a necessary place to visit during this stage.

★ **HUNT HIGH AND LOW:** Get the Power Pack from Surface Area #9 (through Alien Corridor 6/door C) and place it in the Generator in Medic Bay #15 (door B). You'll have to blow through about a dozen eggs to get to the Power Pack, but there's a few power-ups and first aid kits along the way. The toughest part is jumping across the moving platforms to reach the far right side of the second floor, then making more daring leaps to reach the far left side with the Power Pack. One fall can land you back on the ground floor ready for another attempt. It's times like this that you should remember one important fact: there is *no* time limit! Take your time and make your jumps carefully. Once you get the pack you must travel back to the air ducts, then through to the Medic Bay (filled with plenty of first

Jumping across these moving platforms is the toughest part of this mission.

The Generator is in the bottom-right corner of the Medic Bay.

aid kits). The Generator is in the bottom-right corner of the room.

★ **AMP CRAMP:** Repair the Junction Box in Weapons Room #10 (deep in door B). To reach the Weapons Room you must go into door B and go through the Medic Bay and Bugwash. At least there are plenty of first aid kits and weapon power-ups on the way! If you grab first aid kits on the way to the Weapons Room, you can grab them again on the way back to the terminal. The Junction Box is on the top floor of the Weapons Room, guarded by doberman-sized aliens.

Stage 6

★ You'll have to destroy a bunch of eggs just to get to the terminal. Only six more missions and you'll get to see the ending, but it ain't gonna

Alien 3

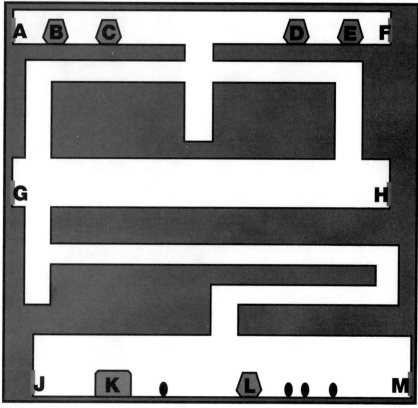

STAGE 6 AIR DUCTS MAP
Terminal is located at position K.
DOOR A <> Weapons Room 20
DOOR B <> Furnace Area (left side)
DOOR C <> Alien 7 <> **DOOR D**
DOOR E <> Furnace Area (right side)
DOOR F <> Assembly Hall 10
DOOR G <> Waste Area 15
DOOR H <> Hangar Bay 2
DOOR J <> Alien 8 <> Mine 5 <> Surface 10 <> **DOOR L**
DOOR M <> Medic Bay 12

be easy! The map is complicated (at least you can refer to it here), and the aliens are very tough. You may want to visit the Weapons Room before *and* after each mission to build up your ammo as much as possible – you'll need it! Use the flame thrower on anything bigger than Ripley, and remember where the Medic Bay is located.

★ **BLACK OUT:** Repair five junction boxes in Furnace Area #1. The Furnace Area is split in two by a solid beam. There are no junction

Alien 3

boxes in the left side, so go to door E to enter the right side. Watch for dripping slime in the top-left area of the room. You can reach the items hidden in the wall by jumping through the fake wall to the left of the items.

★ **RAPID RESCUE:** Release four prisoners in Assembly Hall #10 (door F) and three in Waste Area #15 (door G). The Assembly Hall is a bit tricky,

Rapid Rescue: Jump against the left wall to land on the platforms below to the right.

because you must use the slow elevator along the right wall to reach the different floors. The good news is there's only a small population of aliens. Once you reach the top, go to the far left and jump against the wall to land on the floor below. Go down each floor one by one while searching for prisoners. If you miss a floor you'll need to go back up the elevator and try again.

★ **SECURE AND TORCH:** Destroy all 11 eggs in Alien Corridor #7 and seal the door at the far right of the corridor. If you enter through door D, you can seal the door right away and then plow through the eggs to reach door C. Otherwise, you'll have to backtrack through the corridor after sealing the door, risking attack by several face huggers.

★ **SMASH AND GRAB:** Get the Ignition Unit from Hangar Bay #2 (door H) and take it to the Generator in Furnace Area #1, right side (door E). The Ignition Unit is in the bottom-right corner of the Hangar Bay (it's blue). The Generator is in the top-center area of the room in the Furnace Area. Directly below it is the hidden power-ups and two first aid kits, which you can access by jumping through the fake wall to the left of the kits.

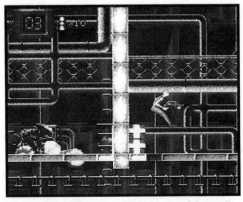

★ **CONFUSED:** Repair five fuse boxes in Mine Area #5 (through Alien Corri-

Don't forget to jump through this fake wall for goodies in the Furnace Area.

Alien 3

dor #8/Door J). At the far right side of the Mine Area there's a wall you can jump through while standing on the bottom-left elevator. Inside is a first aid kit and ammo.

★ **RED HOT:** Destroy the Mother Alien in Surface Area #10 (of course!). The easiest path to Surface Area #10 is through door L, but there are more power-ups if you take the other path, through door J (Alien Corridor #8), then through the Mine Area. Stick to the floor if you enter from the left door. The Mother Alien is about three screens over to the right. She's no tougher than the past mothers (at least she doesn't seem to be). Return to the terminal and enjoy the ending sequence, which ain't bad. You'll also get a password that lets you view the ending as often as you want. Check out the nicknames on the programming team!

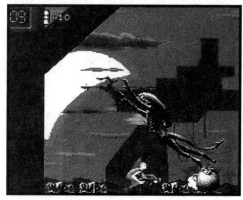

Destroy the final Mother Alien and you'll be treated to a fairly cool ending sequence.

Awesome Secrets!

★ **PASSWORDS:** Mission 2: QUESTION; Mission 2: MASTERED; Mission 3: MOTORWAY; Mission 5: CABINETS; Mission 6: SQUIRREL; Ending Sequence (Resist! You must resist!): OVERGAME

★ **INVINCIBILITY AND OTHER CHEATS:** Press A, B, Y, X on Controller 2, then press A to turn invincibility on and off; press B to turn damage on and off; press X for unlimited weapon ammunition.

BATTLETOADS IN "BATTLEMANIACS"

BY TRADEWEST

Introduction

So you thought the original NES version of Battletoads was tough? This version's even tougher, probably to make up for the fact that there are only six levels, whereas the NES and Genesis versions had 12 levels. (There are two bonus stages where you can build up much-needed extra lives, but they aren't "true" levels.) The graphics in Battletoads are

Even the bonus stages in Battletoads are incredibly tough.

outstanding—way better than the Genesis version—and the game-play is great, too. So you think you're a game master? Take on Battletoads!

Awesome Strategies

★ In two-player mode, each player should cover one half of the screen and stay away from the other Toad, since you can hit and hurt each other (in Mode A). In desperate situations, you can pick up your fellow 'Toad and use him as a weapon, but he'll take damage.

★ Battletoads is a very reflex-intensive game that requires a lot of memorization, so even with the strategies in this chapter, don't expect to win easily. We highly suggest you use

There are two two-player modes: Choose Mode B for an easier time.

Battletoads in "Battlemaniacs"

the secret code at the end of the chapter to give yourself five lives and five continues (25 lives total), because you'll need all the help you can get.

Level 1: Khaos Mountains

★ The double punch is the most potent attack against the attacking Psyko-Pigs. Try to position yourself between two oncoming enemies and smack them both with a single blow.

★ Twice in this level, active volcanoes in the background start erupting and spewing fireballs at you. Watch the shadows on the ground to see where the fireballs are about to hit and quickly move away.

★ Another danger that appears twice in this level are the burning bridges. When you reach a bridge, run across it without stopping and jump over the enemy guard at the end before he leaps and knocks you into the lava.

★ About halfway through the Canyon, stronger purple Psyko-Pigs start attacking you. The best strategy against a purple Pig is to knock him to the ground, then keep kicking him so that he can't get up.

The double punch is your best attack. Use it as much as possible.

★ The boss at the end of the Mountains is a giant stone Psyko-Pig that jumps into the air and tries to crush you as he lands. The stone Pig stops moving for a moment after he lands, so run and head-butt the Pig two or three times to cause damage. If the stone Pig moves off the left side of the screen, stay on the far right side and watch for his shadow to appear on the ground. Keep head-butting until he blows up.

Wait for the Psyko-Pig to land and then head-butt the sucker.

Battletoads in "Battlemaniacs"

Level 2: Forest

★ The first—and most common—enemies in the tree are the robotic wasps. You can punch them or move against the wall and kick your sled across the screen to hit them. If you hit a wasp and then keep hitting its body into the air, you eventually get a 1-Up. (This is very similar to a trick in the original NES Battletoads.)

★ If you try to punch the tree snakes, they're almost guaranteed to hit you back once or twice. It's safer and smarter to kick your sled at the snakes.

Kick your sled at the Tree Snakes instead of punching them.

★ Cannons start shooting Daredevil Rats at you about halfway through the Tree. You can punch the Rats out of the air, but you'll get hit a few times, so memorize when and where the Rats shoot out at you and avoid them instead.

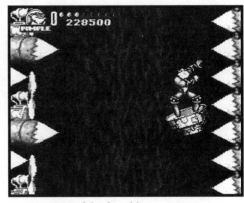

★ The last obstacles before the bottom of the tree are powerful fans. Most of the fans blow you away from them, but a few of them will suck you toward them. Stay close to the middle of the screen as you fight the wind.

Most of the fans blow you away, but a few suck you in. Watch out!

★ After you pass the fans, you start moving downward at tremendous speed. Stay at the top of the screen and away from the spikes.

Level 3: Speeder Bikes

★ There are five sections of the Turbo Tunnel, each one harder to pass than the last. Watch the right side of the screen because that's where

Battletoads in "Battlemaniacs"

the blinking walls appear. Dodge the walls by moving to the opposite side of the tunnel. When the short walls appear on the ground, jump over them, but don't jump too soon. Wait for a moment before you press the jump button.

Don't jump over the short walls too soon.

Level 4: Karnath's Revenge

★ There are four pits in this level. The first pit is just a warm-up, with only a few snakes and no spikes to avoid. The spikes appear for the first time in the second pit, and they're deadly; one touch and you lose a life. Always stay near the back of a snake, and let it crawl ahead of you and move through any spikes in the way.

Let the snakes crawl ahead of you and move through the spikes.

Level 5: Tracktors

★ This level is a long race against a bad guy named Fuzz. You have to steer your vehicle along a road that goes in all directions: up, down, left, and right. Fuzz is slower than you taking the turns, but faster than you on the straight-aways, so you have to take the turns quickly to stay ahead. Using a joystick instead of a standard control pad might help you take the turns faster.

★ When you see a "DANGER" road sign, a low wall is about to appear on the track ahead of you. Press Down and Left or Right (depending on what direction you're driving in) to duck under the wall.

★ The "RAIL OUT" sign means that a break in the track is coming up. Jump over the break or you take a nasty fall and lose a precious life.

★ At the end of the level, you have to duck walls and jump breaks in the

Battletoads in "Battlemaniacs"

track. There's only one jump after the first wall, but two jumps after the second wall. Be ready for them!

Level 6: The Dark Tower

★ You'll race against three kangaroo Rats in the Tower, one Rat at a time, down to TNT plungers. The guy who reaches the plunger first blows up the other guy. The Rats run faster than you on the long ledges, but they fall behind in the sections of the Tower with moving ledges (the ones with holes in them). There's a trick you can use against a Rat to slow him down for

The rats run faster than you on long ledges, but they fall behind on moving ledges.

a moment. Let the Rat overtake you near the end of a long ledge, then punch him. He bounces off the wall and starts running backwards. The best time to use this trick is just before a section with moving ledges. Beat all three Rats and you'll go up against the Dark Queen.

The Dark Queen

★ There's no real pattern to the Dark Queen's movements and no safe place on the screen to avoid her. You just have to dodge her as she teleports, then dodge the mask she fires at you, then hit her before she teleports again. If the Queen is standing on one of the high ledges, stand below and slightly to the side of her, then jump and hit her. If she's standing on the ground, stand as far away from her as possible,

Dodge the Dark Queen's mask, then clobber her with your hammer-fist.

Battletoads in "Battlemaniacs"

wait for her to fire, then jump over the mask and hit her. It takes 20 to 25 hits to defeat the Queen.

Silas Volkmire

★ After you beat the Queen, Volkmire tries to escape in his spaceship and the Battletoads fly off in pursuit. When they catch up, a gun sight appears on the screen and starts moving up and down. Fire at Volkmire's ship when the sight is in the middle of the screen. It doesn't have to be exactly in the middle, just close enough to

Fire at Volkmire's ship when the sight is in the middle of the screen.

hit the ship. Score three hits and you're rewarded with one of the lamest endings in Super NES history. C'mon, Tradewest, you can do better than that!

Awesome Secrets

★ **FIVE LIVES AND FIVE CONTINUES:** Hold A, B, and Down at the title screen (with the stars in the background), and keep holding them while you press START. The Battletoads flag appears and the screen flashes red to indicate that the cheat worked. Start the game and you'll have five lives and five continues instead of three lives and three continues. That's 25 lives instead of nine!

B.O.B.

BY ELECTRONIC ARTS

Introduction

We still don't have a clue what B.O.B. stand for – it's not in the manual or the game – but regardless it's a fun platform adventure game. B.O.B. is trying to find his way off a planet he crash-landed into, and his Inspector Gadget-like body is his only weapon. There are over 45 grueling levels, each jam-packed with enemies and bosses. By collecting power-

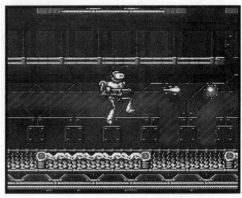

It's Inspector Gadget without the expensive licensing fees. B.O.B. is a fun platform adventure.

ups and using fast reflexes, B.O.B. can find his way off this crazy planet just in time for a date with his galactic babe. B.O.B. also features a pass-word system (three cheers for Electronic Arts!).

Awesome Strategies

★ **Controls:** Use B to jump, A to punch, X to activate current remote, and Y to shoot current gun. The L button lets you choose which weapon is active, and the R button chooses the active remote. Hold Up when jumping to grab overhead vines or poles. Press Start to see your inven-tory of weapons and remotes. Grab the 1-Up icon for an extra life, the wrenches (a red and grey icon) for energy, the flash bulb freezes all nearby enemies, and the shield icon surrounds BOB with a force field. When your time clock runs out, your energy will quickly de-plete, then you'll burst into pieces (you shouldn't let that happen).

★ Watch the background for

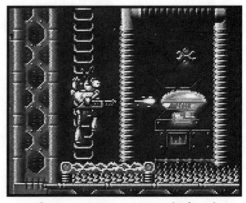

There aren't many 1-Ups to be found, but an energy icon can be just as valuable.

B.O.B.

what looks like a doorway. By pressing up you'll stand in the "recharger" and have your energy totally refilled.

★ You'll receive a **password** after every third stage you complete. Since the stages aren't labeled, we must use passwords to refer to them here in this chapter.

★ If you're having trouble staying alive, there are a few things to remember about platform games.

Stop and shoot each enemy the moment you see them, and avoid their bullets.

First, always **stop and shoot** each enemy the moment you see them. Don't walk up to them and attempt to shoot, because you risk getting hit and losing energy. You should also duck down when you stop to avoid any bullets shot your way. Second, always **look up or down** before jumping or falling. There are many lava pits and other hazards throughout this game, which you're bound to jump into if you don't look before you leap.

★ **THE WEAPONS:** Hit Start to pause the game and bring up the inventory list. The weapons are on the left side, and from the top they are: **Single Shot** – a very weak weapon, but you'll find plenty of ammo and it will pulverize any enemy...eventually; **Triple Shot** – shoots bullets out in a three-bullet spray. Great for shooting down halls where enemies hang from the ceiling; **Flame-Thrower** – Ammo is scarce, but

this powerful weapon will destroy most enemies with a quick blast; **Rocket** – these guided missiles are excellent for hitting enemies that move around too much; **Bolt** – also scarce, but it blasts through enemies with one hit. Save them for the final bosses; **Wave** – strong enough to pierce through several enemies at once.

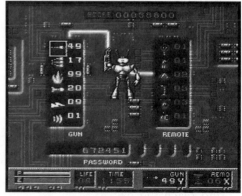

★ **THE REMOTES:** From the top, they are: **Flash** – the

Hit Start to see the inventory screen, then refer to the text at left for a description of each.

B.O.B.

brightness of this light bulb will freeze enemies in place; **Shield** – surrounds BOB with a force field for a brief amount of time; **Umbrella** – allows BOB to fall from high ledges without hitting the ground too hard (which stuns him and allows easy enemy attacks); **Trampoline** – this springboard will shoot you up about the height of one screen, but can be used rapidly to climb up to very high ledges; **Helicopter Hat** – BOB can fly up or down for a short amount of time. It's okay to hit walls, but if you hit the floor or ceiling the propeller will stop; **Floating Bomb** – activate one of these and then clear the area before it explodes.

Stage 1

★ Use **punching** on the first few levels and save your weapons for later. Be sure to grab every weapon and remote icon you see, because you can store a lot of extras. You can **walk while ducking**, which allows you to squeeze through tight spaces and search for icons.

★ **STAGE 1-2** (green blobs): From the start, jump across to the right to find a three-way weapon icon. On your way up the final side-by-side ladders, take the left corridor and shoot the crab to collect a weapon icon and energy fill up, then finish the climb up to the exit.

★ **STAGE 1-3** (second blue dome): When you reach the **elevator,** go down one floor, then duck and shoot the pod while avoiding the fireballs it spits. Go left a few steps and stand under the rocket weapon icon near the ceiling, then activate one of the springboard remotes to grab the icon. There's a recharger on the next floor down (looks like a door), which you can press Up to enter and restore your energy. If you get hit while fighting the creatures below, you can always return and recharge again.

★ Watch for an electric **forcefield across the ceiling**, and a shorter one along the floor. You're very near the end. Climb the ladder, then jump to the right wall and hold right to reach a safe ledge below. If you fall to the pit with the forcefield below, you'll have to use a springboard (quickly) to escape and reach the exit to the upper-right.

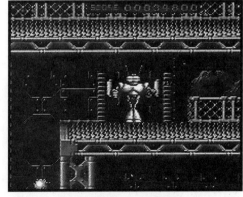

Step up into the rechargers to get your energy refilled.

B.O.B.

Stage 2 [Password=171058]

★ Just in case you missed the last message, we're using the passwords to title the stages because the stages are not labeled in the game. The only way to tell which stage you're on is by comparing the passwords.

★ **STAGE 2-1** (green blob): Jump across to the right until you see the red flame icon below. Drop to collect it and the one below it, then duck and crawl to the right. Keep going until you reach the ladder, then go down and keep leaping across to the left to find another flame icon and an energy. Keep crawling to the right, then follow the direct twisting path to the exit. Climb a ladder near the end to find energy and a weapon icon.

At the beginning of Stage 2-2, crawl through the lower path to find a 1-Up.

★ **STAGE 2-2** (blue dome): Take the lower path through the crawl space to find a 1-Up. If you lose a life, you can always return to grab the 1-Up again. After collecting the only triple-shot icon, drop down to fight a robot then go left and use springboards or helicopter hats to climb up and find a helicopter hat and flame thrower icons. Go back down and hit the exit to the right.

★ **STAGE 2-3** (green bee-hive): Head to the upper-right wall, then drop and hold up to grab a vine. Keep going left until you reach the next wall, then drop and hold up to grab another vine. The exit is below to the left.

Stage 3 [Password=950745]

★ **STAGE 3-1** (blue dome): Time for a ride! Go right and jump into the space buggy then guide BOB up and down to avoid obstacles. You must make it to the exit within one minute, which isn't too difficult on this stage. There are arrows to guide you in the right direction. Stay near the center of the hall to avoid forcefields along the ceiling and floor. Grab the energy power-ups to avoid blowing up. The bottom floor (of three) is a long hallway – race to the right.

★ **STAGE 3-2** (green blob next to green bee-hive): This is one of the larger stages. The path is very linear (only one way to go), with a few

B.O.B.

small rooms containing power-up icons. When you reach the bottom floor you'll have to jump across many small platforms to avoid lava along the floor. Always keep your trampoline remote ready to use so you can get back up to the platforms quickly if you fall.

★ **STAGE 3 BOSS:** Here's the first boss. It's a mechanical dragon head that shoots flames and rockets. It's

Jump on the ladder and fire away at the boss, but hope he runs out of energy before you do.

easiest to shoot the dragon while hanging from the ladder, but it's difficult to move quickly enough to avoid all of his shots. If you have lots of energy, go for the ladder. Otherwise, you should move to the far left and keep your defenses up (jump and duck) to avoid taking hits. Use your stronger weapons, like the Bolt, Flame Thrower, and Wave.

Stage 4 [Password=472149]

★ **STAGE 4-1** (single blue dome): After riding the elevator to the bottom and going to the right there's a long drop that will cause damage to BOB. You can waste an umbrella or helicopter hat if you want to, but if you have even a little bit of energy go for the drop and enter the Recharger to the left (looks like a doorway in the background). Grab the 1-Up to the left. When you reach the bottom-right corner of this area you'll have to use a helicopter hat to reach the exit at the top. You have to guide the copter to avoid hitting the ceiling before you land on the ledge – tap the controller lightly.

★ **STAGE 4-2** (green beehive): The deep pit along the far right wall is empty, but going down it will give you a view of an extra life.

4-2: Use your helicopter hats or trampolines to reach this 1-Up.

B.O.B.

When you get to the second crawlspace (where you have to duck and walk), go to the far right and up into the last room. You'll have to use three or four remotes (helicopter hats or trampolines) to reach it.

★ **STAGE 4-3** (two blue domes): There's a wave weapon icon near the beginning worth grabbing – you'll have to use a remote to get it. Don't miss the Recharger doorway on the second floor down, then jump from the ladder to the left to reach the time bomb icon. Grab the rocket icon left of the elevator (you'll need it for the boss).

★ **STAGE 4-4 BOSS** (green bee-hive): You'll get more rockets on the way out of the last stage and on the way into this one. Stand below the body of the boss, nearer to the head, and use the rockets to shoot into the open hatches along his body. Jump over the creatures that fall

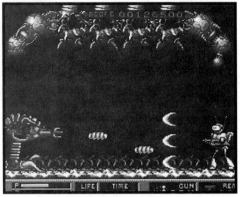

Use rockets to shoot the hatches closed, then avoid the head while blasting it.

from his tail while you're shooting the hatches. When you blow up all four hatches, the head drops off and springs to life on legs. Stay near the center of the screen and leap over the head each time it runs toward you, then quickly run to the opposite side of the screen, turn, and blast him with the most powerful weapons you have (Wave, Rockets, Lightning Bolt or Flame Thrower). Beat the boss and you'll see a short animation, which appears to be the end of the game, but...

Stage 5 [Password=572451]

★ **STAGE 5-1** (pink pyramid): With a new planet comes new (and better) graphics, as well as a host of new enemies to battle. You'll have to use your helicopter hat remote near the beginning to clear a wide lava pit. Keep your eyes peeled for small metal discs on the ground. If you step on the disc a huge steel ball will fall from above, bounce slightly to the right, then continue to fall down. Always run and jump over the activating disc to avoid being crushed.

★ **STAGE 5-2** (red dome): When you get to the bottom floor of this stage you'll walk down steps to the center, then climb up more steps to the right. Stand on the first step up and use the trampoline remote to reach a ladder above. Use trampolines or helicopter hats to reach a 1-Up in

B.O.B.

the upper left corner above. After working your way back down and heading to the right, you'll have to climb another ladder guarded by several laser cannons. You can climb this area more quickly (and safely) if you use trampoline remotes. As you fall down the next pit to the right, you'll be landing on deadly energy beams. Use a shield remote to protect yourself during the hard falls and energy beams.

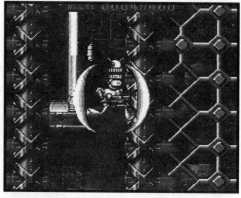

At the end of 5-2 activate a shield to protect yourself from hard falls and energy beams.

★ **STAGE 5-3** (big lava pit): As expected from the representation of this stage on the map, there's a lot of lava. Watch for collapsing blocks near the beginning, and throughout the rest of the stage. Jump across them quickly to avoid falling into the lava with them. After climbing up the first area you'll find a ladder on the right wall. Climb up the ladder past the first floor and up to the top floor (as high as you can climb). The floor below has a Single Shot weapon icon and an energy icon, but there are many dangerous obstacles in the way.

Stage 6 [Password=272578]

★ **STAGE 6-1** (pink pyramid): You'll have to climb out of the top of a pyramid, then find the exit in the huge top chamber. From the top of the pyramid, go right and use helicopter hats to reach the top (there are plenty of copter icons to grab). At the top, go left, but when you drop off hold right to enter the center of the chamber. If you need an energy icon, there is one just a little ways down the left pit, but be ready to use a helicopter hat to get

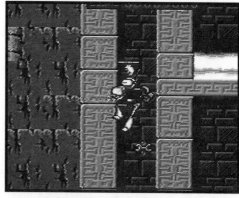

Use a helicopter hat to grab this energy icon in the left pit of the top chamber.

B.O.B.

back up. At the bottom of the pit is lava and a triple-shot icon, but you can collect two icons in the main chamber on the way to the exit. The exit is at the bottom-right – use helicopter hats to safely get around the lava pools. There's an energy icon above the exit.

★ **STAGE 6-2** (red dome): From the beginning, go right. The yellow and black steps will explode when you step on them, so get off of them quickly. Also keep firing rapidly to the right to destroy the incoming missiles. Go up and left, then up to the top. Go right and grab the energy, then down as far as you can go. Go right and shoot the red robot, then down the next ladder to the bottom. Go down the ladder to the left and climb across to the right using the ladders. You may want to have your shield remote ready to activate. The path to the exit is straightforward from here.

★ **STAGE 6-3** (big lava pit): Use an umbrella remote to go down into the first pit, and hold right at the end to avoid falling into the lava at the bottom. At the top of the next area is a triple shot, which requires the use of a trampoline or

End of 6-3: You almost always need to use a Trampoline Remote wherever you find it.

helicopter hat to reach. Watch for small collapsing steps in the next area. At the bottom-right you'll have to climb across five cyclops heads spewing lava, then use three trampoline remotes to reach the top-right area and the exit.

Stage 7 [Password=652074]

★ **STAGE 7-1** (red dome): Take the elevator down and go all the way to the right, then go back to the ladder second from the far left and climb up. Go right and down, then look down to see a 1-Up worth grabbing. Just hold left to grab the 1-Up, then hold up to grab the ladder below it. Quickly climb down the ladder to avoid getting burned. Climb back up to the right to find the passage leading to the top of this area, then head to the lower-right to find the exit.

★ **STAGE 7-2** (floating pink pyramid): The first area of this stage is a maze filled with a few goodies. Grab the Single Shot icon on the way down the first ladder, then use your helicopter hat or trampoline

B.O.B.

remotes to enter any of the upper rooms. The first room has a trampoline icon (it will take you two to gain an icon that gives you three, so it's worth doing). The second room leads up to an energy icon. The last three rooms are empty, but go all the way right to find the ladder to the next area. On the way up is a crawl space with two Triple Shots and a helicopter hat.

Sometimes you can't avoid hitting a trigger, but you can quickly move to avoid the ball!

Go back to the left, up, then right to head toward the exit. You'll have to use a helicopter hat to clear the lava, then jump across ladders to avoid more lava. Jump to the top block, then hold right to fall to the lower right block. Climb halfway up the ladder and jump right to the lower block, then jump across to the lower block on the right and quickly move off of it to avoid the large silver ball. When you reach the ladder against the far right wall, climb up to grab a Bolt icon, then go all the way down and right to find an energy and shield icon. Go left, down, then right to find the exit (left is a dead end). When you find the trampoline icon, use it or the helicopter hat remote to get up to the exit.

★ **STAGE 7-3** (no landmark on map): Hop across to the right to grab a helicopter hat icon, then go back and up through the passage above with a copter or trampoline icon. You must climb all the way to the ceiling, which may require a combination of several trampolines or copters. Go to the far right and use an umbrella to reach the bottom floor. Hop across all the way to the right and climb up the ladder. Hop across all the way to the left and use trampolines or copters to reach the ladders above. Go to the far

To reach the ceiling you might need to use a combination of helicopter hats and trampolines.

B.O.B.

right and down, then hop across to the far right and activate a shield, then drop off to the right and keep dropping until you reach the bottom floor. Go to the far right and use trampolines to reach the exit at the top.

Stage 8 [Password=265648]

★ **STAGE 8-1** (red dome): Oh no, it's another wild ride in the BOB-mobile. The clock starts at the beginning of the of the stage, so don't waste any time getting to the vehicle. Go right and all the way down, then all the way right, then all the way up, then follow the path. The next choices are in a corridor that scrolls to the left. Go all the way left, then back up to the last passage down and take it to the bottom. Follow the passage all the way to the end (there are only a few minor dead ends).

★ **STAGE 8-2** (obelisk with ball spinning around): Go down the first ladder then left to the next ladder. Climb down to the Three Shot icon, then go back to the first ladder and continue climbing down to the bottom. Go all the way to the right and use and umbrella to go down. Follow either path at the bottom to the exit above.

★ **STAGE 8-3 BOSS** (pink factory): Whenever you find this many weapons in one place, you know you're in trouble. The boss is a monster that attacks with his tongue while crawling across a ledge above. Shoot him with your strongest weapons (Wave or Bolt). Save any Rockets you have for the second part of the attack. He moves randomly a few steps, then stops for a second. That's the moment to shoot him – before he drops his tongue. Shoot, then move out of the way. After a few shots he'll drop to the ground, and look defeated, but then he jumps back up to his feet and begins phase two of his attack. He leaps in a high arc back and forth across the screen, and shoots two small sparks that probably won't hit you unless he's on you. During this phase use your shields and rockets. If you rapidly shoot him, you should beat him before needing to activate a third shield.

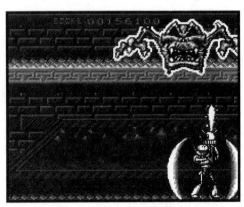

During the second phase of the boss's attack shoot rapid rockets and use a shield.

B.O.B.

Stage 9 [Password=462893]

★ **STAGE 9-1** (two red domes): Go all the way to the right as far as you can go, then go down the ladder. Go left two ladders, climb down and go to the right to the next ladder. Climb across the ceiling to the right and drop down on the third ladder from the left. Drop off the bottom of the ladder and hold up to grab the girder below. Go all the way to the left and climb up the ladders. Climb across the platforms to the far left and get the rocket icon from the top-left corner. Climb all the way down the ladder, then go right and jump across the collapsing platforms. The exit is below.

★ **STAGE 9-2** (bouncing pyramid): Go down the ladder and go to the right, then climb the next ladder and go right. Climb down and go right until you come to the triple-shot and energy icons. Go left until you get the trampoline icon, then climb up the ladder and jump across to the left. Fall down to grab the energy icon and hold up to grab the pipe, then go to the far left and climb down to get helicopter hat. Go to the next ladder to the right and climb across the ladders to the right. Keep going right to find the exit.

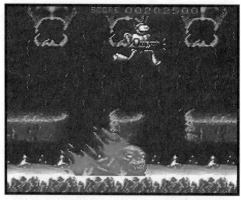

Watch for the back of the boss to pop up, then jump in the direction the flames point...

★ **STAGE 9-3 BOSS** (volcano): Have a copter or trampoline remote ready in case you fall off of a platform. Go to the far right to meet the boss. He looks similar to the lava creatures that pop up throughout the other stages, only this guy is much bigger. Select your strongest weapon for this battle. Before the boss pops up he'll expose a bit of his back. Stand on the center platform and watch

...shoot him rapidly with your strongest weapon (wave, rocket, triple-shot).

B.O.B.

for him, then jump to the left or right, attempting to end up safely behind him rather than in front of him. The flames on his back point in the direction you should jump. He spits a Triple Shot of fireballs, which are very hard to jump over or avoid. If you have a shield, save it until you're almost out of energy, then use it and attack him quickly before it runs out.

Stage 10 [Password=583172]

★ **STAGE 10-1** (two red domes): Go to the right and climb up the right side ladder. You'll need a trampoline to reach the gap between the ladders. When you reach the second gap, get off the ladder and fight the laser cannon, then continue climbing up as high as you can. Work your way to the left wall, then fall off and hold up to grab the poles on the way down. Keep falling down from each pole until you reach the exit at the bottom.

★ **STAGE 10-2** (pyramid with lightning): Watch for red Mr. Potato Heads as you head to the right. Jump up the steps that lead to the upper-left, then keep going left until you reach the middle of the pyramid (there's a pyramid window in the background). There are icons along the ceiling worth collecting, then head to the right across the small ladders over the lava. In the next area you'll collect a lot of trampolines while jumping over small lava pits. Keep going right until you hit the far right wall. Use the trampolines to get up to the next floor, then use a few more to reach the next floor up. Climb up and fight the Mr. Potato Head to the right for a Bolt icon, then go to the far left (planets float by) and go down the first hole. Go right and keep following the somewhat linear path to the exit.

★ **STAGE 10-3 BOSS** (one red dome): This is the final boss of this planet, but you still have an entire final planet to conquer. Walk to the right and shoot the robot. The background will lift and the insect-like boss will attack. Use a strong weapon to destroy his hands quickly before they smash you, then activate a shield and attack his head from below. Once

Destroy the boss's hands quickly before they grab you, then use a shield and attack from below.

B.O.B.

you knock his head off, it will come off and bounce from side to side like a ball. The stronger the weapon you shoot it with, the shorter the battle will last. You'll be treated to a short animation when you conquer him.

Stage 11 [Password=743690]

★ **STAGE 11-1** (red crater): Be careful when you go to grab the first Wave weapon icon. The machine blowing bubbles will blow you all the way to the farthest wall. There are more of these throughout this stage that sometimes help and sometimes hurt. Go down and left to grab a time bomb, then go right and up to find an energy icon. Go all the way back down, right, down, then all the way left to find a shield icon. Punch while crawling to the right, then go down and left. When you reach the left wall, jump toward it and use a trampoline to reach a 1-Up in the top-left corner. Use the umbrella to go down. Go right and jump into the air stream, then go right and up (using trampolines). Go all the way right and jump around until a bubble appears and lifts you to the exit.

Stage 11-1: Use a trampoline to reach this 1-Up in the upper-left corner.

★ **STAGE 11-2** (blue dome): This stage has fewer threats to BOB, and there are lots of useful weapons to find along the way. Save a few trampolines and/or helicopter hats for a climb near the exit (there's one trampoline icon at the bottom of the climb). When you reach the top, you may want to spend a flash or shield remote while running to the right. An umbrella

Save trampolines and/or helicopter hats for the final climb to the exit.

B.O.B.

icon is immediately before the final descent to the exit. Use it and guide yourself down the center.

★ **STAGE 11-3** (forest): The graphics change rather dramatically, but the gameplay is the same. Climb up to the highest point you can, then go right to find an umbrella. Use the umbrella to float down to the first ledge on the left. Fall off and use another umbrella to hit either of the next two holes on the left. The exit is directly below.

Stage 12 [Password=103928]

★ **STAGE 12-1** (two large blobs): Go right and climb up for a Rocket. Go down as far as you can, then go left and up to find a trampoline icon. Go up and right until you find a moving platform that resembles a roach. Before the second roach platform, jump and use remotes to climb up, then go left as far as you can. The exit is above.

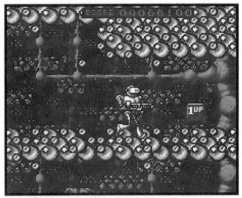

Stage 12-2: A 1-Up is up for grabs in the far upper-right corner of this area.

★ **STAGE 12-2** (big forest): Go right and climb up the steps, shooting the BOB-eating plants as you climb. The area to the left has a few valuable weapon and remote icons, and a few energy icons, so feel free to explore. When you get over the stone steps and into the area to the right of them, head for the upper-right corner to find a 1-Up. The exit is directly below, but you have to head down a ways to enter the maze that leads up to it.

★ **STAGE 12-3 BOSS** (two blobs): An evil skeleton attacks with punches and

Ten skeletons will attack, each leaving behind their heads, then the heads attack. Use rockets!

jumping. When you blow him up, another skeleton appears to fight. This repeats 10 times, then all of the skeleton heads laying on the ground start bouncing from side to side. As you blow up each skeleton, an icon for a weapon or remote will appear when the next skeleton appears. Always try to grab it, and keep switching to your most powerful weapon so you can destroy the skeletons quickly. Save all of your rockets for the attack of the heads. Also try to save your shields for when the heads attack.

Stage 13 [Password=144895]

★ **STAGE 13-1** (blue towers with dome): Time for the next Mr. BOB's Wild Ride. Rush to the left to find the spaceship below, then go to the right. There's only one passage you can take until you go up and face left. Take the last passage down, then at the next junction take the lower path. You'll probably run out of time, but an energy icon near the end will keep you alive for a few seconds until you reach the exit.

★ **STAGE 13-2** (really big forest): Climb the steps leading up to the right, and keep climbing toward the upper-right corner of the forest to find the exit. The biggest threat along the way are the exploding plants. Use a shield if you have one, or shoot up with a Three-Shot weapon. When you reach the far right wall, go to the left a few steps and use the trampoline to get up into the limbs above, and the exit.

★ **STAGE 13-3** (big red blob): Go to the right and jump into the airstream. When you land, crawl right. Use an umbrella to float down, then go left at the bottom. Activate a shield to avoid the lava pits, then keep going left and down. When you reach the bottom floor, go left and watch for a blue hole on the floor. Jump up and down to get inside a bubble, then tap left as you float up to the top. Climb up using remotes and go left, then jump to the left wall and back to the rocket icon. Go right and down to the ladders, then climb down and left to find a passage below. Crawl through the passage to the right and follow it to find a trampoline icon. Use it to go up and left, then use another to go up to the exit.

Watch for a blue hole on the floor, then jump into the bubble for a ride upward.

B.O.B.

Stage 14 [Password=775092]

★ **STAGE 14-1** (blue towers and dome): Go left and climb up the ladder, then go right and down the next ladder for a rocket icon to the left. Go back up and right to the far right ladder and go down. Go right and up the next ladder, then right. Keep following the only path there is, covered wall-to-wall with lots of enemies. Near the end you'll come across five ladders in a row leading up. Go up the last ladder (far left) and go left, then use trampolines to climb up. Go right to the exit.

★ **STAGE 14-2** (red mushroom blob with three blobettes): Go left and climb up to the ceiling, then go to the right to collect an umbrella. Jump back up to the ceiling and go left all the way. Use an umbrella to float down to the bottom floor, then go left and climb up the ladder to the very top. Go to the right and climb up the next ladder. Go right and climb all the way up for an energy icon. Go to the right on the top floor to the next ladder, then grab the pipe and climb across to the right. Go down the ladder and up to the top in the next room to find a trampoline. Use the trampoline to go over to the right, then continue going right and down. Go left to find another energy icon, then go down and right for another trampoline. Climb up the ladder and use the bubble to reach the top floor. Go left and follow the path.

★ **STAGE 14-3 BOSS** (bigger red mushroom blob and blobettes): The boss is a slightly decomposed skeleton (he still has a few internal organs intact). He'll hover mostly along the ceiling while shooting down missiles and blobs. Grab the triple-shot icons and use them to shoot up at him. It's important to shoot diagonally up at him as he moves across the screen so you can get

Using diagonal shots is extremely effective in destroying this boss quickly.

enough hits in before he drops too much stuff on you. When his energy runs out his body explodes and his head remains. Mouths appear in random locations across the screen and vomit a green liquid. Activate a shield and keep moving away from the mouths as they appear, then shoot or jump and punch the skull. Use your strongest weapons first so you can end the battle as quickly as possible.

Stage 15 [Password=481376]

★ **STAGE 15-1** (two blue domes with three towers): Go left and use an umbrella to float down to the first passage on the right. Enter the spaceship and prepare for your final wild ride. Go all the way down and right, then take the next passage down and the first passage to the right. Go down and all the way right and up the steps. Take the first passage to the right and follow it down, right, up, and left. Take the small upper passage and go up, then take the lower of the three small passages to the left. Take the first up, then go all the way up to the ceiling and go right. Keep following the passage and skip the first left to take the lower left. At the next junctions leading right, go up to the third passage and go right to find an energy icon below. Go back to the left one passage and go down to the next right. At the next junction, go up and work your way through the maze (stick mostly to the right when given a choice). From the top, go right and down to the sixth passage to the left (directly below the double passage to the left). The exit is a few screens ahead.

★ **STAGE 15-2** (two blue domes and two towers): Hop across to the far right and go down. Go right and up, then right across the ceiling to find an energy icon. Go left along the floor and down, then left again. Use trampolines to go up and grab a 1-Up, then go all the way to the right and use trampolines to reach the top. Go right and down the ladder, then up the next ladder and climb across the ceiling. Drop down to the bottom floor and go right, then drop and go right again. Get the energy icon below to the left, then crawl right and follow the path to the flame thrower. Go all the way left as far as you can until you see an umbrella icon in a passage above. Use trampolines to shoot up into the passage twice and grab an energy icon and flash weapon. Drop back down and go left to the end of the hall, then jump and use an umbrella to float down to the bottom. Go right to the second ladder and climb up to grab a Three-Shot icon. Go right to the next ladder and climb up, then go right all the way and back down. Go right and up the next ladder, then right

Trampolines are the key (once again) to collecting this 1-Up on Stage 15-2.

B.O.B.

to find a rocket icon. Keep going right and down, then left to the exit.

★ **STAGE 15-3** (large red mushroom blob with blobettes): Jump up to the first ladder and climb up to the right for a shield, then go to the left for a Three-Shot. Climb up to the top and go right, then climb the first ladder and jump into the airstream to be pushed to an energy icon at the far right. Go back to the same ladder and climb past the airstream, then jump to the upper-left ledge and climb. Keep climbing upward and watch for a big bubble to jump into. Ride it up and go left, then climb down the ladder to find a helicopter hat and rocket. Go back up the ladder and use the helicopter hat near the left wall, go up and right with the copter. Use another copter to go up and left for single-shot and helicopter hat icons, then go right and use another copter to go right and up (above the air stream). Go down the next ladder to the right, then climb up the ladders to the right corner for a Flash icon. Go down and left on the ladders to find a shield and single-shot icon. Go right and drop, holding up to grab a rope, then go left and drop again, holding up to grab another rope. Go right and hit the airstream, and let the airstreams blow you in about 10 different directions until you've hit the last one. There are a lot of enemies through the final air stream, so you may want to activate a shield if you have one. Go to the upper-left corner for a Three-Shot, then drop down and hold up to grab a rope. Drop to the right and go right as far as you can. Jump into the bubble and go up to grab a shield, then continue up and right through the steps, then left at the

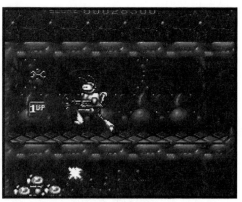

This ledge in the upper-left corner has a valuable 1-Up and energy icon.

top to reach a ledge. Go left and jump across the collapsing platforms, then go up the ladder and use a remote to reach the upper-left ledge (1-Up and energy icons). Go back down the ladder and jump across to the left. Use a copter to get over the lava pit, then ride a bubble to the left corner for an energy icon. Go back up to the right ledge and grab the umbrella and trampoline icons. Go down and right for an energy. Drop down and climb the ladder for the exit.

STAGE 15-4 THE FINAL BOSS! The key to success is staying alive. Seems obvious, and you've already had some experience with that

B.O.B.

way of thinking on the last few bosses. At the beginning of the battle, move to the far left and jump while shooting to the right. When the boss appears spinning at the top of the screen, move underneath him, activate a shield, and shoot straight up with a powerful weapon. Keep firing rapidly as he moves around the screen. When his energy hits zero, he'll recharge a bit of his energy and go ballistic. Grab the icons that appear (especially energy and shields), then activate another shield and keep shooting. When his energy is totally exhausted he'll fall to the ground. But then he vibrates a bit and eventually rises to the top of the screen in the form of a three-armed octopus (tripus?). Grab the icons that appear, activate a shield, then

When the boss appears, stand beneath him and shoot straight up with a powerful weapon.

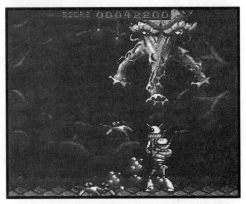

During the bosses final phase, use a shield and stand at the center. Shoot each time the boss hits the center of the screen.

stand at the center and shoot once each time he hits the center of the screen. As long as you grab the icons you should have enough weapons and remotes to outlast him. Once he's defeated you're off this planet and on your date! ...I mean you're on a date with your girlfriend. The ending animation is decent, with great graphics.

COOL SPOT

BY VIRGIN GAMES

Introduction

Originally released for the Sega Genesis, Cool Spot has been enhanced nicely for the Super NES. The graphics are better, the music is better, and there's even a special reward sequence built into the game if you beat it at the Hard difficulty level with using any continues, which is a *major* challenge. In the game, you control the wonderfully animated Cool Spot

Cool Spot includes several ultra-cool animations starring this cute little guy.

(the cute little red guy from the 7-Up commercials) through 11 levels of run/jump/shoot action. Be cool! Play Cool Spot!

Awesome Strategies

★ **Controls:** Press Y to shoot and B to jump. Easy!

★ You don't need to get 100% of the **Spots** on each level. 90% or so is usually enough to get you the 1-Up, and 95% is always enough to get you into the bonus level where you can earn a continue.

★ In the **bonus levels**, the continue letter is always at the top of the bottle. Be sure to grab the clocks to increase the amount of time you have to collect all the Spots.

★ **Explore everywhere** to find Spots. They're scattered all over every level. Always look for enemies to find areas you haven't explored before. Jump behind objects in the foreground (pipes, shoes,

You need 95% of the Spots to gain access to the bonus level.

Cool Spot

blocks) to find hidden Spots.

★ There are **three major differences** between the Hard difficulty level and the Normal difficulty level: the Hard mode has more enemies, there aren't any recharging 7-Ups after you defeat enemies, and there aren't any hands to point you in the direction of the caged Cool Spot in each level. The same strategies work in both Normal and

You don't get any 7-Up recharges in the Hard difficulty level.

Hard; you just need to play more carefully (and know your way around) in the Hard level.

Level 1: Shell Shock

★ Search behind the **7-Up bottle** at the beginning of the level for two Spots.

★ Jump off the 7-Up bottle to grab onto a **balloon**, then start jumping to the right to grab onto more balloons and collect Spots. If you fall to the beach, you can walk left to the 7-Up bottle and jump up to the balloon again, or walk to the beach chair in the middle of the level.

★ There's a **beach chair** in the sand about halfway through the level. Search around the chair, in the

Before shooting the lock off the cage of the Cool Spot, collect any nearby Spots.

green chair seat, and on the back of the chair. Jump behind the chair's armrest to find a few more hidden Spots. And just so you know, there's nothing interesting about the **CHEAT CODES book** next to the chair. The programmers just threw it in there for fun.

★ The **caged Cool Spot** is in the upper-right corner of the level. Jump up and right on the balloons to find it.

Cool Spot

Level 2: Pier Pressure

★ Don't fall off the **bottom of the screen** or you'll lose a life instantly.

★ **Shoot up or down** when you're climbing up or down a rope to hit any worms that might be crawling on the rope.

★ There's usually a **crab** at the bottom of the rope. Shoot the crab while you'll still on the rope so you don't get pinched!

★ Look for **holes in the pier poles**. You can walk through these holes into the next part of the level. Jump while you're in a hole to grab hidden Spots.

Be careful as you're climbing down ropes. Most crabs are waiting to pinch your butt!

There's also a **1-Up** hidden in one of the poles.

★ The **caged Cool Spot** is in the upper-right corner of the level.

Level 3: Off Da Wall

★ There are no 7-Up symbols in this level, but plenty of **hidden Spots** behind the pipes. Keep jumping behind the pipes to boost your Spot total.

★ Use small jumps to grab Spots placed over **barbed wire**.

★ You can shoot the pieces of **cheese** that the mice throw at you. It's better to shoot the mice while you're climbing up or down a wire, to totally avoid the cheese.

★ If you jump onto the left side of a **mousetrap**, you'll take damage, but if you jump onto the right side of the trap, you'll be flung into the air without taking damage.

★ Don't always go in the

The left side of the mousetrap is dangerous, but jumping on the right side shoots you into the air.

Cool Spot

direction that the **hands** point you in. Search all over the place to find more pipes and more Spots.

★ There's a **1-Up** close to one of the checkpoint flags in this level. Look for barbed wire (and a wire leading down) to the right of the flag. Jump past the barbed wire and climb up the next wire you find, then go left past the mousetrap to find the 1-Up.

Level 4: Wading Around

★ The beginning of the level is a bunch of **tricky jumps** to the right. Look down after each jump to see how far you have to jump to the next object. If you fall into the water, you instantly lose a life, so take your time.

★ There are several places in this level where you have to **intentionally fall** to grab Spots. The first place is the far right side of the level. Bounce up the big bubbles to the tiny bubble and float to the top of the blue blimp, then jump right and grab the Spots as you fall. You'll land on top of a rubber duck.

If you're trying to collect Spots, there are several areas where you'll have to fall to grab one.

★ After you touch the first checkpoint flag, start jumping left. The small **UFOs** tilt when you jump onto them, so jump off again before you fall. Keep going left to reach a **green spaceship**. Slide off the right side of the spaceship to collect a 7-Up symbol and land inside a tiny bubble. Float back up to the spaceship and keep jumping to the left.

★ When you reach the **red blimp** on the far left side of the level, jump left and fall to grab lots of Spots. You'll land on a UFO, so jump to the right and bounce off the bubble before you drop back to the start of the level.

★ There's a **red spaceship** to the right of the third (and last) checkpoint flag. Slide off the ship to grab a 7-Up symbol, then float back up to the ship in the bubble.

★ When you reach the **caged Cool Spot** in the upper-right corner of the level, drop off the left side of the blimp below the cage to collect two Spots and two 7-Up symbols. Float back up to the blimp and open the cage.

Cool Spot

Level 5: Toying Around

★ There are **two Spots** behind the **shoe** at the beginning of the level.

★ The **colorful blobs** explode into pieces when you blast them. Shoot the blobs ASAP, because they're the peskiest enemies in this level.

★ Search behind everything to find **hidden Spots**: cards, dice, fire trucks, wooden blocks, and shoes. If you can't walk behind a wooden block from one side, try the other. Slide down the ladders of fire trucks to find even more Spots.

★ Climb up the **shoelaces** to make your way through the level. You can't hold onto the bottom of a shoelace, so jump and grab as high as you can.

★ There's a **1-Up** hidden inside a **yellow block** with the letter B on it (there are two dice on top of the block). Look for it near the bottom of the level.

The blobs will explode into pieces when you blast them. Shoot or avoid the pieces.

★ If you don't have 100% of the Spots when you reach the **caged Cool Spot** in the upper-right corner, don't panic. Jump up and left into the block to the left of the cage to find some hidden Spots and a **1-Up**.

Level 6: Radical Rails

★ There are **no enemies** in this level, so all you have to do is collect Spots and open the cage in the upper-right corner of the level. Use small jumps to climb up the rails, and search the rails at the bottom of the level (below the rails) to find Spots. You'll also find a **1-Up** at the bottom of the level.

★ There's a **7-Up** symbol at the beginning of the level, in the upper-left corner.

Use small jumps to climb up the rails while searching them for Spots.

Cool Spot

★ It's almost impossible to find all 100% of the Spots before time runs out, so go for 90% and head for the cage. Jump behind the elevator to the right of the cage for a few more Spots (and a **1-Up** in the upper-right corner) before you shoot the lock.

Level 7: Wound Up

★ This level is a lot like **Level 5**, with the same graphics and Spots hidden in the same types of locations.

★ Look for **four stacks of blocks** in the upper-right corner of the level (one block, then a 2-block stack, then 3 blocks, then 4 blocks) just below the caged Cool Spot. Go left from the stacks to find a **1-Up** on a small ledge, then jump back to the stacks.

Find the four stacks of blocks, then go left to find a 1-Up on a small ledge.

Walk into the bottom blocks in the 3- and 4-block stacks to find Spots, then jump onto the left side of the cage to find another Spot.

Level 8: Loco Motive

★ Walk through each **train car** to collect the Spots inside, then jump on top of the car and collect the Spots on top. There's one train car with a **tennis ball** on it. Jump behind the ball to grab two hidden Spots, then jump above the ball for more Spots.

★ There's a **7-Up recharge** at the end of the train (on the far right side of the level). Take the recharge and then jump onto the weird-looking balloon (with red pants!) above the

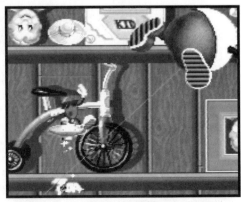

Don't miss the two 7-Up symbols on the far left side of the level (worth 14 Spots!).

Cool Spot

train. Jump up and right from the balloon to grab a **1-Up**.

★ There are two 7-Up symbols (**14 Spots!**) on the far left side of the level, about one screen above the train engine. After you hit the first checkpoint flag, jump onto one of the UFOs on the far left side of the screen and let yourself fall down the UFOs to grab the 7-Ups. Jump back up before you fall down to

Jump above the tennis ball to find a few spots.

the train engine and have to walk all the way back to the right.

★ When you reach the **caged Cool Spot** in the upper-right corner, drop down the UFOs below the cage to find a 7-Up symbol and a Spot. Jump to the left on the UFOs or you'll drop down to the train.

Level 9: Back To The Wall

★ Remember Level 3? If you do, you'll suffer some major deja vu playing through this level. The only new enemies are the bouncy **lightning bolts**. Watch out for the bolts when you're climbing down a cable.

Keep jumping around behind the pipes to find all of the hidden Spots (and there are plenty of them to find).

★ When you reach the **caged Cool Spot** in the lower-right corner, you won't have enough Spots to reach the bonus level. Walk to the right, past the cage, and bounce off the bubble into an area with lots of Spots (some hidden) for the taking.

The bouncy lightning bolts are the only new enemy. Watch for them on the cables.

Level 10: Dock and Roll

★ Jump up the **nails** at the beginning of the level to find a 7-Up symbol.
★ This level is a lot like Level 2, so use the same strategies that you did before. The **caged Cool Spot** is in the upper-right corner.

Level 11: Surf Patrol

★ Most of the Spots in this level are in the air. Grab onto the **balloons** and let them float to the Spots instead of trying to jump for the Spots yourself.

★ Search the **beach chair** for some hidden Spots. There are two hidden Spots behind the 7-Up can under the chair, and behind another 7-Up can to the right of the chair.

★ Look for two more hidden Spots behind the **7-Up bottle** to the right of the cage.

★ Complete this level and you get to watch the **ending animation**. If you fin-ished on the Hard level

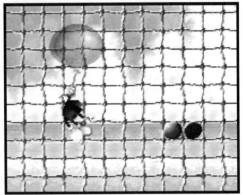

You'll have to perform some creative acrobatics to reach most of the spots.

(and you're an incredible player if you did), you'll get information on how to enter the contest. Otherwise, you'll get a screen telling you to try again at the Hard level. And that's it!

Bonus Levels

★ **Bonus Level 1 (U):** Bounce to the top of the bottle to find the letter U. There are two clocks on the far left and far right sides of the bottle, near the top. You need to get them both to have enough time to grab all of the Spots and 7-Ups.
★ **Bonus Level 2 (N):** Bounce to the top of the bottle and grab the clock, then bounce to the far right side of the bottle to find the letter N.
★ **Bonus Level 3 (C):** The mines appear for the first time in this bonus level. Shoot the mines to destroy them. Jump into the tiny bubbles and you can float upward in them for a few seconds before they pop. (You can also jump out of the bubble to pop it.) Look for clocks in the upper-left corner of the bottle and the right side of the bottle, near the

Cool Spot

top. The letter C is in the upper-right corner.

★ **Bonus Level 4 (O):** The letter O is in the upper-left corner of the bottle, surrounded by mines. There are two clocks: One of them is just below the O, and the other is in the upper-right corner.

★ **Bonus Level 5 (L):** To get the letter L, you have to bounce to the middle (and top) of the bottle, then fall through the mines. There are clocks on the left and right sides of the bottle, both about halfway up.

★ **Bonus Level 6 (A):** There are two clocks in the upper-left corner of the bottle. The letter A is in the upper-right corner, below two bubbles and some mines. Pop the bubbles and steer to the left of the mines, then steer right to touch the A.

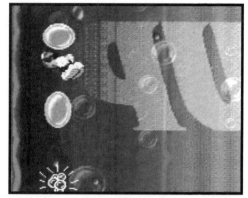

Use the bubbles to bounce up, aiming for the top where valuable items float.

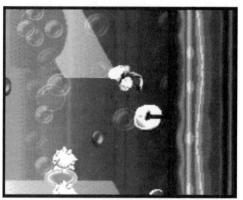

Each U-N-C-O-L-A letter you collect will earn you a continue.

GOOF TROOP

BY CAPCOM

Introduction

Goof Troop borrows parts of *The Legend of Zelda: A Link to the Past* and the obscure puzzle game *Boxxle* to make a very fun action/adventure game. In case you don't know, Goof Troop is a Disney TV cartoon series starring the freakish man/dog hybrid Goofy and several other folks: Goofy's son Max, Goofy's friend Pete, and Pete's son, PJ. Pete and PJ are

Goofy can pick up and throw objects just like the adventurous Link.

kidnapped by pirates and taken to Spoonerville Island, and Goofy and Max have to save them by solving puzzles and defeating big bad bosses.

Awesome Strategies

★ If you've messed up a puzzle room, leave the room and then go back in. The room will be reset and you can try to solve the puzzle again.

★ Items like diamonds and food appear randomly when you pick up pots or dig holes in the ground, so keep picking objects up to find goodies.

★ We've written solutions for the puzzles in each room. Here's a typical sentence from a solution: "Kick the first block from the right Up." This means to walk to the first block from the right side of the screen and kick it upward. Here's another typical sentence: "Kick the second block from the right Down and Right." This means to walk to the second block from the right side of the screen and kick the block down, then to the right. Got it? Good!

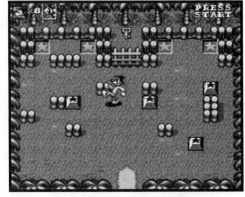

If you mess up a puzzle room, leave and come back to try again.

Goof Troop

Stage 1

★ **Room 1:** The "boss" is a group of 7 pirates that pop out of the holes in the ground and throw three different items at you: barrels, mines, and bombs. You can grab the bombs after they hit the ground and stop moving; don't try to grab them when they're still bouncing or you'll take damage. You can tell if a bomb's going to hit the ground if it's thrown high into the air. Low throws always go off the screen. You can also grab the barrels and throw them back at the pirates. It's safer to grab and throw the barrels and avoid the bombs.

★ **Room 2:** There's a Bell and three pirates in this room. You need Key 2 to open the North gate.

★ **Room 3:** Key 2 is here. Puzzle solution: Kick the lower-left block Left. Kick the third block from the left Right. Kick the second block from the right Down and Right. Now kick all the blocks onto the markers and take Key 2.

★ **Room 4:** Key 1 is here. Puzzle solution: Kick the first block from the left Left. Kick the second block from the left Left. Kick the first block from the right Left. Kick the third block

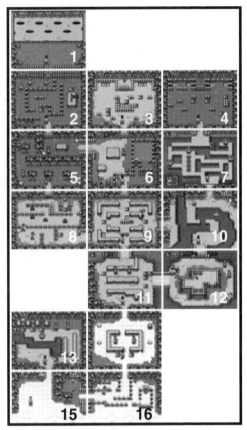

STAGE 1 MAP

Room 1: Catch the barrels and toss them back at the seven pirates.

Goof Troop

from the left Down. Kick the fourth block from the left Up and Right. Kick the first block from the left Down and Left. Kick all the blocks Up and take Key 1.

Room 6: Dig around in the field to find random items.

★ **Room 5:** There are three pirates here. Beat them all to open the North gate.

★ **Room 6:** A Shovel is here. Dig in the field to find some random items. Defeat the pirate to open the North gate.

★ **Room 7:** There's a Blue Diamond here.

★ **Room 8:** There's a Rope Gun and a Red Diamond here. You need Key 1 to open the North gate.

★ **Room 9:** Kick the blocks onto the markers to open the North, West, and East gates.

★ **Room 10:** A Board is here. Use the Board to cover the hole in the bridge so you can walk across to the North door.

★ **Room 11:** A Rope Gun is here.

★ **Room 12:** There are three pirates and a Rope Gun here. Defeat them all to open the North and South gates.

★ **Room 13:** There are two Diamonds and three pirates here. Grab the barrel with a Rope Gun so you can kick the brick out of the way to take the Diamonds.

★ **Room 14:** A Bell is here.

★ **Room 15:** You start the stage in this room.

★ **Room 16:** A Rope Gun is here.

Stage 2

★ **Room 1:** The boss starts by throwing torches at you, then he breathes a stream of fire across the screen. Avoid the torches, grab the barrels, and throw them at the boss. When he breathes fire, get as far away as you can. When you run out of barrels, a few nice guys will walk onto the screen and throw barrels down to you, but you have to catch them and then throw them. Don't get too close to the top of the screen or the boss starts twirling and running left and right rapidly.

★ **Room 2:** There are two Red Diamonds here. You need Key 3 to open the North gate.

Goof Troop

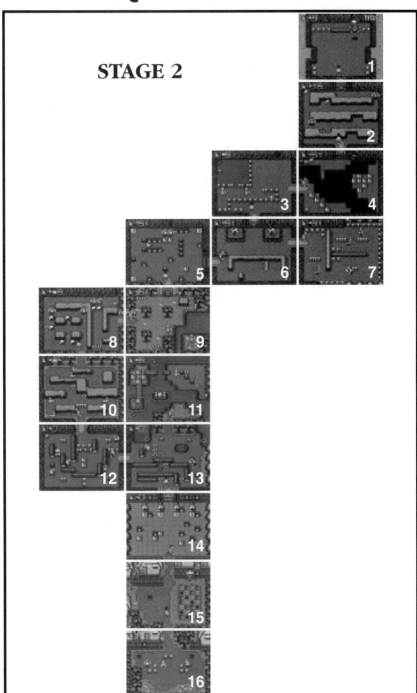

STAGE 2

Goof Troop

★ **Room 3:** Key 3 and a Shovel are here. Use the Shovel to dig around in the field and find a few items.

★ **Room 4:** You need two Rope Guns to cross the hooks in this room. Use a Rope Gun to hit the gray button on the right side of the North gate and open it. There's a Red Diamond and a Rope Gun near the North gate.

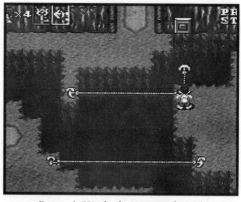

Room 4: Hit the button on the side of the gate to open it.

★ **Room 5:** This room is tricky, because the pirates can kick the blocks and make it impossible for you to kick them onto the switches and open the East gate. Kick the top two blocks onto the top two switches, and the bottom two blocks onto the bottom switches.

★ **Room 6:** Pick up and throw the cannonballs at the cannons to destroy them. You can also catch the cannonballs in the air

Room 6: Two cannons rain down cannon balls at you.

if you stand close enough to the cannons. Destroy the first cannon, then run past the rolling logs and destroy the second one. You need Key 2 to open the North gate.

★ **Room 7:** A Rope Gun is here.

★ **Room 8:** A Rope Gun is here. This is the first room in the game with blocks that start blinking when you kick them and eventually explode. Tricky!

★ **Room 9:** Key 1 is in this room, and you need it to open the North gate. Use a Rope Gun to connect the hooks on the right side of the room and walk across to take Key 1.

★ **Room 11:** Key 2 is here. Use a Rope Gun to connect the hooks, then use a Board to cross the hole in the bridge.

★ **Room 12:** There's a Board and Rope Gun here.

Goof Troop

★ **Room 13:** There's a Rope Gun and two pirates here.
★ **Room 14:** Puzzle solution: Kick the first block from the right Up. Kick the second block from the left Right and Up. Kick the second block from the right Up. Kick the first block from the right Right, Up, Right, Up. Kick the first block from the left Right, Up, Left, Up.
★ **Room 15:** There's a field here you can dig into with the Shovel to find random items.

Stage 3

★ **Room 1:** There's a field here you can dig into with the Shovel to find random items.
★ **Room 2:** There are stairs leading upward, and two Diamonds next to the stairs, but you have to come in from Room 9 to get to them.
★ **Room 4:** A Candle is in the upper-left corner of this dark room. There are two Shovels, one in the middle of the room and one in lower-right corner, next to a Red Diamond.
★ **Room 5:** Pick up a pot and throw it into the mirror to smash it and open a hole.
★ **Room 6:** A Candle, Bell, and Blue Diamond are here.
★ **Room 7:** A Rope Gun is here. Some of the suits of armor come to life and chase you. Hit the armor once to disable it, and twice to destroy it. Hit all four switches to open the North door.
★ **Room 9:** Key 1 is here and you need it to open the door. Grab the Key

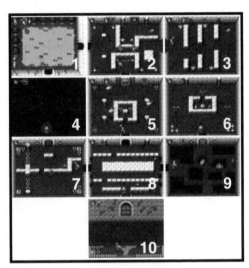

STAGE 3 – FLOOR 1

Room 5: Smash through the mirror by throwing a pot into it.

Goof Troop

and open the door while avoiding the bad guys.

★ **Room 10:** Grab the plants and then walk onto the switch in the lower-left corner to create a bridge and open the door of the castle.

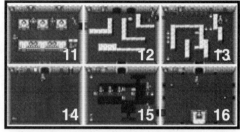

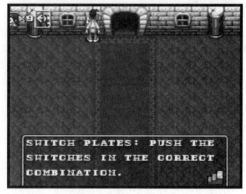

STAGE 3 – FLOOR 2

FLOOR 2

★ **Room 11:** Key 3 is here, and you need it to open the door.

★ **Room 12:** You need Key 2 to open the West door.

★ **Room 13:** A Board is here. There's a crack in the upper-left corner of the room. Pick up and throw a jar at the crack to make a hole.

★ **Room 14:** There's a note on the upper wall, just to the left of the door.

Room 14: Read the note next to the door for a little advice.

There's also a Rope Gun and stairs leading up.

★ **Room 15:** Key 2, a Bell, and a Board are here. You need two Boards to get across to Key 2.

★ **Room 16:** Destroy the cannon to open the West door.

FLOOR 3

★ **Room 17:** Walk onto the switches in this order: upper-right, lower-left, upper-left, lower-right. This opens the East door.

★ **Room 18:** Key 5 and a Rope Gun are here. You need Key 4 to open the door.

★ **Room 19:** Key 4 is here. Walk onto the switches in the order O, P, E, N to open the North door.

★ **Room 20:** Key 6 is here. You need Key 5 to open the door.

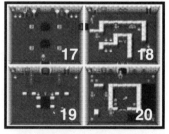

FLOOR 4

★ **Room 21:** Destroy both cannons to open the East door.

STAGE 3 – FLOOR 3

Goof Troop

★ **Room 22:** Key 7 is here.
★ **Room 23:** A Diamond is on the left side of the room.
★ **Room 24:** A Candle is here. You need a Rope Gun to connect the hooks, and you need Key 6 to open the door.

FLOOR 5

★ **Room 25:** The bosses are two skeletons that throw their bones and skulls at you. Avoid the bones as they bounce around, then grab and throw the bones when they stop bouncing. The skeletons don't start throwing their skulls until you've hit them a few times. You can't hurt a skeleton when its skull is flying around, so throw bones at the skull until it returns to the skeleton, or just avoid the skull until it flies away.

★ **Room 26:** The West wall in this room starts moving as soon as you walk inside. Run to the North door and use Key 7 to get through before the wall crushes you.

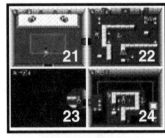

STAGE 3 – FLOOR 4

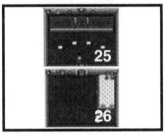

STAGE 3 – FLOOR 5

Stage 4

★ **Room 1:** The bosses are two centipedes that crawl along the ledges. When the screen shakes, watch for shadows on the ledges. Avoid the shadows and pick up the rock that falls to the ground. Throw the rock at either centipede's head to hit it. There's a safe spot at the bottom of the screen next to the door; the centipede can't get you here. Only one centipede attacks you at first, then two of them appear. Defeat the red centipede first, because he's tougher.

★ **Room 2:** Defeat all the pirates to open the North door.

★ **Room 3:** You need to solve the puzzle in Room

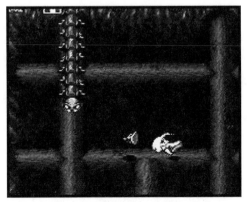

Room 1: Avoid the shadows, then pick up a rock and heave it at the centipede.

Goof Troop

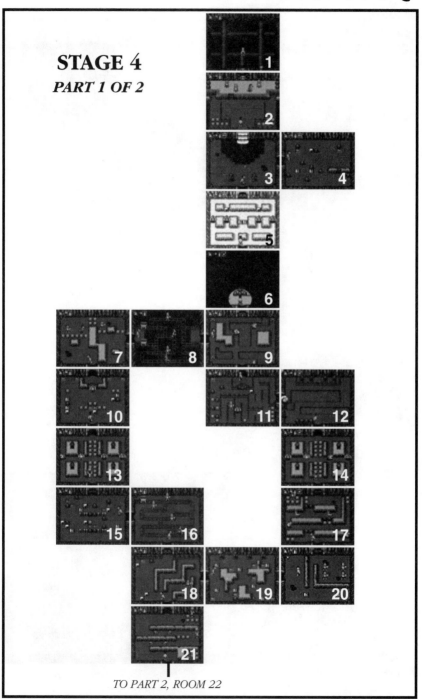

STAGE 4
PART 1 OF 2

TO PART 2, ROOM 22

Goof Troop

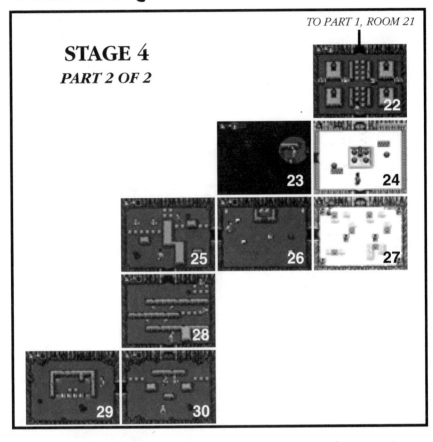

TO PART 1, ROOM 21

STAGE 4
PART 2 OF 2

22

23   24

25   26   27

28

29   30

4 to open the door behind the waterfall, and you need a Rope Gun to get across to the door.

★ **Room 4:** Puzzle solution: Kick the exploding block Down, Left, Down, Right. Kick the right block Left, Up, Right, Down, Right. Kick both blocks up to "open" the waterfall in Room 3.

★ **Room 5:** Trick the four rolling pirates into running into the blocks you kick to open the North door.

★ **Room 6:** A Rope Gun is in the upper-right corner of

Room 5: Trick the pirates into the blocks you kick at them.

Goof Troop

this dark room, and you also have to solve a tricky puzzle.

★ **Room 9:** A Candle is here. Hit all four switches to open the North door.

★ **Room 11:** Pick up and throw all the barrels, and defeat all the pirates, then kick the green block Left. Go through the maze and kick the block Up and Left to open the North door.

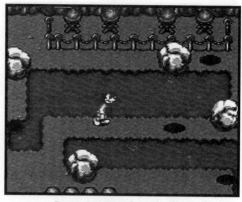

Room 12: Stand on the spots where the boulders aren't bouncing!

★ **Room 12:** When you first enter the room, watch where the boulders bounce and where they don't, then hide on the spots where the boulders don't hit.

★ **Room 15:** Puzzle solution: Kick the first block from the right Left. Kick the second stone block from the left Right. Kick the first stone block from the left Right and Up. Kick the first green block from the left Up. Kick the first yellow block from the left Left and Up. Kick the first stone block from the left Left. Kick the middle green block Left. Kick the first green block from the right Down and Left. Kick the first stone block from the right Up. Kick the first green block from the right Down. Kick the first yellow block from the left Down and Right to open the North door.

★ **Room 17:** Defeat all the pirates to open the North door.

★ **Room 18:** Puzzle solution: Kick the green block Left. Kick the first yellow block from the top Down. Kick the first yellow block from the bottom Left and Up to open the North door.

★ **Room 19:** Kick the blocks onto the switches. No solution necessary because it's so easy to figure out!

★ **Room 20:** A Bell is here. Kick the highest block on the right side of the screen Left. Use the Bell to lure all four pirates into

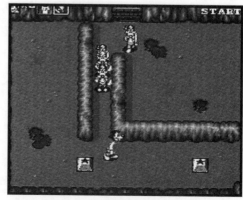

Room 20: Lure the four pirates into the passage and knock them out with the block.

Goof Troop

the narrow passage, then kick the block Up to hit them all and open the North door.

★ **Room 23:** There's a Red and a Blue Diamond in the lower-left corner.

★ **Room 24:** Defeat pirate to open the North door.

★ **Room 26:** There are two Red Diamonds and a Candle here. Puzzle solution: Kick the stone block Up. Kick the green block Up and Left. Kick the first

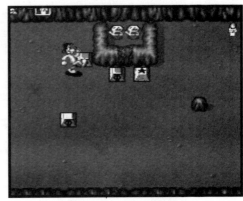

Room 26: Solve the puzzle for two handy Red Diamonds.

yellow block from the left Right. Kick the green block Up and Right. When block explodes, it destroys the wall so you can take Diamonds.

★ **Room 27:** Hit all six switches as fast as you can to open the North door. If you don't hit them all fast enough, the switches pop up and you have to hit them again.

★ **Room 29:** Puzzle solution: Pick up all the barrels. Kick the fourth block from the left Up. Kick the second block from the left Up. Kick the fourth block from the left Right. Kick all the blocks onto the switches to open the North door in Room 30.

★ **Room 30:** You need to solve the puzzle in Room 29 to open the North door.

Stage 5

★ **Room 1:** Pirate Pete is the final boss, and he has several different attacks. In the first attack, he spins around the screen and hurls bombs at you. Catch the bombs and throw them at Pete when he's not spinning to cause damage. In the second attack, Pete reaches at you with a *long* arm. Stay far away from Pete and walk away from the arm

Room 1: Pirate Pete has plenty of attacks and takes a lot of hits.

Goof Troop

as it reaches for you. In the third attack, Pete jumps up and shoots a gun at you. Stay at the bottom of the screen and move between the bullets. In the fourth (and final!) attack, Pete whistles and calls two pirates onto the screen. Avoid the pirates and Pete will hit them by accident when he attacks you. It takes 12 bombs to defeat Pete and win the game.

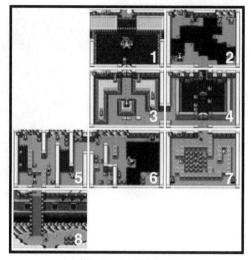

STAGE 5 – FLOOR 1

★ **Room 2:** You need two Rope Guns to get to the South door.

★ **Room 3:** Use the buttons to aim and fire the cannon at the four pirates. Defeat all the pirates to open the North door.

★ **Room 4:** Puzzle solution: Kick the lower-right block Left. Kick the second block from the left Down and Left. Kick the first block from the bottom Left. Kick the upper-left block Down. Kick the upper-right block Right and Up. Kick the middle block Up. Kick the new middle block Left, Up, Right, Up.

★ **Room 6:** A Rope Gun is here. Use the Gun to walk across to the stairs going down.

★ **Room 7:** There are two Rope Guns and a Blue Diamond here.

FLOOR 2

★ **Room 9:** A Rope Gun is here. If you enter this room from the stairs, you have to use the arrows to "walk" across to the East door. When you walk on an arrow, the platform moves in that direction, so step on the Up and Right arrows to keep moving to the door.

★ **Room 10:** Holes appear in the floor of this room

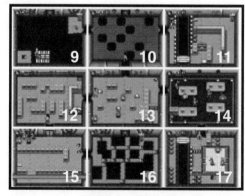

STAGE 5 – FLOOR 2

Goof Troop

in three different patterns. Watch the patterns and run to where the holes aren't!

★ **Room 11:** Pick up the barrel next to the West door. Walk down and throw the barrel onto the gold button to make the bridge move so you can walk across. There's a Rope Gun behind the door. You need Key 2 to open the door.

Room 9: Use the arrows to walk across the room to the door.

★ **Room 12**: Puzzle solution: Kick the block Right, Up, Right, Up, Right.

★ **Room 13:** A Rope Gun and Bell are here. Defeat the pirates to make the spikes disappear so you can take the Bell.

★ **Room 15:** Hit the arrow switch to make a row of barrels slide onto the screen. Throw the barrels at the pirates. Walk onto the gold switch in the upper-left corner to open the North door.

★ **Room 16:** Kick the bricks off the walkways to clear a path across the room.

★ **Room 17:** Hit the pirates with barrels to lower the spikes in front of the stairs going down. There are two Candles on the other side of the spikes.

Room 15: Hit the arrow switch to bring some barrels onto the screen.

FLOOR 3

★ **Room 18:** Key 2 is in the upper-left corner of this dark room. The stairs in the lower-left corner go up to Room 12.

★ **Room 19:** There's food in the corners of this dark room.

★ **Room 20:** Use the Bell to lure the pirate onto the gold button and open the door. There are two Rope Guns behind the door.

★ **Room 21:** You need a Rope Gun to get to the North door, and you need Key 1 to open it.

Goof Troop

★ **Room 22:** A Bell is here. Grab the barrels with a Rope Gun and throw them at the gold buttons at the top of the room. Hit both buttons to open the North door.

★ **Room 23:** Key 1 is here. Push blocks onto the middle two switches to open the door to the Key.

★ **Room 24:** There's a Bell, two Candles, and a Blue Diamond here, guarded by pirates.

★ **Room 25:** Puzzle solution: Kick the lowest block Right and Up. Kick the highest block Down, Right, Up. Kick the new highest block Left, Up, Right. Kick the lowest block Right and Up. This opens the North door.

★ **Room 26:** You need one Rope Gun to get to the West door, and two Rope Guns to reach the North door.

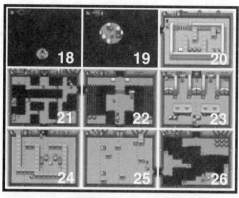

STAGE 5 – FLOOR 3

Room 24: There are plenty of items for the taking in this room.

Awesome Secrets

★ **PASSWORDS:** Stage 2: Banana, Red Diamond, Cherry, Banana, Cherry; Stage 3: Cherry, Red Diamond, Blue Diamond, Cherry, Banana; Stage 4: Red Diamond, Cherry, Blue Diamond, Blue Diamond, Red Diamond; Stage 5: Banana, Cherry, Blue Diamond, Red Diamond, Banana.

LUFIA

BY TAITO

Introduction

Lufia is a *big* role-playing game in the style of Final Fantasy II. It's aimed at beginner and intermediate role-players—with only a few puzzles to solve and lots of combat—but even advanced players will get some fun out of it. The Japanese-to-English translation is also quite good (with a few exceptions, of course). You control the ancestor of a long-dead war-

Lufia's interactive opening sequence puts you right into the heat of the action.

rior who defeated four evil beings called Sinistrals almost 100 years ago. When the Sinistrals return, you're called upon to save the world by finding the long-lost Dual Blade that your relative used. Buy this cart and prepare for a good 30 to 40 hours of role-playing madness!

Awesome Strategies

★ Your characters will swing at where a monster was even if it's dead, so estimate how many more hits a monster will take before assigning your characters to attack it. Especially near the end of the game, you can't afford to "waste" attacks. You must eliminate each monster as efficiently as possible. (An efficient adventurer is a happy adventurer!)

★ We don't have room for maps in this book, but you really don't need 'em as long as you follow this simple guideline: **explore everywhere**! In towns, keep pressing the A button to find hidden stuff, especially inside drawers and dressers. In dungeons, the best way to keep track of where you've been is by looking for chests that you've opened. Open chests indicate that you've been that way already.

★ Whenever you visit a town for the first time, **visit all of the Shops** and see if they have items for sale that you need. It's important to keep constantly buying new weapons and armor to keep up with the strength of the monsters in each new area.

★ In this chapter, we use a few terms you may not be familiar with. *XP* stands for **Experience Points**; *HP* stands for **Hit Points**; *MP* stands for

Lufia

Magic Points; *Overworld* refers to the map of the world that you use to travel from town to town.

Adventure Walkthrough

★ **DOOM CASTLE:** You start the game with the four heroes **Maxim, Guy, Selan,** and **Artea**, inside the palace of the Sinistrals. The goal here is to climb up to the top of the Castle to battle the Sinistrals. All the characters start with not much more XP needed before reaching the next level, and they are already very strong.

★ Go downstairs in the Castle to find **three chests** and a potion inside. You already have a sackful of them, of course, but you should explore to get the feel of the game (and the feel of the Castle layout— you'll be back here twice more later on). Since you're so powerful, you'll never be in danger from the attacking monsters.

Walk around the walls of the Sinistral chamber to find Miracle Potions in the chests.

★ When you reach the top floor, explore around the border of the room to find three **Miracle Potions** in chests, then go across the glass to the four Sinistrals. Remember, you don't really need to explore the Castle at all, you can win the battle by coming straight here, but you might as well get training now, when you're super-strong, instead of later.

★ The **Sinistrals** attack one at a time. All of them have *thousands* of HP and therefore take quite a bit of time to defeat. Because you have so many of them, go ahead and use your Miracle Potions on party members with low HP or MP or both. The

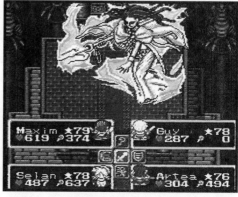

Use your Miracle Potions during your battle against the four Sinistrals.

Lufia

best attack strategy is for Maxim and Guy to hack away with their swords while Selan and Artea cast spells. When the fourth and final Sinistral is destroyed, the Castle starts to collapse, and Maxim and Selan are left behind in the chaos. Sob, sob.

★ **ALEKIA:** Now the real adventure begins. Explore the town to talk to everyone and to find items. Some of the things you should do: Buy a

Dagger at the Weapon Shop and sell the wimpy Knife. Buy two or three Potions. Get the **Cloth Helm** out of the dresser in the Knights' Room, and search outside in the bush to find a Potion. Search Lufia's room at the inn upstairs to find a **Dress**. Go into the cleric's house and take the underground path to the church so you can open the chest behind the cleric and get the item inside. Future towns don't

Take the secret path from the cleric's house to the church and open up the chest.

have quite this much stuff to do, but it's important to explore thoroughly! When you're done in town, walk north to Alekia Castle.

★ **ALEKIA CASTLE:** Again, explore everywhere to find treasure chests and items. Talk to the **Commander** in the upper-left corner of the ground floor. The **Princess Estea** is on the top floor. Talk to her for 100 Gold, then search her bedroom (ahem) to find a **Bracelet** and

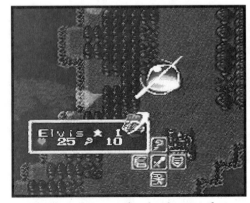

Stuffed Bear. Talk to the **King**, who can't do anything about Sheran yet. Walk into the upper-right corner of the top floor and go down the stairs to find a room with three chests. When you're done pillaging the Castle, walk back into Alekia, save the game, and leave town. Walk north to Chatam.

★ **OVERWORLD:** You'll get into one or two battles on the way to Chatam. Attack

You'll get into your first battle going from Alekia to Chatam. Hope you bought a Dagger!

with your Dagger and use a Potion if you get low on energy.

★ **CHATAM:** Look in the **fields** and the trees below the field to find hidden Potions. Stay at the Inn, then go just outside of town and walk in a circle until you encounter a monster. Keep fighting walking in circles to fight monsters and build your experience and gold. Stay at the Inn whenever you're

Get the hidden item out of the field in Chatam. Search the bushes for another item.

running low on HP. You should build to at least Level 4 before continuing north to the North Caves.

★ **NORTH CAVES:** There are two entrances to the North Caves. Walk up and right as far as you can go to find the first entrance. This leads to several Gold-filled chests in the Caves that you can't normally reach. The second entrance is northwest of Chatam. Use the second entrance to get to Sheran.

★ **SHERAN:** All of the people have been attacked by monsters, so it's no surprise that they're panicking and telling you to leave. Don't let the poor guys rush you, though. Explore the town thoroughly and walk north into Sheran Castle.

★ **SHERAN CASTLE:** There are tons of chests inside the Castle, and no monsters around. A nice combination! There's a room in the basement with a strange **dark spot** on the floor. Remember where it is. You'll also find two doors in the throne room that are locked. You can unlock them later. Leave Sheran and return to Alekia.

★ **ALEKIA:** Talk to **Lufia** in her room (she's still mad), then go to the Castle and talk to the Commander, Princess, and King. Leave Alekia and walk north. Lufia runs out of town and

Explore Sheran Castle to find a basement with a strange dark spot on the floor.

Lufia

joins you after a long conversation. Now hang around Alekia and power Lufia up to Level 4 the same way you powered yourself up. It's too dangerous for her in the North Caves until she's at Level 4 or higher.

Elvis, knight from the Kingdom of Alekia. I've come to help.

Rescue the royalty from the basement of Sheran Castle.

★ **NORTH CAVES:** Inside the Caves is a man looking for his sister **Lilah**, who works in Sheran Castle. The man also has a **Sheran Key**. How convenient! Take the Key and go to the Castle.

★ **SHERAN CASTLE:** Go to the throne room and unlock the two doors. Throw the **switch** behind the left door and open the chest behind the right door. Now go down to the basement room with the **dark spot** on the floor. The spot will have turned into stairs! Go down the stairs to find the King and Lilah in a prison cell. Rescue everyone and escort them out of the Castle.

★ **SHERAN:** When you leave the Castle, you're attacked by the **Sinistral** of Destruction. Lufia runs off with the people, and you stay behind to fight. Have some laughs and take a few swings before the Sinistral knocks you out. Lufia shows up just in time to save you by chasing away the Sinistral.

★ **ALEKIA:** Find **Lilah** in Alekia Castle and take her up to Chatam.

★ **CHATAM:** Lilah is reunited with her brother, who steers you southwest to Treck, where someone is supposed to know about the Sinistrals. It's a long trip, so bring along Potions. Once you're at Treck and have saved the game in the church, you can wander around outside to build up levels.

★ **TRECK:** Visit the Weapon and Armor Shops and buy better equipment. You'll

You'll be attacked by the Sinistral of Destruction when you leave Sheran Castle.

Lufia

find **Cloth Shoes** in one house. Buy some **Cider** if you can afford it. Talk to the old man next to the dock. He takes you to his house and asks his son to escort you to the East Caves.

After the heroic Guy passes away, plunder his grave to get the Short Sword.

★ **EAST CAVES:** Leave Treck, walk east, and enter the Caves. Open the chests along the way. On the other side of the Caves, go into Guy's House (although you don't know it's Guy yet).

★ **GUY'S HOUSE:** After a brief chat with **Guy**, he kicks the bucket! After his burial, search his grave for a powerful **Short Sword** and search his house for a Great Potion. Return to Treck.

★ **TRECK:** Power up outside of town until you and Lufia hit Level 8 or 9, then walk into town and talk to the old man, who points you to the soldiers at the dock. Talk to the soldiers and you're attacked by four **Demon Lords**! The soldier **Aguro** fights at your side, so it's not too tough a battle. When you win, go up to the top floor of the bar and talk to the sailor about his ship, the **Maberia**. Go west of town into the Caves to find the Maberia.

★ **CAVES:** There's a pit about halfway through the Caves. Drop into the pit to find a **magic fountain** where you can recharge all of your HP and MP by walking on the blue circles. You should hang around the Fountain and build a few levels since it's so easy to get HP and MP back.

★ **MABERIA:** When you find the ship, you're attacked by three **Goblins**. They can be nasty opponents if your levels aren't high enough. If you lose the battle, power up one or two levels and try again. Defeat the Goblins and

Look for the magic fountain in the Caves and use it to build up your levels.

Lufia

you sail the Maberia to Treck.

★ **TRECK:** Talk to the sailor and tell him you have his ship. Now he can take you between Treck and Lorbenia for free. Sail to Lorbenia.

★ **LORBENIA:** Explore the town and buy new equipment for both yourself and Lufia. Go to the top floor of the dress shop and Lufia gets pickpocketed by a little kid named **Lou**. (You

Only Lufia can get the Fairy Kiss from the 2nd level of the Old Cave.

automatically catch the kid before he runs away.) Stay at the **Inn** to find out more about Lou. When you leave the Inn, Aguro comes to see you and joins your party. Power up outside of town before beginning the journey to Grenoble to build up Gold so you can buy good equipment for Aguro.

★ **GRENOBLE:** Explore the town and find the guy who asks you about the **rumor**. Pay him 50 Gold and walk down the stairs into the basement room. Talk to one of the men to be assigned a mission. Also talk to the man who wants the **Fairy Kiss** on the 2nd level of the Old Cave. No problem!

★ **OLD CAVE:** Go down to the 2nd level and open every single chest to find lots of items and the **Secret Map**. (The open chests help you keep track of where you've been.) Send Lufia through the door to get the Fairy Kiss and a few other items, including the **Heeled Shoes** that give her a better attack but lower her defense slightly. Return to town with the Kiss and the Map.

★ **GRENOBLE:** Give the Fairy Kiss to the man for info and give the Secret Map to the treasure people. The old man tells you to search out the **NW Tower** and gives you a letter to give to the person inside. Before you leave, get assigned a mission for the 3rd level of the Cave. You can complete the mission or visit the Tower; the Tower has tougher monsters, so go for the Cave first.

★ **OLD CAVE:** Look for the **Silver Wick** in one of the chests. The monsters here are very tough, but that makes this a great place to power up levels. When you find the **Brone Sword**, *don't* equip it or you'll be cursed and take damage whenever you hit a monster with it. If you don't read the last sentence and *do* equip the Sword, go to the church and pay the cleric 600 Gold to lift the curse, then sell the Sword at the

Lufia

Weapon Shop. The church only lifts the curse from you, not the Sword, and you'll be cursed again if you try to use it again.

The Apprentice won't tell you what he knows until you defeat him in one-on-one combat.

★ **NW TOWER:** Finish up at the Cave, save the game in Grenoble, and go north to the Tower. Explore as you usually do to find several chests. The best item to be found is the **Sonic Ring**, which boosts your Defense and especially your Agility. If the Tower is too tough for you, look for a window and jump out of it (!) to drop back to the ground without taking any damage.

★ The man you're looking for (named the **Apprentice**) is on the top floor of the Tower, and he won't give you any information until you beat him in a **one-on-one battle**! We weren't able to beat him until we reached Level 16, and we did that by powering up in the Old Cave. The Apprentice casts **Fake** spells on himself to increase his Agility, so he can get in several attacks in a row unless your Agility is high enough. Use lots of Potions to recharge during the battle. The Apprentice usually chugs a Potion in the same turn as you, but your hits take away more energy than his Potions give back, while his hits are less than what your Potions give back. Defeat the Apprentice to learn about **Elfrea** and to get a Speed Potion. Return to Grenoble and get assigned the mission for the 4th level of the Old Cave.

★ **OLD CAVE:** The **4th level** is a great place to build XP. Stay near the entrance and fight the monsters to earn 200+ XP per battle. Don't explore the level until your guys are strong enough! The Red Orbs are the nastiest monsters in this level; they cast a Dread spell that lowers your Defense ratings.

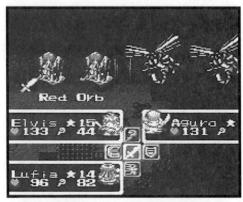

Fight the monsters on the 4th level to build your levels, but watch out for the Red Orbs.

Lufia

Open all the chests, find the **Crown** (use your Float spell to hover over the poison squares), and take it back to Grenoble. Time to head for the town of Kirof!

Go to Elfrea, though it's far. You must pass three towns to reach it.

The mysterious old man in the shrine gives you some info on how to find Elfrea.

★ **OVERWORLD:** Walk up near the NW Tower, then go around the mountains to the west and head south. Go across two bridges, then head north to find a small **shrine**. Enter the shrine and look around to find the **wise old man**. Talk to him for more info on Elfrea. He also uses a strange flashing power on you. You'll be meeting this guy several more times before the game is over! Leave the shrine and walk south until you find Kirof.

★ **KIROF:** Explore the town, then listen in on the conversation between **Reyna** and **Mark**. When Mark leaves, talk to Reyna, then leave town. Walk east to the town of Medan.

★ **MEDAN:** This town has well-stocked Armor and Weapon Shops, and you should have plenty of Gold, so buy some new equipment for your party (they deserve it!). Walk north into the Medan Castle.

★ **MEDAN CASTLE:** Walk into the chamber of the **Hope Ruby** and talk to everyone. Walk outside of the room, then go right and up to find stairs going down. Take the stairs and follow the path until you overhear the Princess and a soldier talking about the fake Hope Ruby. Leave the Castle and you see Mark running away from several soldiers. Looks like he "borrowed" the Ruby! Leave Medan and return to Kirof.

★ **KIROF:** Talk to Mark and he joins your party. Leave town and go north to the Haunted Cave. The guard lets you pass to rescue Reyna.

★ **HAUNTED CAVE:** The **Willowisps** are very tough to defeat with swords, but Lufia's **Bang** spell works great against them. Use the Bang whenever two or more Willowisps are attacking.

★ The path to Reyna can be found by staying on the upper paths of the Cave and walking to the right until you find a door. Go through the door to find two stairs leading down. Go down the right stairs first to find several chests and a man who tells you the "secret" of the Cave. Go down the left stairs to find five more sets of stairs. Go down the middle stairs at the bottom of the room to appear on a cliff. Walk north off the cliff to walk onto an **invisible bridge**! The other bridges col-

Lufia

lapse when you try to cross them, so the invisible bridge is the only way across. Go across and through the door to find Reyna.

★ Reyna is possessed by an evil **Phantasm** that you have to fight. Attack the Phantasm with your character and Aguro while Lufia casts one or two Drain spells on the Phantasm to lower its Defense. Lufia should also cast

Poor little Reyna is possessed by an evil Phantasm. Kill the creature to save her soul!

spells and use Potions to heal the party during the battle. Defeat the Phantasm and you automatically return to Kirof. Talk to Reyna and Mark. Leave town and go east to Medan.

★ **MEDAN:** The Princess confesses the secret of the Hope Ruby to the townspeople, and everyone agrees to work harder to restore the town to its former glory. Awww. Talk to the Princess, then talk to the innskeeper for a free stay at the Inn. Save the game at the church, leave Medan, and walk north past the lakes to the old Medan Mines.

★ **MEDAN MINES:** Take a quick tour through the Mines. Find the **old man** and talk to him briefly about the Hope Ruby. He thought it was real, huh? Hmmm. Leave the Cave and go south to Medan, then east into the Caves.

★ **CAVES:** The guards let you pass now that you've talked to the Princess.

Don't forget to open the chests before you leave. (Float over the poison squares with a spell or Potion to find the chests.) Once you're on the east side of the Caves, walk south to Belgen.

★ **BELGEN:** Explore the town and buy better equipment for the party. Talk to everyone to find out that poor **Jerin** has been given up as ransom (don't they mean "sacri-

We don't have the strength to fight. We have to leave Jerin up to fate.

Talk to the people in Belgen to find out about the sacrifice--er, ransom of Jerin.

Lufia

fice"?) to the monsters. Find the **room with the maidens** and one of them tells you of her brother in the cave southwest of town. You *must* find this maiden before you leave. Save the game and walk southwest to the Cave.

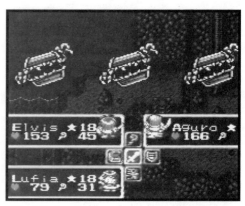

★ **DIAS KEY CAVE:** There's a complete set of **Brone armor** in the Cave chests, but what you're *really* looking for is the maiden's brother. Look for an **inter-**

The Mimics give you tons of XP, but they usually run away before you can kill them.

section with paths in all directions and a staircase in the middle. Take the south path to find the brother. Open the chest he's guarding to get the Dias Key. Leave this cave and go to Belgen to save the game, then go straight west into the Caves. Use the **Dias Key** to open the door blocking your way. Open all the chests on your way through. On the way, you might be attacked by a few **Mimics**, which are weak creatures that give you a huge amount of XP if you can defeat them before they run away from the battle. When you make it through the Caves, head west to the Altar.

★ **ALTAR:** Poor **Jerin**! There's nothing you can do right now, so talk to the cleric to save the game, then walk up to the pots on either side of the Altar and press the A button to refill your HP and MP. When you leave the Altar, a huge dragon swoops onto the screen and takes Jerin away to the North Tower. Go get her!

★ **NORTH TOWER:** Climbing up to the top floor isn't that hard, but once you're there, you need to walk on certain **teleport circles** to reach Jerin. *Don't* walk on the circle at the north end of the room or you'll be teleported back to the bottom of the Tower. Here's what to do to reach Jerin: Walk onto the circle on the right side of the room

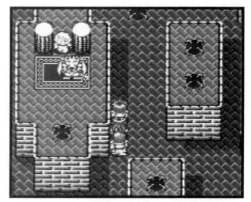

You have to walk on the teleport circles in a certain order to get to Jerin.

Lufia

(next to the stone pillars). Walk north into the next circle. Walk north again.

★ Jerin's being guarded by a dragon named **Follower**. Have your character and Aguro hack away while Lufia casts her Drain spells to weaken the Follower. Use Shield spells if the Follower casts Drain spells on your party. The Follower can cast Stronger spells to recharge its HP, so keep hacking away. When you

Jerin makes a surprise appearance in the Guide Station and makes Lufia jealous.

win, you automatically return to Belgen. Talk to everyone in town to hear their guilt at sending Jerin off to be dragon dinner. Save the game, leave town, and walk east across the desert to Surinagal.

★ **SURINAGAL:** Buy better equipment at the Armor and Weapon Shops, save the game, and talk to everyone to learn about the Lost Forest south of town. Go south and walk across the bridge, then walk west until you find a small building. Go into the building, *not* the Forest.

★ **GUIDE STATION:** Talk to the old man and ask for the guide. It's **Jerin**! After a very funny intermission sequence, Jerin joins your party. Search the Guide Station for items, then talk to the old man again and rest. Now leave the Station and head back to **Surinagal**. You need to buy Jerin some equipment for the journey ahead. Use whatever it takes to keep her alive on the way back to town, even Smoke Balls to run away from battles.

★ **SURINAGAL:** Buy a **Glass Cap** and **Brone Breast** for Jerin, then power up outside of town. Get Jerin up to **Level 17** before heading for the Lost Forest.

★ **LOST FOREST:** Listen to Jerin as she calls out directions through the Forest. You're attacked by monsters on the way through, but it's a short journey. When you come out of the Forest, walk west into the

With Jerin in your party, getting through the Lost Forest is a breeze.

Lufia

building. Talk to the old man and rest. Leave the building and walk east to the tower. Go inside and follow the passage to find an old man. Talk to him and keep going east until you're back on the Overworld. Go north to the town of Jenoba.

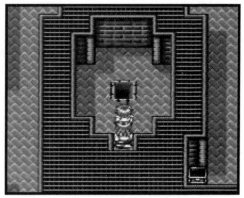

Drop into the pit at the top of the Blue Tower to find the chest with Green Jade inside.

★ **JENOBA:** Visit the Armor and Weapon Shops to buy new and improved equipment. Sell your old weapons and armor for extra Gold. Go into the building with the stairs going down. Take the stairs all the way down to a pub. Talk to the old woman and buy her drinks until she tells you about **Elfrea**. Buy a drink from the **bartender** for more information about the Green Tower. Once you're ready, leave town and walk southeast to the Blue Tower.

★ **BLUE TOWER:** There's a note on the 2nd floor of the Tower that says "Go to the red tower last." Good advice! The **Dark Elves** are by far the toughest creatures in the Blue Tower, thanks to their deadly Water spell. Attack them first. Go up all of the stairs to find chests. Only one set of stairs on each floor leads to stairs on the next floor, however. At the top of the Tower is a **pedestal**, but you can't do anything there yet. For now, look for the room with a **pit**. Drop through the pit, open the chest, and drop down the pit again. Open the second chest for the

Green Jade. That's it! Leave the tower and head back to Jenoba to save the game and buy supplies. Leave town, walk south across the bridge, and walk east to the Green Tower.

★ **GREEN TOWER:** Go through the right door on the 1st floor to find an Inn! Stay there to recharge your HP and MP. Now go through the left door (for treasure) and the middle

There's an Inn at the bottom of the Green Tower if (and when) you need to recharge.

door (to find stairs up to the 2nd floor).

★ There's a room with a **switch** on the left side of the 2nd floor. Move the switch down and you can climb up the stairs to the treasure chests on the 3rd floor. Move the switch up again in order to climb up to the 4th floor. On the 4th floor is a man who tells you the **secret of the Towers**, but you don't need to pay him since we

The jeweller in Ruan tells you the difference between rubies and sapphires.

already tell you the secret in this chapter! Might as well give him some money since you came this far, though. Leave the Tower and head northeast to the town of Ruan, next to the Red Tower.

★ **RUAN:** Talk to the Jeweller to find out some interesting information on **jewels**. Save the game and head into the Red Tower.

★ **RED TOWER:** Go through the second door from the left and down the stairs into the basement. Use a **Float** spell to hover over the poison and open the chests for Potions. Climb back to the 1st floor and start making your way up.

★ The evil **Dark Ghost** is at the top. He's one tough cookie, with super-powerful **Water** spells that suck away your HP like they're going out of style, so you should be up to Level 23 or 24 before taking him on. Keep using the Strong and Stronger spells to keep everyone alive, and using the Drain spells on the Ghost to make him weak. Beat the Ghost to free the **Water Fairy** and restore purity to Ruan's waters. Drop off the top of the Tower and walk to Ruan.

★ **RUAN:** The Innkeeper lets you stay for free, so take advantage of it. Save the game, because you now have to walk all the way back to the Medan Mines to talk to the old man!

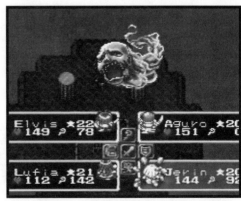

The Dark Ghost is the boss at the top of the Red Tower. Defeat him to free the Water Fairy.

Lufia

★ **MEDAN MINES:** Find the old guy and talk to him to get a **Red Sapphire**. Go into his treasure room and open the chests for more items. Now return to Ruan, save the game, and go into the Red Tower.

Take the long trip back to the Medan Mines to get the Red Sapphire from the old miner.

★ **RED TOWER:** Go into the basement of the Red Tower. Remember how it was flooded with poison? The poison's gone and there's a chest on the floor. Open it to find **Blue Jade**. You now have all three items and can open the way to Elfrea.

★ First, go to the top of the Blue Tower and put the Blue Jade inside the pedestal. Then go to the top of the Green Tower and put in the Green Jade. Now head for the top of the Red Tower and use the Red Sapphire. You'll be magically transported to Elfrea.

★ **ELFREA:** The Innkeeper's so surprised to see humans that he lets you stay for free. Buy equipment from the Weapon Shop. (You might need to fight monsters outside of town to build up your Gold.) Go upstairs in the house at the north end of Elfrea to find **Artea**. He can't help you, alas, but he gives you the **Shrine Key**. Just as you leave his room, Artea gives his **bow** to Jerin.

★ Buy Tridents for yourself and Aguro, Quilted Silk for Lufia and Jerin, and Heeled Shoes if you want to boost up Jerin's or Lufia's Attack strength. When you're equipped, go downstairs in Artea's house and use the Shrine Key to get into the Shrine. Walk onto the circle to warp to the shrine.

★ **OVERWORLD:** Use the **Shrine Key** to unlock the other shrine and walk onto the circle. Go outside to the Overworld. From here, walk west and go into the shrine surrounded by poison squares. Search the

The once-great Artea is now blind and feeble, but hey, at least he gives you a cool weapon!

shrine for the old man. Talk to him for guidance and advice. He also gives you power for a future battle. Use the lower-right door to leave the shrine and walk southeast until you find the town of Ranqs. (There's a cave to the east of Ranqs, but you don't need to visit it.)

Read the steps below to get through the force field in the Mountain Tunnel.

★ **RANQS:** Women are running the town because all the men are working in the Mountain Tunnel to Odel. Buy weapons and armor from the Shops and save your game at the church. There's a **Power Potion** hidden in the bush next to the old woman's house. When you're done exploring, leave town and walk west to the Mountain Tunnel.

★ **MOUNTAIN TUNNEL:** There's an invisible **force field** blocking the Tunnel. If you want a clue about how to get through here, visit the old man in the cave east of Ranqs. Better yet, just use our directions! From the tunnel entrance (just past the sign), go Up 1, Right 2, Up 1, Right 2, Up 4, Left 3, Down 1, Left 2, Down 1, Left 2, Up 2, Right 1, Up 1, Right 2, Up to the stairs. To go back south, just walk straight through the tunnel. Once you pass through the Tunnel, walk southwest to Odel.

★ **ODEL:** Explore the town and buy weapons and armor at the Shop. Walk to the building in the **northwest corner** and go down the stairs. Talk to everyone in the basement to learn about the architect in Odel Castle. Leave the building and enter the Castle.

★ **ODEL CASTLE:** Search the bushes on the east side of the Castle for **three Potions**, then enter the Castle and climb up to the throne room. Talk to **Piron** and he'll send you to get his friend in Lyden. Leave the throne room and leave Odel. You might

Elvis found Mind Potion.

Pilfer the bushes on the right side of Odel Castle for Potions before you go inside.

Lufia

want to level up outside of Odel until you're strong enough for the journey to Lyden. When you're ready, go southeast from Odel to find Lyden.

★ **LYDEN:** Talk to the man in the **restaurant** and he heads back to Odel. Explore the town to find another restaurant with an old man near the entrance. Walk down into the basement of the restaurant to find—well, nothing, really,

There's a man called the "Wizard of Taste". His dishes are unbelievable!

Remember the location of the restaurants in Lyden. You'll be coming back here later.

but you need to come back here later, so remember the place. The monsters outside of town are exceptionally strong, so power up and keep saving. Return to Odel when you're ready.

★ **ODEL CASTLE:** Talk to Piron and he sends you into the Arus Caves to find the broken bridge.

★ **ARUS CAVES:** There are four ways into the Caves, but only one of them takes you to the bridge. The other entrances just lead to chests. Go southwest until you find a bridge going north. Cross the bridge and into the entrance. This Cave takes you to the bridge. Walk into the bridge so that the characters talk about how smashed up it is, then go back to Odel Castle.

★ **ODEL CASTLE:** Talk to Piron and he goes to the Caves.

★ **ARUS CAVES:** Go back into the Caves and talk to him at the bridge. He asks you to watch his work from the cliff on the right. Aargh! Can't this guy just fix it already?! Anyway... Leave the Cave and walk east to Odel, then go west across the bridge. Go into the first or second entrances from the right, then walk south along the path until it turns west. Walk west to find the cliff. Piron (finally) fixes the bridge when you're in position. Go back to the

After an amazing amount of hassle, Piron finally fixes the bridge while you watch.

Lufia

first entrance and cross over the bridge. Keep going until you're through the Caves.

★ **ARUS:** The Professor's not here, of course, but in the Tower of Grief west of town. Explore the town and talk to everyone. Get the Potion out of the bush at the north end of town. Save the game and head west through the small cave to the Tower.

Climb to the top of the Tower of Grief to boost Lufia's magical potential.

★ **TOWER OF GRIEF:** To get to the chests on the **2nd floor**, fall through the crevice surrounding the chests and go up the stairs in the room you fall into. There are four sets of stairs on the 3rd floor. Go up the lower-left and upper-right stairs to chests. The other ones lead to more stairs. There are **MP and HP circles** on the 5th floor, next to the stairs to 6th floor. Power up here, then climb the stairs and talk to **Flake** (nice name!). He increases Lufia's MP by 10. Open the chest next to him for a **Miracle Potion**. The Prof has returned to his lab, so go back to Odel Castle.

★ **ODEL CASTLE:** Go down the stairs in the **Castle courtyard** to find **Shaia Lab 2**. Shaia's gone to Lab 1. Walk into the southeast corner of the room and down the stairs, then follow the tunnel to a warp square. Talk to the man and he explains how the square works. Walk onto the square, then take the west tunnel to Lab 1.

★ **SHAIA LAB 1:** Go upstairs to find the **Prof** at last! After an unusual conversation, he takes you to see his submarine named **Falcon**. You end up at the dock of Shaia Lab 1 with the Falcon.

★ Instead of heading for Shaia Lab 3, it's time to take a journey to the **Isle of Forfeit**. To get there, sail around the peninsula, then sail east along the coast until you reach

Take your spiffy new boat around the coast to the mysterious Isle of Forfeit.

Lufia

Lyden. Save the game there and sail north, staying along the coast, until you reach the Isle. You'll fight some tough sea creatures on the way, so you better be powered up!

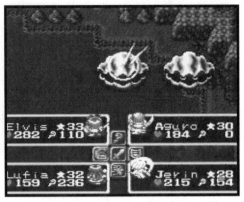

On the way to the Isle of Forfeit, you'll encounter a barrage of sea monsters.

★ **ISLE OF FORFEIT:** The only really interesting items for sale are the **Gladius** at the Weapon Shop and the **Knife Shoes** at the Armor Shop (they raise Attack and Defense). On the 2nd floor is a shop with everything you've ever sold at other shops! There's also a shop with two girls who force you into buying something. Once you've walked into the shop, you can't leave until you buy something. Get something very cheap and you get kisses from both of them as you leave the shop. Hubba hubba!

★ See those stairs next to the trees on the north side of town? Here's how to get to them. When you first enter town, walk east behind the trees, then go east and north to the stairs. Go down the stairs and walk north into the **House of Magic**, where the magician talks about Long Nails and Straw Dolls. Hmmm. Now walk south and follow the path to find a chest with a **Mind Ring**. Take the Ring, leave town, and sail back to Shaia Lab 1. Once you're there, sail due west to Shaia Lab 3, on the middle of the three islands.

★ **SHAIA LAB 3 (CARBIS):** Go into the basement to find **Professor Shaia** along with a cleric! Talk to the woman against the west wall and smell the oil to recover all your HP and MP (it's like staying at an Inn). Save your game with the priest and talk to the Prof. He sends you on a mission to get his friend Copper from the town of Bakku. Go back to the ship and sail due west to

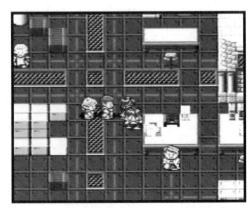

Look for Shaia Lab 3 on the middle of the three islands west of Lab 1.

Lufia

find Bakku. (It's on the south coast.)

★ **BAKKU:** The Weapon Shop doesn't have anything new, but the Armor Shop has cool new stuff for all the characters. Buy it! Talk to the **cleric** to find out that Cooper is at the fifth level of the Old Cave, way back near Grenoble. Geez! Leave town and get back into the Falcon.

Shaia's pal Cooper is way back at the Old Cave near Grenoble. Go get him!

★ **OVERWORLD:** Sail east around the peninsula and straight north until you see a **temple**. Go into the temple. It's the **mysterious old man**! Talk to him and go into the upper-right door to warp to the temple near Kirof. From here, go south, east, and north to Treck, then south to Grenoble. This is familiar territory, so you shouldn't get lost.

★ **GRENOBLE:** Go to the Old Cave assignment room and get assigned a mission for the 5th level. Go to the old cave.

★ **OLD CAVE:** Go down to the 5th level. the monsters are pretty weak, so you won't have any problems here. Head for the eastern side of the Cave to find **Cooper**. He's behind a door surrounded by poison squares. Don't talk to him until you've explored the entire level, because you automatically use the Escape spell to leave the Cave. Especially look for the Mind Ring and Luck Blade (which is cursed, so sell it and don't use it).

The Mind Ring boosts your Intelligence by 30 and slightly decreases other attributes.

★ **GRENOBLE:** Return here and drop off the item at the assignment place for some Gold. Leave town and walk back to the shrine. Go inside, talk to him, and use the lower-left door to return to the temple next to your ship. Set sail for Shaia Lab 3.

Cooper's behind this door in the Old Cave. Use the Float spell to get over the poison squares.

Lufia

★ **SHAIA LAB 3:** Save the game and talk to the Prof. He asks you to hunt down seven pieces of **Alumina**. You have to travel to **Linze** and talk to a guy named **Brant** who knows where the Alumina is. Leave the lab and sail to Bakku. Save the game there and walk north to the Tower of Light.

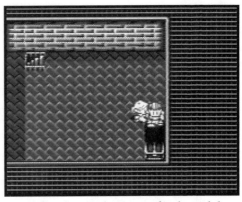

Find this chest in the Tower of Light and drop through the trap door to greater treasures.

★ **TOWER OF LIGHT:** Drop into the pit when you first walk into the Tower and open the chests for several Potions, then climb back up the stairs. There are several trap doors in front of the treasure chests in the Tower, and there's one of them on a high floor that you *want* to fall through. You'll land in a small room with no doors. Walk around the floor to fall through another trap door and open the four chests for great stuff!

★ When you reach the floor with the red carpet, you've almost reached the **Guardian** at the top. Attack him by using your character and Aguro to attack while Lufia and Jerin cast spells. The Guardian casts plenty of spells, so keep using the Boost spell. After you defeat the Guardian, the Sinistral **Amon** appears. Eeek! When Amon and his bud leave, open the chest for the Light Key and jump off the north side of the Tower. Walk north into the Tower, then to the north end of 1st floor. Use the Light Key to open the door. Walk northeast to Linze.

★ **LINZE:** You'll find out from the people in town that Brant went to **Gayas Island** to get Alumina. Buy new weapons and armor at the Shops, then save the game and go down the stairs in the house in the northeast corner. Talk to the woman and go down the stairs again. Walk down the red

The Great Reunion draws nigh! Even now, our brother Daos awakens!

Amon is waiting for you at the top of the Tower of Light. Don't let him scare ya!

tunnel and talk to the old man, then open his chests. Walk down the green tunnel and up the stairs at the end. You're now on Gayas Island!

★ **GAYAS ISLAND:** Walk east to the Gayas Cave and go inside.

★ **GAYAS CAVE:** In the first level of the Cave, you encounter the same monsters as in the Tower of Light. The worst new enemies by far are the **Were-frogs**. Unless you get in a surprise attack, run away from the Werefrogs or just be prepared to use lots of spells.

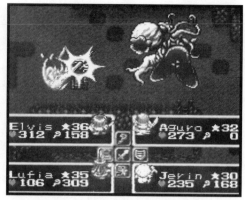

One of the monsters in the Gayas Cave might give you the Buster Sword when he dies.

★ There are several trap doors in the Cave, along with a much-needed **piece of Alumina**. Look for the wall with three doors. Go into the left door to find a chest, the middle door to find a switch, and the right door to climb on top of the wall.

★ Once you've got the Alumina, move the switch down, then go through the left door and walk onto the warp circle. You'll appear in a new area of the Cave. Don't miss the **Silver Sword**; walk into the southeast corner and through the door. Go onto the warp circle to find a chest with the Sword inside. You might also get a **Buster Sword** while fighting the monsters in this cave. It's *very* powerful, so use it!

★ After you cross the bridge near the end of the Cave, you can go north or east. Go east to find a shrine where you can restore HP. Go north to find a man named **Clack**. Ask him questions about all four topics in the list. When you go to leave, Clack takes you to his room and gives you the **Wave Ring**, which used to be Maxim's. Coolness! Equip the ring to heavily boost your Attack and Defense ratings. Leave the Cave and go back to Linze.

Ask Clack what he knows about the four topics on the list, then get the Wave Ring.

Lufia

Save the game and go north to Marse.

★ By the way, if you die in the Gayas Cave and restart in Linze, your ship appears in the lake! To get to Marse without sailing, walk south through the Tower of Light, then east to the shrine, then north across the bridge. Go through the cave and north to Marse, then inten-tionally die after saving at Marse and the ship

Take a cruise from Marse to scope out the Fargo Islands north of town.

appears there when you restart. Weird, huh?

★ **MARSE:** Take a cruise to get acquainted with the **Fargo Islands**. Save the game and get ready to sail yourself! Instead of heading for the Islands, however, go west to the river and then sail into it. Follow the river south to the town of Herat.

★ **HERAT:** There are great Weapon and Armor Shops here. One person here tells you that if you take eight **Dragon Eggs** to the **Dragon Shrine** southeast of here, you get a wish granted. You should have seven Eggs when you reach here. If you don't, you haven't been exploring the dungeons enough! Go north into Herat Castle.

★ **HERAT CASTLE:** Talk to everyone to figure out that the King wants something very tasty. That something is the **Purple Newt** in the cave to the east of Herat. Leave town and sail out of the river, then go west

and follow along the coast for a bit. Land the boat and start walking south along the coast to find the Dragon Shrine. From here, go east and north to the Newt Cave.

★ **NEWT CAVE:** Go to the switch room in the upper-right corner and throw the **switch** down. Go to the teleport circle in the lower-left corner and walk into it to teleport to an area with two chests. One of them

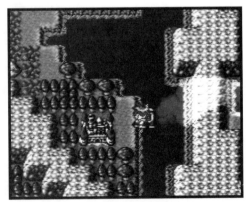

Sail down the river west of Marse to find the well-hidden city of Herat.

has the **Purple Newt** inside. Now get the heck out of this Cave (use an Escape spell for an easy exit), return to your ship, and sail to Marse. Save the game and take a long sail south and east to the town of Lyden.

Give the Magic Flavor to the King of Herat in exchange for mondo treasure.

★ **LYDEN:** Go to the restaurant with the old man and keep going down the stairs until you find the **Wizard of Taste** (he's dressed in red). Give him the Newt in exchange for the **Magic Flavor**. Leave town and sail back to Herat.

★ **HERAT CASTLE:** Give the Magic Flavor to the chef in the kitchen. See the King and he sends you down to his jewel collection in the Castle basement. Enter the basement and open the chests for all kinds of great stuff, including a **piece of Alumina**. Two pieces down, five to go! Save the game and set sail for Elba Island, to the north of Marse.

★ **ELBA ISLAND:** There are **three pieces of Alumina** in this huge cave, which is also linked to **Ulaff Island**. The **blue** section of the cave is Elba; the **red** section is Ulaff. There's an **Inn** at the bottom of the blue cave if you run low on energy. Walk into the lower-right corner and go up the huge ladder, then go into the door and teleport to an area with chests. Alumina is inside one of them. The eighth Dragon Egg is also somewhere in this cave.

★ To find the second piece of Alumina, go into the door to the right of the huge ladder and press the switch down. Climb up the ladder and teleport to the red section of the cave. Remember, you need to find three pieces of Alumina. Once you have, leave the island. Sail back to Marse, save the game, and then sail northeast to Loire Island.

There are three Alumina pieces in the caves below Elba and Ulaff Island.

★ **LOIRE ISLAND:** Walk into

Lufia

the door in the upper-right corner of the cave for **Alumina** inside a chest. That's **six** pieces! Explore the rest of the cave, then go down the stairs on the west side of the cave near the bridge. Look for a chest in a small enclosed area. Walk toward the chest to fall through a pit and land in a new area of the cave. Look! It's **Brant**! Talk to him and you automatically cast the Escape

Fall into the lowest level of the cave to find Brant and get the final Alumina piece.

spell to leave the cave. Brant gives you the last piece of Alumina before he leaves. You can go to Shaia Lab 3 now, but before you do, take a detour to the Dragon Shrine that you passed by earlier on the way to the Newt Cave.

★ **DRAGON SHRINE:** The Dragon gives you a choice of four wishes: Raise Everyone Two Levels, Give Each 3 "~ Potions", We Want A Might Shield, and We Want A Might Bow. The first two wishes are pretty lame, since your levels are always increasing anyway and you're always finding Potions in treasure chests, so get the **Might Shield** (which we did) or the **Might Bow**. Go back to the ship and sail to Shaia Lab 3.

★ **SHAIA LAB 3:** Enter the Lab and the assistant tells you that the Prof went to Aisen Island alone! What a doofus! Now you have to go rescue him. Sail back to Marse and save the game, then sail northwest to the pirate tower on Aisen Island.

★ **AISEN ISLAND:** There's nothing too tricky in here until you reach the **door with four buttons** in front of it. You have to hit the buttons in a certain order or you'll be attacked by a group of four very angry Pirates. Hit them in this order: upper-left, lower-right, lower-left,

Walk on the buttons in the right order to open the door at the top of Aisen Tower.

upper-right. Now hit the fifth switch to open the door without setting off the alarm.

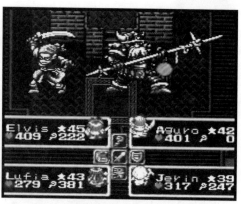

Bosun is weak, but he casts healing spells on Pirates. Take Bosun out first.

★ Behind the switch door are **two bosses**. **Bosun** is the weaker of the two, but he casts healing spells on the stronger guy, **Pirates**. Concentrate your attacks on both of them at same time. Use Boost spells to keep the party healthy, Drain spells on both bosses, and attack spells just for fun. Beat the bosses and open the chests behind them for the Pirate Key and a strange object. Find the Professor's prison cell (if you didn't stumble upon it earlier). Open the chest first for the Heavy Ring, then free the Prof. (The Heavy Ring heavily boosts your Attack skill, but your other skills suffer big declines.) When the Prof is free, he sails for Shaia Lab 3. Follow him there.

★ **SHAIA LAB 3:** Talk to the Prof and he fixes **Falcon**. Now you automatically take the Falcon to the surface of the ocean. Sail due north to find **Linze Island**. Go to the north end of the island and dock in Soshette.

★ **SOSHETTE:** Enter the cave to the north and talk to the old man about the lagoon inside the island. Leave town and sail into the **swirling eddy** on the east side of the island. Now you're **underwater**!

★ **UNDERWATER:** All three eddys around Linze Island are passages that lead to the sunken Doom Island through underwater caves. You can explore all of them to find treasure chests, or just get through one quickly to reach Doom Island. The **blue squares** on the floor are **flowing currents**. Don't get caught in a current or it might wash you down a tunnel you don't want to go down!

★ **DOOM ISLAND:** You explored this Castle at the beginning of the game, so make your way back up to the room of the Sinistrals. The monsters here are nastier than ever! There are no chests to be opened, so just head for the top of the Castle to find the **Dual Blade**. When you get the Blade, a very long sequence of events takes place, but the point of it all is that Lufia is one of the Sinistrals. Yikes! Once the long intermission is over, set sail for Shaia Lab 3.

★ **SHAIA LAB 3:** Talk to the Prof to find out how to make the Falcon fly. You need **Power Oil**, which is for sale only in Epro. Leave Lab 3 and set sail for Epro, which is due north of Marse.

Lufia

★ **EPRO:** Buy weapons and armor. The **Sword Shoes** and **Cat Heels** might be the only things you need, but you should have more than enough gold to buy whatever you want. Talk to everyone to find out about **Hedge**, the man north of town who's looking for a way through the mountains. You can walk up to Hedge, but it's much faster and easier to sail the route. Talk to Hedge to get the **Oil Key**. He also mentions eddies in the **East Lagoon**. Ah-ha! Sail east and north into the swirling eddy.

Sail up to Hedge and talk to him in exchange for the Oil Key.

★ **EAST LAGOON:** The exit eddy is in the northwest corner, but explore the cave before you go through it. It's a good way to power up on the sea monsters while you round up treasure. When you hit the northwest eddy, you appear back in the ocean. Go west and hit the next eddy to appear in the mountain lake. Sail north and hit land, then walk north, west, and south over the poison squares to find the Oil Cave.

★ **OIL CAVE:** Hover across the poison and use the Oil Key to open the door. Go into the Cave and explore, then go down the stairs in the southwest corner to the 2nd level. The **Oil Dragon** is in the northeast corner of the 2nd floor, and you have to fight it to get the Power Oil. Use the same boss technique you've been using up to now to defeat it easily. Open the chest for the Power Oil, then use an Escape spell and go back to the ship. Sail back to the eddy and go through it to the East Lagoon. Now go due east to find Frederia.

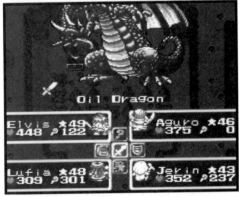
You can't get the Power Oil without first defeating the Oil Dragon. Makes sense.

★ **FREDERIA:** Save the game, buy weapons and armor, and go into the basement dock to find the Prof. Talk to him and he refits the Falcon to fly. Once you appear outside of Frederia, press A to take off and fly straight west over the mountains to Arubus. Land in the water and walk into town.

★ **ARUBUS:** Buy armor and weapons if you need them. Walk into the cave at the north end of town and buy lots of healing **Apple Cider**. It's expensive, but you can afford it. Walk back out of the cave and talk to the man at the north end of town. He

Give some Apple Cider to the man in Arubus in exchange for some information.

asks for some cider, so give it to him and he tells you where the Glasdar Key is hidden. Save the game and fly to the North Cave. Park next to the Cave and go inside.

★ **NORTH CAVE:** There's a **White Ring** on the west side of the 1st floor, through the door. Go down the stairs after you get the Ring and you'll eventually come to two doors. Go into the left door to find a chamber

with a warp circle and a door. Go through the door and pull the switch down. Now go back to the two doors and take the right door to find a warp circle. Hit the warp circle to teleport next to some stairs. Go down the stairs and open the chests to get the **Glasdar Key**. Yes! Use the Escape spell to leave, fly back to Arubus, and save. Now fly west and slightly north to find the Glasdar Cave. Land the Falcon and go inside.

Use the altars in Glasdar Cave to power up. This is the last chance you'll have to do it!

★ **GLASDAR CAVE:** There's a **Black Ring** in this cave, along with an altar where you can restore your HP and MP. You might want to power up in this area before going through the Cave. Once you get through the Cave, walk north and into the Glasdar Tower.

★ **GLASDAR TOWER:** You've explored plenty of towers up to now, but

Lufia

this one's the biggest of them all. Walk through the hallways to find your way to the stairs up to each new floor. There's a **door** near the top of the Tower with **three buttons** in front of it. Hit the middle button and walk through the door. hit the wrong button and you're teleported back down to a lower floor of the Tower.

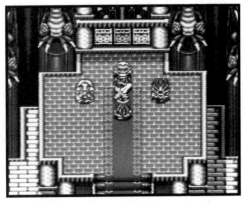

Defeat Nazeby and the Sinistrals take Lufia away from you. This means war!

★ A creature named **Nazeby** attacks you at the top of the Tower. He's *very* powerful, with spells that can kill your party members instantly. Use the Boost spell constantly to keep your party healthy as you fight. If you lose a party member, use a **Miracle Potion** or cast a spell to bring him back to life. You need all four characters to survive!

★ When you defeat Nazeby, the **Sinistrals** appear and take away Lufia! Yikes! Doom Island flies southeast and parks in the air just north of the **Tower of Grief**, which is due east of Linze island (where Doom Island erupted from in the first place). Save the game and get yourself a powerful weapon to replace the Dual Blade, then fly the Falcon to the Tower of Grief and fly into Doom Island.

★ **DOOM ISLAND:** Land on the pad and walk north to the temple. Speak to the old man and he gives you power for the final battle. Save the game, then walk north to leave the temple and climb up to Doom Castle.

★ **DOOM CASTLE:** This is your third time in here, so you better know your way around by now! The chests have items in them, so search them all. You especially want the **Miracle Potions** for the final battle. The creatures here are extremely tough, so use your **Sweet Water** to keep them away (or at least to

The monsters in Doom Castle are extremely tough. Use Sweet Water and get to the top!

try and keep them away).

★ At the top of the Castle, you'll get the Dual Blade back and be attacked by the three Sinistrals in order: **Gades**, then **Amon**, then **Daos**. Amon casts a lot of **Dread** spells instead of attacking you, so he's very easy to beat. Daos is much tougher. Have Jerin cast a few Trick spells to increase your attack power when fighting Daos. Remember to keep using

The individual Sinistrals are easy to beat if you keep using the Boost spell.

Boost spells to keep the party's HP up. And if you're in *real* trouble, have your character cast a Valor spell to recharge everyone's HP.

★ When you beat Daos, he unites the Sinistrals into a giant creature called a **Guard Daos**. Luckily you have **Lufia** fighting with you again! Use the same fighting technique you've used against all the bosses: you and Aguro attack while Lufia and Jerin cast spells. The only difference is that Jerin should cast her **Mirror** spell on everyone in the party to

protect them from Daos, who loves to cast Figual (confusion) and Flood spells. With the Mirrors up, the Flood spells will backfire and hit Daos.

★ Defeat the Guard Daos and you get to watch an extremely long **ending sequence** where all the loose plot twists (except that strange old guy who kept helping you!) are tied up. When "THE END" appears, don't turn off the SNES. Keep pressing the

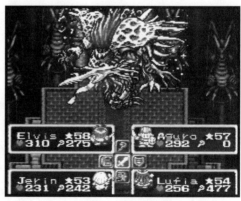

The Guard Daos is the final boss. Use the Mirror spell to deflect his barrage of magic.

buttons until a statistic screen appears with all kinds of stats about how well you did during the game. Neat!

MORTAL KOMBAT

BY ACCLAIM

Introduction

The biggest fighting game since Street Fighter II has made it to the SNES, but it's not a perfect conversion of the arcade game, since Nintendo make Acclaim take all the blood and gore out. Three of the fatalities are the same—Liu Kang, Scorpion, and Sonya—but the other four have been toned down. Still, it's the game-play that matters, and Mortal Kombat's just as fun without the blood.

This version of Mortal Kombat has modified fatalities.

If you've never played Mortal Kombat before (and where have you been?), it's a fighting game where you take control of one of seven different characters and guide him or her through a martial arts tournament. Each character has several special moves and a finishing move used to finish off your opponent in gruesome fashion.

Awesome Strategies

★ This chapter has everything you'll ever need to know about Mortal Kombat. It's divided into several easy-to-read sections. Keep in mind that almost all of the strategies in this chapter also work on the arcade version:

★ **Basic Moves** details the simple moves that all the characters can do.

★ **Character Profiles** details each character's special moves and finishing move.

Learn basic moves like the skull-denting High Punch.

Mortal Kombat

★ **Attacks and Counter-Attacks** details the best ways to retaliate against each character's special moves.

★ **Two-Player Tips** tells you strategies to use against a human opponent.

★ **One-Player Tips** tells you strategies to use against the computer.

★ **Boss Tips** tells you strategies to use against Goro and Shang Tsung.

★ **Awesome Secrets** tells you how to make the mysterious secret character Reptile appear.

Basic Moves

★ This section assumes that you're using the default control method.

★ **High Punch**: Press Y repeatedly. This is a fast attack and does good damage, but it can't hit a crouch-blocking opponent. The High Punch is best used to hit an opponent in the air, since it knocks them higher into the air and gives you time to set up for a special move.

★ **Low Punch**: Press B repeatedly. It doesn't do as much damage as the High Punch, but it's just as fast, and can hit crouch-blocking opponents (except for Sonya). If your opponent isn't blocking away (by pressing the controller Down/Away or Away), you'll throw him.

★ **Jump Kick**: Jump at your opponent and press X or A. If your opponent doesn't jump in response, don't press the Kick button until late in the jump so that you don't get tagged by an Uppercut, and so your Kick doesn't fade out by the time you reach the opponent.

★ **Sweep Kick**: Press Away and A. The farther away from your opponent you start the Sweep, the harder it is for him to hit you with a counter-attack if he blocks.

★ **Weak Kick**: Press Down and X or A. This is the only move that can always hit an opponent who's close to you and using Low Punches.

Tag a low-punching opponent with the Weak Kick.

You can also use the Weak Kick to kick an opponent out of the air if he finished a Jump Kick too soon or if he's using a jumping Punch.

★ **Knee**: Stand right next to your opponent. Press Toward (or leave the control pad centered) and A. This works best against opponents who are crouching but not blocking (to avoid Low Punches).

★ **Roundhouse Kick**: Press

Mortal Kombat

Away and X. Looks cool, but isn't too effective.

The Uppercut is one of the most powerful moves in the game.

★ **Kick**: Press B or C when you're not doing any other Kick move. Use this to retaliate against a Sweep Kick or to kick opponents out of the air.

★ **Throw**: Move close to your opponent and press X. If you don't throw your opponent, he's blocking and pressing Down/Away or Away.

★ **Close Attack**: Move close to your opponent and press Toward and B. Each character has a different close attack. Johnny Cage strikes his opponent with an elbow, Kano head-butts his opponent, and so on.

★ **Uppercut**: Hold the joystick Down and press Y or B. Liu Kang and Johnny Cage are the best with the Uppercut, and can knock jumping opponents out of the air almost every time. Try this method: when an opponent jumps at you, block and crouch (hold L Button or R Button and press the controller Down and Away) and use the Uppercut when your opponent hits your body. The Uppercut is also useful right after blocking a special move (such as Scorpion or Rayden's Teleport).

Character Profiles

★ In the moves listed for each character below, **Toward** means to push the controller toward your opponent, and **Away** means to push the controller away from your opponent.

Johnny Cage

★ A martial arts superstar trained by great masters from around the world, Johnny Cage is also the star of such (fictitious) films as Dragon Fist and Sudden Violence. His "real" name is listed in the Mortal Kombat manual as John Carlton. There's a real-life John Carlton working at Midway in Chicago; he's an artist who also worked on the NBA Jam coin-op.
SPECIAL MOVES AND FINISHING MOVE:

★ **Fireball**: Press Away from your opponent, then push Toward and B.

★ **Shadow Kick**: Press Away from your opponent, then push Toward and A.

Mortal Kombat

★ **Split Punch**: Hold R Button and press B. Usually followed by a Throw or by jumping away to get clear of the opponent.

★ **Finishing Move**: Stand right next to your opponent and press Toward, Toward, Toward, Y. Johnny does a Low Kick so strong it penetrates into his opponent's chest.

COMBINATIONS:

The Shadow Kick is easy to execute and very fast.

★ **Combination #1**: Jump Kick/Shadow Kick. Jump Kick an opponent on the ground and then Shadow Kick (or a regular standing Kick if your opponent is trapped on the side of the screen).

Kano

★ A criminal member of the Black Dragon Organization, Kano has a metal implant on the right side of his face that includes an infrared eye.

SPECIAL MOVES AND FINISHING MOVE:

★ **Roll Spin**: Press the controller Away and then spin the controller in a circle back to Away. If you hold down the Block button while using the Spin, Kano hovers in midair.

★ **Knife**: Press the controller Away, Away, Toward, R Button.

★ **Finishing Move**: Stand close to the opponent (but not too close) and press Away, Down, Toward, B. Kano plunges his hand into the opponent's chest and feels around for his or her heart.

COMBINATIONS:

★ **Combination #1**: Jump Kick/Roll Spin. Jump Kick an opponent on the ground and follow up with a Roll Spin. A tough combo to execute. To

Kano hurls an energy knife at his opponent.

Mortal Kombat

make it even tougher, try doing two Jump Kicks in a row, then the Roll Spin.

★ **Combination #2**: Jump Kick/Knife. Jump Kick an opponent on the ground and follow with a Knife throw.

★ **Combination #3**: Low Punch/Roll Spin. Use the Low Punch to lure your blocking opponent into attacking, then use the Roll Spin.

Kano does an impromptu chest examination on his opponent.

Liu Kang

★ Once a member of the super-secret White Lotus Society, Liu Kang is the only fighter in Mortal Kombat who doesn't draw his powers from the "dark side"—that's why the screen doesn't darken when you perform his finishing move.

SPECIAL MOVES AND FINISHING MOVE:

★ **Fireball**: Press Toward, Toward, Y.

★ **Flying Kick**: Press Toward, Toward, X.

★ **Finishing Move**: Press the controller Down and then spin the controller in a circle at your opponent and back to Down. If your opponent is on your right, spin the controller clockwise. If he's on your left, spin it counter-clockwise. Liu Kang does a spinning flip and a massive uppercut. It's easier to execute this move if you hold down Block while rotating the directional pad in the coin-op version.

COMBINATIONS:

★ **Combination #1**: Jump Kick/Flying Kick. Jump Kick an opponent on the ground (or in the air) and immediately follow with a Flying Kick.

★ **Combination #2**: Fireball/Flying Kick. Stand at least half a screen away

Liu Kang takes to the air with his ferocious Flying Kick.

Mortal Kombat

from your opponent and hit him with a Fireball, then follow up with a Flying Kick. If he tries to jump over the Fireball, you'll smash him with your Flying Kick. The computer Liu Kang uses this combo all the time.

Rayden

★ Though his name has been changed from the spelling in the coin-op version (Raiden), this mythical thunder god hasn't lost any of his deadly moves and supernatural powers.

SPECIAL MOVES AND FINISHING MOVE:
★ **Lightning Throw**: Press Down, then Toward and B.
★ **Teleport**: Press Down, then Up.
★ **Flying Attack**:Press Away, Away, Toward.
★ **Finishing Move**: Move next to your opponent, and press Toward, Away, Away, Away, Y. Rayden uses lightning to electrocute his opponent.

COMBINATIONS:
★ **Combination #1**: Jump Kick/Flying Attack. Jump Kick an opponent on the ground and immediately follow with the Flying Attack. Another tough combo, but it can be done.

The Flying Attack pushes your opponent to the edge of the screen.

Try doing the Flying Attack before your opponent has hit the ground.
★ **Combination #2**: Jump Kick/Lightning Throw. Jump Kick an opponent on the ground and strike with the Lightning Throw.

Scorpion

★ An undead warrior who is said to have perished at the hands of a Lin Kuei assassin, Scorpion harbors a deep hatred of Sub-Zero that can be traced to these rumors.

SPECIAL MOVES AND FINISHING MOVE:
★ **Harpoon**: Press Away, Away, B. This should always be followed up by an Uppercut for maximum damage. This is a great move to use after blocking Kano's Roll Spin, or after an opponent jumps right next to you.

Mortal Kombat

★ **Teleport**: Press Down, Away, Y.

★ **Finishing Move**: Stand about a body length away from your opponent and press Up, Up. Scorpion pulls his hood off and uses his fire breath to toast his opponent. You can also hold down Block while doing the finishing move, but this keeps you from reaching Reptile in the coin-op version.

Scorpion throws his Harpoon straight into Johnny Cage's throat. Ouch!

COMBINATIONS:

★ **Combination #1**: Jump Kick/Harpoon. Jump Kick an opponent on the ground, then Harpoon him and finish with an Uppercut. Tough.

Sonya

★ A member of a top-ranked Special Forces unit, Sonya and her companions were tracking the mercenary Kano when she was captured by Shang Tsung's army and forced to participate in the tournament. The Mortal Kombat coin-op was already being tested in the Chicago area when the designers decided to add Sonya to the game; the original lineup only included six fighters and the two boss characters.

SPECIAL MOVES AND FINISHING MOVE:

★ **Ring Toss**: Press Away and B.

★ **Square Wave Flight:** Press Toward your opponent, then Away and Y.

★ **Scissors Grab**: Press Down, then press B + A + R Button at the same time. One of the cheapest moves in the game. If you keep getting Grabbed, don't hold down Block— wait for Sonya to slam you to the ground, then let go of Block, and press Block again when you start to get up.

Sonya's Scissors Grab is about to pound Rayden into the ground.

Mortal Kombat

★ **Finishing Move**: Toward, Toward, Away, Away, R Button. Sonya blows a "kiss of death" that burns the flesh off her opponent. You can't reach Reptile with Sonya in the coin-op since her finishing move uses the Block button.

Sub-Zero

★ The actual name of this warrior is unknown; he is believed to be a member of the Lin Kuei, a legendary clan of Chinese ninja assassins.

SPECIAL MOVES AND FINISHING MOVE:

★ **Freeze**: Press Down, then roll the controller Toward your opponent and press B. Using the Freeze attack on an opponent who's already frozen causes a Double Ice Backfire, which freezes Sub-Zero instead.

Here's a Freeze technique to try: Throw your opponent and do a Freeze just as he's getting up. If your opponent isn't blocking, you can throw him again.

Sub-Zero puts the Freeze on Rayden while Rayden blasts Lightning back at him.

★ **Slide**: Hold Away, then press B and A and R Button at the same time.

★ **Finishing Move**: Move right next to your opponent and press Toward, then roll the controller Down, then roll the controller Toward again and press Y. Sub-Zero freezes his opponent and then smashes him into ice cubes with a backhand fist.

COMBINATIONS:

★ **Combination #1**: Jump Kick/Slide. Jump Kick an opponent frozen in the air, then Jump Kick again and then Slide.

★ **Combination #2**: High Punch/Slide. Move next to an opponent frozen in the air, then jump and hit with

Sub-Zero's finishing move is the hardest one to execute in the game.

Mortal Kombat

a High Punch on the way down. Immediately follow with a Jump Kick and Slide. Easier than Combo #1 but does less damage.

★ **Combination #3**: Jump Kick/Uppercut. Freeze an opponent trapped against the side of the screen, then Jump Kick him and follow with an Uppercut as he gets up.

Attacks and Counter-Attacks

★ The most important skill in Mortal Kombat is being able to counter-attack. When someone comes at you with a particular move, you respond with a particular move of your own. We've listed a variety of attacks and counter-attacks in this section, including special moves. These will definitely help you against human opponents, and will also help against the computer.

Fight defensively and know which moves to use against your opponent.

ATTACK: Your opponent is using a **Sweep Kick.**
★ Johnny Cage: Block and use the Shadow Kick.
★ Kano: Block and use the Rolling Attack.
★ Liu Kang: Block and use a Sweep Kick. If they're far enough away after their Sweep Kick, use a Flying Kick instead.
★ Rayden: Block and use the Lightning Attack.
★ Scorpion: Block and use a Sweep Kick or Harpoon.
★ Sonya: Block and use a Sweep Kick or Scissors Grab.
★ Sub-Zero: Block and use a Sweep Kick or Freeze.

ATTACK: Your opponent is using **Low Punches**.
★ Any character: Hold the controller Down/Away and press Low Kick rapidly. It's best to do this while your opponent is still approaching before he starts Low Punching. Don't always respond with Low Kicks; block the Punches once in a while. Block more often if your opponent uses a Sweep Kick when you try to Low Kick.

ATTACK: Your opponent is **jumping toward you**.
★ Any character (method #1): Block the opponent if you have more ener-

gy and time is running out.

★ Any character (method #2): Block the opponent and then Uppercut after he hits you. If he pressed the Kick button too early, he'll hang in the air and give you time to Uppercut.

★ Johnny Cage, Liu Kang, Rayden, or Sonya: Uppercut him in the air. This works better if the opponent is jumping from close range.

The best technique against a jumping opponent is to block and uppercut.

★ If your opponent jumped from far enough away, use a special move.

★ Johnny Cage: Use the Shadow Kick at close range or the Fireball at long range.

★ Kano: Use the Rolling Attack at close range or the Knife at long range.

★ Liu Kang: You *could* use a Fireball, but you'll walk into your opponent since you need to press Toward twice. Stick with Uppercuts.

It's almost impossible to Jump Kick over Rayden's lightning.

★ Rayden: Use the Lightning Attack. It's *very* difficult to Jump Kick Rayden when he's using the Lightning.

★ Scorpion: Use the Harpoon *if* you're far enough away so that you won't be kicked if you mess up the move. Otherwise, use the Teleport, or just Block.

★ Sonya: Use the Square Wave Flight as early as possible, hopefully at the same time your opponent starts his jump.

★ Sub-Zero: Use the Freeze and follow up with a combination move.

ATTACK: Your opponent is **jumping away** from you.

★ Any character: Use your missile weapon and anticipate when your opponent is going to jump. If an opponent jumps back once, he'll probably jump back again, so try to execute a combo on him.

Mortal Kombat

ATTACK: Johnny Cage's Shadow Kick.

★ Any character: Quickly duck and Uppercut. If you can't duck fast enough, Block and try to throw Cage instead.

ATTACK: Kano's Roll Spin.

★ Any character: Block and counter with any special move you like. Or duck and use the Uppercut as soon as Kano comes out of the Spin in front of you or behind you.

ATTACK: Liu Kang's Flying Kick.

★ Any character: Block and Uppercut.
★ Johnny Cage: Use a Shadow Kick, which is easier than the Uppercut but does less damage.
★ Rayden: Use the Flying Attack.
★ Scorpion: Use the Harpoon, which is easier than the Uppercut and more damaging.
★ Sonya: Use the Scissors Grab, but this is harder to do and less damaging than the Uppercut.
★ Sub-Zero: Use the Freeze. It's *very* hard to pull this off before Liu Kang hits you.

Counter the Flying Kick with a Scissors Grab as Sonya or you'll get your teeth kicked in. (ouch!)

ATTACK: Rayden's Flying Attack.

★ Johnny Cage: Block and *quickly* use a Fireball.
★ Kano: Block and use a Roll Spin (without holding Block, because you need to hit quickly).
★ Liu Kang: Use the Flying Kick.
★ Rayden: Use the Lightning Throw.
★ Scorpion: Use the Harpoon (tough) or use the Teleport (easier).

Block the Flying Attack and quickly use a Roll Spin (if you're Kano, of course).

Mortal Kombat

★ Sonya: Use the Square Wave Attack.
★ Sub-Zero: Use the Freeze.

ATTACK: Rayden's Teleport.
★ Uppercut as soon as he Teleports. This is easy to do if you were crouching and not blocking when he Teleported.
★ If you're walking or standing up, press Low Kick or High Kick immediately.
★ If Rayden's on the other side of the screen and you think he's about to Teleport, keep doing the controller motions for a special move, and press the button as soon as he Teleports.

When Rayden starts the Teleport, use an Uppercut.

ATTACK: Scorpion's Teleport.
★ Any character: Block and throw him after he teleports. Or just walk around without blocking until he teleports, then quickly block, crouch, and Uppercut. This works just like when you block a Jump Kick; Scorpion stays in the air after he hits you, giving you enough time to wail him with the Uppercut.

Scorpion started his teleport too closely, so you can block and throw him when he lands.

ATTACK: Sonya's Scissors Grab.
★ Any character: Block and Uppercut.

ATTACK: Sonya's Square Wave Flight.
★ Any character: Wait until she's about to land next to you, then Uppercut.

Mortal Kombat

ATTACK: Sub-Zero's Slide.

★ Any character: Jump back and kick the sliding Sub-Zero, if you can anticipate when he's going to start his Slide. Another method is simply to block Sub-Zero and try to throw him, or hit him with Low Punches.

★ Johnny Cage: Use the Shadow Kick. The best counter-attack to the Slide.

★ Kano: Quickly use the Roll Spin.

★ Scorpion: Jump back and kick, then Teleport, then use the Harpoon and Uppercut.

★ Sonya: Quickly use the Scissors Grab. Very tough to do, so don't try it unless you're way ahead on energy.

★ Sub-Zero: Use the Slide.

Johnny Cage should've countered with the Shadow Kick. Big mistake.

Two-Player Tips

★ **Always fight defensively**! Wait for your opponent to make a mistake, and then make him pay for it. If your opponent is too aggressive, you'll beat him easily. If he's playing defensively, you have to force him into making a mistake by reducing his energy until he gets aggressive. Try any of these methods to annoy a defensive opponent:

★ **Low Punch him** several times, then stop and be ready to block any Small Kicks, then Low Punch several more times.

★ Use one **Small Kick** and back away from your opponent. He won't be able to retaliate.

★ Walk up to an opponent until you're at the limit of your sweep range, and then **Sweep Kick**. Don't get too close or your opponent can easily

Use the Sweep Kick from as far away as possible. It'll drive your opponent nuts.

Mortal Kombat

counter-attack.

★ **Use a missile attack.** This is the safest and easiest way to reduce a blocking opponent's energy, but don't use it too much or he'll jump over the attack.

★ If your opponent isn't good with Uppercuts, use **Jump Kicks** at long range. Start the Kick early so he can't counter-attack.

★ Walk up to an opponent who is crouching and use a few Low Punches. As

Keep walking back and forth so you can quickly jump or block.

soon as the opponent releases Block to try for a Small Kick, press Low Kick to knee your opponent.

★ Keep walking back and forth without blocking. This way, you can quickly switch to jumping, crouch-blocking, or using a special move.

★ **Always block Away or Down/Away**, or you'll be thrown. When doing a special move, or using the Uppercut, always push the pad Away while you're recovering from the move, then push Down/Away once you've recovered.

★ You can **avoid being thrown** even if you can't block (because you've been harpooned, frozen, etc.) Just push Away and you won't be thrown.

One-Player Tips

★ This version of Mortal Kombat is much tougher than the Genesis version and maybe even harder than the arcade version. Start with the Very Easy or Easy difficulty level and work your way up the ranks as your skills improve.

★ Almost every attack works once or twice against the computer, but after that, the computer **"learns"**

The Jump Kick works beautifully against the computer. Use it as much as possible.

Mortal Kombat

your attack pattern. For example, if the computer Kano uses the Roll Spin on you as you do the Sweep Kick, he'll use the Roll Spin every time you Sweep for the rest of the round.

Use your missile weapons from as far away as possible.

★ The attacks that **work at least once** are: Jump Kick, Sweep Kick, Small Kick, most special moves, and the Roundhouse Kick.

★ At the beginning of a round at a higher difficulty level, the computer usually shoots a **missile weapon** right away. Use a Jump Kick at the start to hit him, then jump away.

★ Use your missile weapon once or twice. The first time, it doesn't matter how far away you are from the opponent. After that, do it from very far away or at medium range. If you do it from far away, the computer can't counter-attack even if he jumps over the missile. If you do it from medium range, the computer has to block or crouch, and you can block before he counter-attacks.

★ Use the **Roundhouse Kick** at the limit of your range. Sub-Zero, Scorpion, and Rayden have the best ranges. If the computer Sweep Kicks you when you try the Roundhouse, don't use it any more in the current round.

★ The **Jump Kick** is the most effective attack against the computer. Press the button early enough and the computer opponent (except for **Goro**) almost never blocks. Try this attack pattern: Jump Kick, jump back, back up a bit, and Jump Kick again. The Jump Kick is the only reliable way to win **Flawless Victories** against the computer (which you need to do to reach Reptile).

★ If you try a Jump Kick and the computer blocks, don't jump away. Instead, block

If the computer blocks your Jump Kick, block standing up.

while standing up. The computer will usually try a special move, which you can block and counter-attack.

★ If the computer doesn't use a special move, block until he approaches to try Low Punches. When he starts attacking, crouch and the computer will have to use the Small Kick to get you. Block the Small Kick, then stand up and block. Keep switching between standing blocks and crouching until the computer tries for a Round-house, Kick, or Sweep Kick. Now you can tag him with an Uppercut.

The Uppercut does more damage, but the Split Punch looks more painful!

★ If the computer has you **pinned on the side of the screen**, use High Punches, or use a Sweep Kick and jump over your opponent. Don't use your Sweep Kick until you're forced into the corner, or the computer will "learn" it.

Wait for the computer to try a kick, then knock him silly with an Uppercut.

★ **Johnny Cage**: Don't use the Shadow Kick unless it's as part of a combo. Against anyone but Cage or Sonya, the Split Punch works very well. Wait for the computer to try a Small Kick, then block and wait until the computer starts walking toward you, then use the Split Punch. Block and hold Away after using the Punch to avoid being thrown.

★ **Kano**: The computer can duck under your Knives easily, so don't rely on them. Use the Roll Spin once or twice by itself, and after that only in combos. Mostly use your Jump Kick, which is *very* effective.

★ **Liu Kang**: Rely on the Jump Kick/Flying Kick combination, and use it from long range. Even if you Jump Kick too early, the Flying Kick will still hit. If you knock the computer down, use a Fireball and the computer will stand up into it. If the computer pins you to one side of the

Mortal Kombat

screen, wait until he gets close, then use the Flying Kick, and you'll fly past him.

★ **Rayden**: Don't use the Teleport; you'll find out why not soon enough. Use the Lightning Throw at medium to close range and the computer opponent will usually stand up into it (he can't jump over it). If you Jump Kick the computer down, follow up with a Flying Attack.

Teleport only when the computer is more than half a screen away.

★ **Scorpion**: The Harpoon is very fast, but only use it as a counter-attack against the computer's mistakes. Don't use the Teleport when the computer opponent is more than half a screen away from you. If you hit with the Teleport, follow with the Harpoon.

★ **Sonya**: The Sweep Kick is very fast, and can catch the computer opponents off guard. When you knock the computer down, follow up with a Scissors Grab and keep using the Grab repeatedly.

★ **Sub-Zero**: Use the Freeze frequently. The computer just doesn't block it as much as it should. Use Freeze when the computer is less than half a screen away, or on the other side of the screen. Follow up Jump Kicks and Uppercuts with a Slide and you'll hit almost every time.

Boss Tips

★ **Goro** is very slow, so you get in **twice as many attacks** as you do against regular opponents. Goro is also very strong, so his attacks do **twice as much damage**. And finally, Goro is very stupid, so he doesn't block when he's getting up from a knockdown.

★ At the beginning of the round, use a Jump Kick. Goro usually shoots a fire-

Start every round against Goro with a Jump Kick.

ball underneath you, and your Kick knocks him down. Follow up with a missile attack, then jump away and crouch block. If Goro fires another missile, block it and Jump Kick him, then use a missile attack and jump away again.

Jump Kick straight up when you reach the edge of the screen.

★ If Goro doesn't fire a missile, jump away again. Keep jumping until you're at the edge of the screen. Wait until Goro is just out of your Sweep Kick range, then Jump Kick straight up. If Goro blocks, try the Kick again. if he fires a missile, your Kick will **hit his arm** as he reaches out to fire.

★ **Shang Tsung** doesn't block, and always teleports when you jump too close to him. He *does* block when he's taken on the form of Goro or another character.

Shang Tsung can change into any other character in the game.

★ If Shang Tsung **changes into another character**, use the strategies earlier in this chapter to defeat him. If he **remains Shang Tsung**, keep jumping at him until he teleports. Now do the motion for a special move as soon as you land, and finish the move when Shang Tsung appears behind you.

★ If you're playing as **Scorpion**, use the Teleport when Shang Tsung is on the other side of the screen and you'll hit him. Wait until he backs away, then use the Teleport again. Repeat until he's defeated.

Awesome Secrets!

★ **REPTILE**: Lurking in the shadows at the bottom of Mortal Kombat's spike-laden Pit stage is the green Ninja master Reptile. His clothing resembles that of the enemy warriors Sub-Zero and Scorpion, and he

Mortal Kombat

can perform the special attacks of both Sub-Zero *and* Scorpion.

★ Appearing only in newer versions of the arcade game (versions 3.0 and up), Reptile was put into Mortal Kombat by programmer Ed Boon, who whipped up the necessary program enhancements in a single weekend. Not even John Tobias—Mortal Kombat's graphic artist— was aware of the presence

Reptile shows up every once in a while to give you hints on how to find him.

of Reptile. In version 4.0 of the coin-op, Reptile occasionally appears on the screen to give you a hint on how you can bring him out of hiding for a battle. These hints also appear in the Genesis version. Here's a list of all ten hints. Use these if you want to try figuring out how to reach Reptile yourself.

★ **HINTS GIVEN DURING THE GAME**
ALONE IS HOW TO FIND ME
BLOCKING WILL GET YOU NOWHERE
FINISHING IS THE KEY
I AM REPTILE, FIND ME!
LOOK TO LA LUNA
PERFECTION IS THE KEY
POINTS IF YOU DESTROY ME
TIP EHT FO MOTTOB (try spelling it backwards)
YOU CANNOT MATCH MY SPEED
YOU MUST FIND ME TO BEAT ME

★ **AND HERE'S WHAT YOU NEED TO DO TO FIND REPTILE:**
1. Start a one-player game and play to The Pit stage **without continuing**.
2. During your Battle on The Pit stage, **never use Block**. That means don't touch the L or R button (or whatever you're using as the Block button).
3. Get a **Double Flawless** victory—win two rounds without getting hit. If you're hit in the first or second round, intentionally lose that round. You can still get a Double Flawless and make Reptile appear even if you lose one round.

Mortal Kombat

4. Perform the **finishing move** on your opponent. You *can* press Block for the fatality if you're playing as Scorpion or Sonya.

★ Do all of this right and Reptile drops onto the screen, then you appear in the bottom of The Pit to fight him. Defeat Reptile for a whopping 10-million-point bonus.

Reptile's ready and waiting for you at the bottom of The Pit.

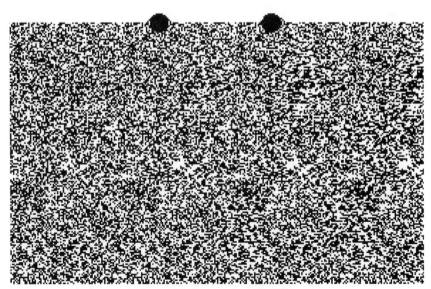

See page 298 for viewing instructions.

REN & STIMPY

BY T•HQ

Introduction

One of the funniest and most bizarre cartoons in the history of TV has been turned into a video game, and it's not bad at all considering it's from T•HQ. Each of the game's four levels is based on an episode of the show, from "The Boy Who Cried Rat!" to "Marooned!" The graphics are perfectly cartoony, and there are several sound bites from the TV

Happy happy, joy joy! (What other caption would we lead off with!)

show (when Ren gets hit by an enemy, he cries out "Stimpy!"). Fans of the show will not be disappointed.

Awesome Strategies

★ **CONTROLS:** Press Y to slap an enemy. Press B to jump. Press X to pick up an item.

★ This game has infinite continues, but no passwords, so you'll need to play all the way through in one sitting (or leave your SNES on until you finish the game).

★ Most stages have a tight time limit, so you can't waste time exploring. Just get through the current stage and on to the next.

Level 1: The Boy Who Cried Rat!

★ **Stage 1-1 (Living Room):** Walk to the right and slap the **television** to break it open and uncover a **piggy bank**. Grab the bank to score a little cash. Now jump and grab the **paintings** above the TV; there's a **safe** full of money behind one of them. Keep slapping open all the TVs and grabbing all the paintings you find on this level.

★ Keep going right to a ringing **telephone**. Jump off the telephone when it rings to make a super-jump onto the spinning clock. Grab onto the clock and jump off to fly forward to the bookshelf. Walk to the end of the bookshelf and you'll be attacked by Stimpy. Grab a flower vase and throw it into Stimpy to get rid of him (for a while).

Ren & Stimpy

★ After a while, you'll run into a **block barrier**. Jump onto the top of the barrier to make it collapse. You can also hit the barrier from the side, but it takes longer to make it collapse this way, and you have a tight time limit in this level. Keep moving!

★ You'll find two **logs** near a fireplace. Grab one of them and throw it at Stimpy when he pops out from behind the fireplace.

"It's Log, It's Log, it's better than bad, it's good!"
Whack Stimpy with your piece of wood.

★ There's a piece of **cheese** on the bookshelf to the right of the fireplace. Grab the cheese and hold onto it until Stimpy attacks you, then eat it and you'll shoot a cloud of bad breath at him. If you miss, just clobber him with a flower vase instead.

★ Continue going to the right until you see Stimpy at the top of the screen holding a cage. Super-jump off the ringing telephone and slap Stimpy silly, then jump up and right behind the curtain to find a **hidden 1-Up**. Keep walking to the right behind the curtain until you fall back to the floor.

★ There's another **extra life** at the end of the level, just before Stimpy's tongue. Pick up the heart (that's the extra life!) and then walk into Stimpy's tongue to enter the next stage.

★ **Stage 1-2 (Stimpy's Mouth):** *Don't* touch any of the **tooth nerves** on the bottom of Stimpy's mouth. If you do, his jaws will bite down and crush you, and there is no way to avoid them. If you touch a nerve, you'll lose a life. Simple as that.

★ The mouth slowly closes during the stage, so run as fast as possible to the left.

★ If a **tooth beaver** jumps and sinks its teeth into you, shake it off by rapidly pressing Left and Right on the control pad.

Avoid the tooth beavers and
especially avoid the tooth nerves.

Ren & Stimpy

★ The first special item in this stage is the **sock**. Grab the sock and use it to gain super-speed. The problem with super-speed is that it makes it harder to control your jumps, so don't go *too* fast to the left or you'll end up jumping onto a tooth nerve.

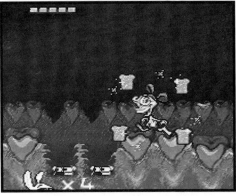

"Powdered--Toast--MAN!" Grab the toast to make yourself invulnerable.

★ The second special item is **Powdered Toast**. The toast gives you temporary invincibility, so you can't be hit by the tooth beavers or falling teeth, but you still have to avoid the tooth nerves even when you're invulnerable.

★ **Stage 1-3 (Stimpy's Tongue):** There are two places on the screen where **rotten teeth** appear: on the far left side of the mouth (next to the tall wooden tooth) and the far right side. Grab a tooth and throw it at the tooth beaver on the tongue. When you take the tooth from one place, the next tooth appears in the other place, so you need to go back and forth to grab the teeth. Once you have a tooth in your hands, wait for the tongue to start pounding against the roof of the mouth. Then move under the tongue, jump, and throw the tooth straight up to hit the tooth beaver. Watch out for the falling teeth! When the tongue is near the bottom of the mouth, stay away from it and wait for it to move back up to the roof. You really shouldn't have any problem against this boss unless you get too aggressive.

★ **Stage 1-4 (Stimpy's Mouth):** The first time you played this stage, you were running to the left. Now you're running to the right, and the mouth is closing faster, so you need to run faster yourself! There are more socks in this level and more pieces of Powdered Toast, so you've got to make accurate jumps to survive. You

Grab the rotten teeth and throw them straight up to hit the tooth beaver on the tongue.

know you're close to the end when you reach **six dollar bills**, and you're *really* close when you reach three tooth nerves placed side by side. Jump over them and finish the stage!

Level 2: In The Army

★ **Stage 2-1 (Basic Training):** Walk to the right and jump up the **tree branches** to collect the dollar bills, then drop back to the ground and walk to the right. Powdered Toast Man flies onto the screen and drops a **Helicopter Beanie** down at you. Jump up and grab the Beanie, then fly to the right. Don't fly *too* high or you might land on a bad guy when the Beanie wears off.

★ The **helmets** in the ground are **soldiers** that hide and wait for you to get close, then jump out of the ground and shoot a plunger at you. Move slowly towards a helmet until the soldier jumps out of the ground, then slap him before he can shoot.

Sneak up to the helmets on the ground and slap the soldiers when they attack.

★ The next ground obstacle is an **unexploded bomb**. You can slap the bomb to make it explode, but if you're not standing far enough away, you'll be hurt by the explosion. Don't jump on the bomb or you'll definitely be hurt (along with your pride).

★ After the bomb is a **bridge**. At this point, you can run across the bridge before it collapses, or you can drop into the hidden passage below the bridge. If you run across the bridge, you can get a **1-Up** by going to the right and jumping over to the heart when you reach the end of the cliff. If you drop into the secret passage, you'll

Run past the broken bridge and go right to find a 1-Up heart.

Ren & Stimpy

find some dollar bills being guarded by some soldiers. You'll also encounter a couple of **bats**. Slap the bats to get rid of them.

★ Whichever path you take, you'll eventually make it to the log-filled lake. Jump across the lake and you'll land in the **fire**. Quick run to the right and go into the water to put out the flames before you start taking damage. Jump into the

"Fire! Fire!" Oh, wait, that's a line from Beavis and Butt-head, *not* Ren & Stimpy...

cannon on the right side of the water and grab the **Umbrella** as you're shot into the air. Glide down and to the right to catch some dollar bills. When you land, pick up the hand grenade and throw it at the wall to blow it up.

★ Run into the passage behind the wall and follow it until you get back outside. Watch out for the **floating clouds**, because they can hurt you. Keep going to the right until you find a cannon. Jump into the cannon and blast yourself up and left to the next cannon. Or, you can always miss the ledge and drop back to the ground to catch the dollar bills in the air. Watch out for those clouds, though! When you reach the second cannon, shoot yourself up and right to land on a black missile flying through the air! Jump to the right to land on a ledge before the missile disappears. Wait for the log in the water to float within jumping range. Leap onto the log and ride it to the right.

★ Use the **tires** to bounce into the trees and grab the dollar bills, along with a band-aid. Drop back to the ground and walk right to find another bomb in your path. Slap the bomb and run right into the water. Keep going right and jump to grab the Umbrella, which shields you from the falling **watermelons**! From here, it's just a few

Hold onto the Umbrella to protect yourself from the falling watermelons.

screens more to the right to finish the stage.

★ **Stage 2-2 (Basic Training II):** Run to the right and grab the dollar bills as you drop into the tunnel. Grab the Umbrella and start gliding down the screen. You'll find several more Umbrellas on the way down, so switch from one Umbrella to the next. You can also just avoid the Umbrellas and fall all the way to the bottom of the

Walk past the tanks and slap the soldier, then take the Helicopter Beanie.

screen, since you won't take damage from the fall. Avoid the ledges on the left or right; just drop straight down to the bottom.

★ Once you land, pick up the **grenade** and throw it into the wall on the right. Walk to the right and keep going until you reach the soldier. Slap him silly and then grab the Powdered Toast dropped by Powdered Toast Man. Run to the right while you're protected by the Toast and keep going until you reach two **tanks** and a soldier hiding behind a bush. Slap the bush to uncover the soldier and then grab the Helicopter Beanie. (Thanks, Powdered Toast Man!) Fly up to the cannon and blast yourself up and left onto the ledge.

★ Grab the Umbrella here, then run left and jump to the left to glide over to the next ledge. Walk left and drop beneath the flying soldier. Grab one of the grenades he drops at you and throw it back up at him to blow him away. You'll have to hold onto the grenade until it's just about to explode, so watch the timing of your throw! When you blow up the soldier, grab his Helicopter Beanie and fly up and left as fast as you can to the dollar bills above the cannons. Fly onto the ledge to the left of the bills, then walk left to find a **1-Up heart**. Jump to get the 1-Up, then go back to the

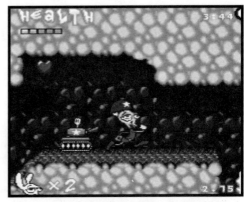

Use the Helicopter Beanie to fly into the tunnel with the 1-Up heart.

Ren & Stimpy

right and drop down to the cannon. Shoot yourself up and right to the ledge. From here, just go right until you finish the stage.

★ **Stage 2-3 (Night Maneuvers):** Walk to the right and you'll see two **flying soldiers**. You can get either soldier's Beanie, but there's nothing in the air other than a few dollar bills. Just stay on the ground and go right until you reach the bombs. Slap

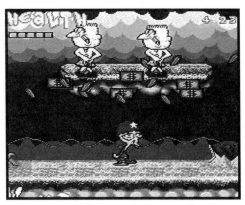

Throw the grenade between the soldiers to blow them both up.

through the bombs and keep going to reach two soldiers hiding in bushes. Pick up the grenade and throw it between the bushes so that the explosion gets both of them. They'll shower you with dollar bills.

★ Go right and slap the **jumping fish** as you jump across the logs. There are several floating clouds on the other side of the logs; jump over them or run under them. Keep going right to find a cannon, but don't jump in it yet. Go to the right and slap the two soldiers, then return to the left and jump into the trees. Jump up and right to the highest branch, then jump right to land on a ledge with a tank.

★ Run to the right and jump over the tanks, then grab the Helicopter Beanie and fly up and right until you see Powdered Toast in the air. Grab the Toast and walk back to the left until another Beanie appears. This time, fly up and right without stopping to land on the ledge. From here, go to the right until you reach a **broken bridge**. Drop through the hole in the bridge and go left past the tanks to find a **1-Up heart**. Grab the 1-Up and then jump out of the hole. You're almost finished with the stage, so just keep going right.

★ **Stage 2-4 (The Sarge):** Jump up and right to grab onto the **helicopter** as soon as the stage begins and you won't take dam-

Grab the helicopter at the start of Stage 2-4 to avoid the grenade showers.

age from the shower of grenades. After the third shower, drop off the helicopter and grab the piece of meat for some energy, then get ready to fight the Sarge.

★ Stay on the opposite side of the screen from the Sarge and jump over the bullets he fires at you. Don't move toward the Sarge unless you need to pick up a grenade off the ground. Jump off the tree branch and throw the grenade into the Sarge's head to hit him. It has to hit his head to cause damage. It's harder to throw grenades at the Sarge from the right side of the screen—there's no tree branch—so you'll have to get close to him and risk getting hit by a bullet. It takes three hits to beat the Sarge.

Level 3: Stimpy's Invention

★ **Stage 3-1:** Walk right and pick up the **spring**. Carry it all the way to the left and jump off it to grab the dollar bills in the air. Now carry the spring all the way to the right and jump over the wall. Watch out for the arcing **electricity** at the top of the wall—touch it and you instantly lose a life. Go right and grab the spring between the electric balls. Carry it to the right and jump over the wall.

★ Go right and pick up the spring. Carry it all the way to the right and use it to jump onto the top of the ledge. Walk right and fall off the ledge, then walk left and grab the spring (the wall opens when you get close). Go right and drop the spring against the wall. Jump over the wall and go right to finish the stage.

★ **Stage 3-2:** Walk right and drag the **safe** to the left, then jump onto the ledge. Jump up and right to the top of the blue wall. Go right to the moving columns in the floor. Jump onto the ledges above the columns to get the dollar bills. Keep going right, past the electric beams, until you reach a wall with a **vial** next to it. Grab the **yellow and blue test tubes** and pour them into the vial to make it explode and blow through the wall. Go right to finish the stage.

★ **Stage 3-3:** Walk right to the switch. Jump into the air and slap the switch to turn it on. Walk right and jump onto the moving

Play mad scientist and mix the test tubes in the vial to blow through the wall.

Ren & Stimpy

platform. Jump right onto the top of the blue wall. Go right until you find a safe. Drag the safe to the left and jump off the safe to hit the switch. Ride the moving platform to the top of the blue wall. Go right until you find a **beach ball**. Pick up the ball and walk left underneath the switch. Jump and throw the ball straight up to hit the switch. Pick up and hold the ball. Ride up the

Beach party, dude! Throw the beach ball straight up to hit the switch.

moving platforms to the ledges, then jump right to the top of the blue wall. Go right until you find a switch. Jump and throw the ball to hit the switch. Jump up the moving platforms to hit a second switch. Ride to the top of the blue wall and go right to finish the stage.

★ **Stage 3-4:** Walk right and carry the spring all the way to the right. Pick up the **blowtorch** and walk into the flame to light up the torch. Bounce off the spring to the blue wall, then jump up the ledges to reach the top of another blue wall. Walk right and use the torch to burn through the **ropes**. When you land on the next ledge, burn through the ropes again. Walk right and carry the spring all the way to the right. Pick up the blowtorch and jump onto the blue wall. Walk right and use the torch to burn through the blocks.

★ Walk all the way to the right and drop the torch, then go back to the left. Pick up the spring and drop it just to the left of the glass tube in the foreground. Now pick up the torch. Bounce up and left off the spring to light the torch in the flame, then bounce up and right onto the blue wall. Go right and hit the switch, then ride up the moving platform and burn through the blocks. (You'll need to ride the platform several times to burn all the way through.)

Pick up the blowtorch and walk into the flame to light it up.

Ren & Stimpy

Go right and burn through the second wall of blocks, then go right to finish.

★ **Stage 3-5:** Walk right and pick up the ball. Throw it onto the left side of the **scale**. Jump onto the left side of the scale, then jump to the right, and the scale will throw you into the air. Jump to the right and onto the blue wall. Jump up and left to grab the vial. Set the vial against the wall of blocks. Pour in

Pick up the beach ball and use it to bounce off the scale.

the blue and yellow test tubes to make the vial explode.

★ Walk right until you reach the safe. Drag the safe to the right and use it to jump onto the scale. Jump off the scale to hit the switch. Ride up the moving platform to the top of the blue wall. Walk right to find a spring. Carry the spring the way to the right. Bounce up and left off the spring and take the blue test tube. Jump over the blue wall and keep

going right until you find a vial. Pour the test tube into the vial and move the vial next to the block wall. Use the ball and the scale to bounce up to the yellow test tube. Grab it and pour it into the vial to blow through the wall. Go right to finish the stage.

Trick the moving platform into going one way, then run in the other direction.

★ **Stage 3-6:** All you have to do is throw the **Happy Helmet** onto Ren's head, but it's a *lot* harder than it seems. There are two platforms in the air above you.

One of them moves slowly left and right, but the other platform *follows* you and blocks the Helmet when you throw it into the air. The best way to trick the platform is to run in one direction, then turn around and run in the other. You'll have a moment to throw the Helmet before the platform gets in the way. Throw the Helmet at the top of your jump to get the most height.

Ren & Stimpy
Level 4: Marooned!

★ **Stage 4-1:** In this stage, press the B button to **flap your arms** and slow down your fall. The faster you flap, the closer you stay to the top of the screen. For the first part of your fall, that's exactly what you should do. Stay at the top of the screen and move left and right to avoid the aliens. When the "wall" of **four aliens** comes onto the screen, stay in the middle and the aliens will move away from you and splat against the walls. Keep flapping until you grab the two green energy items.

★ After you get the items, move down to the middle of the screen, because the aliens start coming from above *and* below you. Be careful not to bounce off the walls or you'll ricochet into the aliens. There aren't any more energy items for the rest of the stage, so you've got to play carefully.

★ **Stage 4-2:** Walk to the right and slap the aliens with your tongue. Grab the **Space Cadet Handbook** and you can use it like a boomerang. You have to catch it on the way back, though! Keep going to the right to find **green spores** in the air. You can grab these spores and throw them at the aliens if you don't have the Handbook. You'll find a heart box at the end of the ledge; jump to grab it and drop down to the next ledge.

Grab the Space Cadet Handbook and throw it like a boomerang at your enemies.

★ Grab the **trash can lid** and run to the left. The lid will deflect the eyeball streams. You'll find several lids as you go left, so grab each one and use it. There's another heart box at the end of the ledge. Jump onto the ledges to get up to the box. From

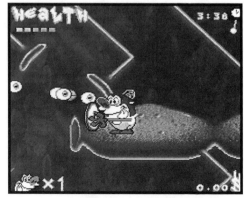

Hold the trash can lid and use it to deflect the eyeball streams.

here, just keep on truckin' through the level until you find a weird-looking **pink creature** in the air. Jump onto the creature and it starts moving to the left. Stay on the creature as it goes left to grab a heart box and a trash can lid. Keep going left to find a couple more pink creatures. Ride left on them to find a **1-Up heart** and a heart box.

Ride left on the pink bubble-gum creatures to find a 1-Up heart in the air.

★ From here, just keep going downward until you reach the ocean of green slime at the bottom of the stage. (Ride on the pink creatures to find more items on the way down.) Go to the right on the pink creatures until you run into a wall. Jump left and land on the creature coming out of the slime. Go upward and jump over the wall. Go right to finish the stage.

★ **Stage 4-3:** This stage is a lot like 4-1. You should *always* stay at the top of the screen, because no enemies will attack you from above, and most of the enemies at the beginning of the stage fly straight across the middle of the screen. The nastiest new enemies in this stage are the **green germs**. If you get hit by a germ, it keeps doing damage until you shake it off by bumping into a wall. As you get closer to the end of the stage, the walls change from red to blue.

★ **Stage 4-4:** There are *three* extra lives in this stage, so you shouldn't have any problems finishing.

★ The **first extra life** is close to the first **green geyser** in the stage. When you reach the geyser, jump up and left onto the hill. Climb up the hill and go left to find the 1-Up heart.

★ On the way to the second extra life, you'll run into what seems like a dead end. Jump into the air and hit the **green object**;

Go up and left from the green geyser to find the first of three 1-Up hearts.

Ren & Stimpy

it turns into a bubble! Float upward to find the next green piece of gum before your bubble bursts.

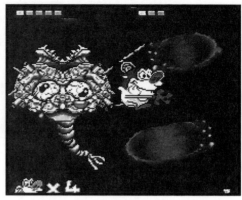

★ The **second extra life** is in a tunnel below four downward-pointing **arrows**. When you reach the arrows, drop into the right side of the hole and hold Right on the control pad to drop into a tunnel. The 1-Up heart is at the end of the tunnel.

Drop vitamins into the final boss's mouth to see the terrible ending sequence.

★ The **third extra life** is near a pink creature facing to the right. (There's a trash can lid just to the left of the creature.) Jump onto the pink guy and let him carry you to the 1-Up heart.

★ **Stage 4-5:** Go to the left and drop down to the bottom of the wall. When the screen rotates to the left, stand between the lumps on the left side of the spikes and wait for the screen to rotate right. When it does, jump to the left and land on the ledge just below the spikes. Jump over the spikes and run to the left. From here, keep going deeper into the tunnel until you reach the final boss!

★ Grab a pink vitamin and jump to the ledges at the top of the screen. Drop the vitamin into the boss's mouth to hurt it. The boss shoots blue bullets at you, so watch out. Stay at the top of the screen, because it's the best place to attack the boss. Feed the boss three vitamins to win the game and get an extremely crummy ending sequence with two programmer credit screens. Lame, lame, lame!

SHADOWRUN

BY DATA EAST

Introduction

The year is 2050. The place is Seattle, Washington. You are—well, you don't know who you are, exactly, because you've woken up in a morgue (!) with a case of amnesia. Your goals are simple: figure out who you are (easy), figure out why someone tried to kill you (not easy), and track down whoever was trying to kill you (definitely not easy). Along

You'll give the morticians a scare when you walk into their office.

the way, you're engulfed in a world of high-tech computers and powerful magic. Shadowrun is easily one of the best role-playing games available for the SNES. Check it out!

Awesome Strategies

★ This chapter is a detailed guide to the secrets of Shadowrun. It's divided into seven easy-to-use sections. **Combat Tips** gives you advice on the best ways to win battles. **Computers** gives you advice for getting through the computers in The Matrix. **Items** is a list of the major items

and weapons in Shadowrun. After each item, we list: Location (where to get it), How Obtained (how to get it), and Function (what to do with it). **Locations** is a list of the major locations in the game, and also describes how to solve some of the puzzles in each location. **Shadowrunners** talks about several special Shadowrunners and lists their statistics. **Spells** lists the items you

From combat tips to spells, everything you need to know is in this chapter.

Shadowrun

need to bring the Dog Shrine to obtain the six different spells. **Walk-through** describes the best path to take through the entire game from start to finish.

Combat Tips

★ You don't need to worry about dodging and re-aiming your weapon. Just draw your gun, aim it at the nearest bad guy, and keep firing until he drops.

★ In the Drake and Aneki buildings, several thugs attack you at once. In the Drake building, they ambush you as soon as you step out of the elevator! There are **two methods to use** in these combat situations. Method #1: Cast the **Invisibility spell** on yourself (and your Shadowrunners), then shoot the thugs while they can't see you. Keep casting and shooting until they're all gone. Method #2: Cast the **Summon Spirit spell** to damage all of the thugs at once. Both of these methods work, but Method #1 is much more effective. You'll especially need to use Invisibility against stronger enemies like the Jester Spirit and Drake the Dragon.

Don't bother with dodging bullets; just aim and shoot.

★ One of the most useful techniques in any role-playing game is **"powering up"**—repeatedly going into an area filled with bad guys and defeating them to build up your fighting abilities and other statistics. If you're having a problem surviving, or just want to boost your Attributes and Skills, use one of the locations below.

★ **The first power-up location** is in Apartments 7

Enter the apartment next to yours and shoot the thugs to build up your stats.

Shadowrun

and 8, which are located right next to your own apartment, Apartment 6. One to three thugs almost always appear and shoot at you. Shoot back!

* **The second power-up location** is in the Caryards. One to four thugs appear in this area and leave behind 20 to 40 nuyen when you defeat them. It's crucial to power up here before taking on the stronger opponents in the Arena.

The docks at Daley are an excellent power-up location.

* **The third power-up location** is the docks area in Daley. The bad guys are plentiful, and they leave behind big bucks when you defeat them, usually 50 or 60 nuyen each.
* **The fourth power-up location** is on Bremerton. There are two screens where bad guys appear every time, providing plenty of nuyen and a Karma point every time you defeat them all.

Computers

* **Make maps of every computer** you explore. If you take too much damage and have to jack out, you can use the maps to avoid IC squares the next time you jack into the computer. The reasons we didn't provide you with maps are that 1) they would've taken up too much space in the book, and 2) making your own is very easy with a few pieces of graph paper (or even without). Actually, if your character is particularly strong, you can probably blunder through computers without needing to make maps at all.

* After you download all the Datastore squares from a

Always check your inventory for data files after logging off a computer.

Shadowrun

computer, check your inventory for new datafiles and read through the files for hints, tips, and "plot development" information.

★ Take the time to **boost your Computer skill** early in the game. This gives you the ability to attack and destroy IC squares (the squares that cause you damage when you walk onto them). There are some computers where you *have* to destroy ICs to reach Datastore squares.

★ Several computers have the same layout as other computers. Always check the maps you've made of previous computers to see if you're in a computer with the same layout.

Items

★ **Beretta Pistol**
Location: Dark Alley. *How Obtained:* Walk into the Dark Alley and you'll see the pistol next to the body of the Decker you talked to when you left the Morgue. *Function:* The Pistol is your first Weapon.

★ **Black Bottle**
Location: Talisman Shop. *How Obtained:* Buy it. *Function:* Use the Bottle to pick up the Pool of Ink left behind when you kill the Octopus in the Docks.

★ **Boosted Reflexes**
Location: Dr. Maple-thorpe's Office. *How Obtained:* Buy it. *Function:* Boosts your reflexes, although it isn't necessary to finish the game. You're better off saving your nuyen for a powerful weapon.

★ **Broken Bottle**
Location: Bremerton. *How Obtained:* Look inside the

Pick up the Beretta Pistol, equip it, and shoot the Orc.

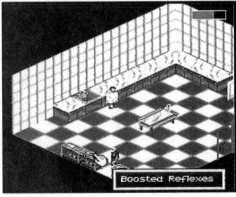

The Boosted Reflexes chip isn't needed to finish the game.

safe guarded by a single Orc. *Function:* Gives you a clue about what you need to destroy the Toxic Oozes.

Shadowrun

★ **Bronze Key**

Location: Dark Blade. *How Obtained:* Talk to Vladimir, and after he runs through the wall, search the bookshelves in the Library to find the Key. *Function:* Unlocks the Bronze Gate in the Dark Blade's kitchen.

★ **Credstick**

Location: Morgue. *How Obtained:* Talk to the mortician who isn't busy about Grinder. He unlocks the cabinets with the Credstick inside. *Function:* Used to make calls on Video Phones.

★ **Crowbar**

Location: Rust Stiletto Hideout. *How Obtained:* Shoot the two Orc guards. One of them drops the Crowbar. *Function:* Pries open a rusty door on Bremerton.

★ **Cyberdeck**

Location: Glutman's Office. *How Obtained:* Pickup the Cyberdeck from the desk. *Function:* Used to access Computers and enter The Matrix.

★ **Detonator**

Location: Bremerton. *How Obtained:* Look inside the safe guarded by a single Orc. *Function:* Combines with the Explosives to create a Time Bomb.

★ **Dog Collar**

Location: Town Square.

Use the Credstick to reach out and touch someone's video phone.

You'll find the Cyberdeck early on, but you can't use it until your Datajack is fixed.

Free the dog in the Town Square to get the Dog Collar.

Shadowrun

How Obtained: Open the Broken Gate and the dog barks with joy and leaves the Collar behind. *Function:* The Dog Collar is one of three items you need to talk to the Dog Spirit at the Dog Shrine.

★ **Dog Tag**

Location: Bremerton. *How Obtained:* Shoot the guard dog. It drops the Tag. *Function:* The Dog Tag is one of two items you need to get the Summon Spirit spell.

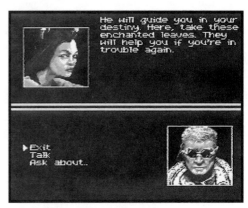

He will guide you in your destiny. Here, take these enchanted leaves. They will help you if you're in trouble again.

▶ Exit
Talk
Ask about..

Talk to Kitsune about Dog to get the Enchanted Leaves.

★ **Door Key**

Location: Agent's Office. *How Obtained:* Examine the body that "Seems familiar..." *Function:* Used to open the door to Apartment 6.

★ **Enchanted Leaves**

Location: Jagged Nails Bar. *How Obtained:* Talk to Kitsune about Dog. *Function:* The Leaves are one of three items you need to talk to the Dog Spirit at the Dog Shrine.

★ **Explosives**

Location: Docks. *How Obtained:* Shoot the Orc guarding the boat to Bremerton. He drops the Explosives. *Function:* Combines with the Detonator to create a Time Bomb.

★ **Ghoul Bone**

Location: Graveyard. *How Obtained:* Shoot Scary Ghouls near the gate and one of them eventually leaves behind a Bone. *Function:* The Bone is one of two items you need to get the Powerball spell.

★ **Green Bottle**

Location: Bremerton. *How Obtained:* Use the Time Bomb to blow open the safe being guarded by four Orcs. *Function:* Used to disintegrate the Toxic Oozes.

Shoot the Ghouls in the Graveyard until you get the Ghoul Bone.

★ **Grenades**

Location: Business Man's

Office. *How Obtained:* Ask the Business Man about Firearms and he offers to sell you Grenades for 100 nuyen each. *Function:* Weapon.

★ **Iced Tea**

Location: Grim Reaper Bar. *How Obtained:* Talk to the Club Manager and he serves you the Tea. *Function:* Give the Tea to the normally rude Club Patron and you can talk to him.

★ **Iron Key**

Location: Daley Station. *How Obtained:* Shoot the two Orcs that attack you the first time you arrive at the Station. One of them drops the Key. *Function:* The Iron Key opens the door to the Rust Stiletto Hideout.

★ **Leather Jacket**

Location: Dark Alley. *How Obtained:* Shoot the Orc and Examine his body to find the Jacket. *Function:* Armor.

★ **Lonestar Badge**

Location: Business Man's Office. *How Obtained:* Ask the Business Man about Lone Star and he offers to sell you the Badge for 150 nuyen. *Function:* Use the Badge at the Morgue to talk to the Mortician and make him unlock the Filing Cabinets.

One of the Daley Station guards has the Iron Key to unlock the hideout.

The mortician talks to you once you have the Lonestar Badge.

Heal the Indian Shaman in exchange for the Magic Fetish.

Shadowrun

★ **Magic Fetish**

Location: Graveyard Crypt with Indian Shaman. *How Obtained:* Use a Slap Patch on the Shaman to heal him and he gives you the Fetish as thanks. *Function:* The Fetish has two functions. 1) It's one of three items you need to talk to the Dog Spirit at the Dog Shrine. 2) Give the Fetish to Vladimir inside Dark Blade and he tells you the (incorrect) name of the Jester Spirit.

★ **Matchbox**

Location: Your Inventory. *How Obtained:* You have the Matchbox at the start of the game. *Function:* None.

★ **Memo**

Location: Agent's Office. *How Obtained:* Pickup the Memo from the desk. *Function:* Provides a clue about why someone tried to kill you.

★ **Paperweight**

Location: Empty Office next to Glutman's Office. *How Obtained:* Pickup the Paperweight from the desk. *Function:* The Paperweight is one of two items you need to get the Powerball spell at the Dog Shrine.

★ **Potion Bottles**

Location: Talisman Shop. *How Obtained:* Buy them. *Function:* Used to take

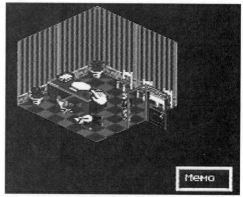

Check the desk in the Agent's Office and read the Memo for a clue.

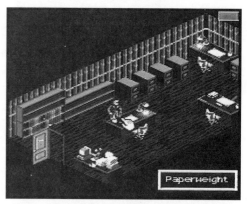

It's really easy to overlook the Paperweight. Don't miss it!

Read the Ripped Note and give Sassie a ring on the Video Phone.

Shadowrun

Water from the Water Fountain and to pick up the Toxic Water on the ship.

★ **Ripped Note**

Location: Apartment 6. *How Obtained:* Pickup the Note. *Function:* The Note has the phone number of your girlfriend Sassie, who has the phone number of Glutman's Office.

★ **Safe Key**

Location: Bremerton. *How Obtained:* Shoot the Orc guarding the safe. He drops the Key. *Function:* Used to open the safe being guarded by only one Orc.

★ **Scalpel**

Location: Morgue. *How Obtained:* Pickup the Scalpel from the middle table on the left side of the room. *Function:* Use the Scalpel to open the Crypt Doors in the Graveyard.

★ **Shades**

Location: Apartment 6. *How Obtained:* Pickup the Shades. *Function:* Use the Shades to disguise yourself before you enter the Morgue so the morticians won't run away.

★ **Skill Software**

Location: Dr. Maplethorpe's Office. *How Obtained:* Buy it. *Function:* The Skill Software gives you the Leadership skill.

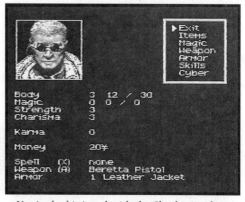

The Scalpel makes a handy crypt lockpick in the Graveyard.

You're lookin' cool with the Shades in place. "I wear my sunglasses at night..."

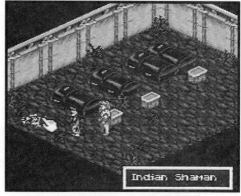

Don't use the Slap Patch right away. Save it for the Indian Shaman.

Shadowrun

★ **Slap Patch**

Location: Morgue. *How Obtained:* Open the right fridge door to find the Patch. *Function:* You can buy Slap Patches later in the game to heal yourself, but this first Slap Patch should be used on the Indian Shaman in the Graveyard Crypt.

★ **Stake**

Location: Talisman Shop. *How Obtained:* Buy it. *Function:* Use the Stake on Vladimir several times to learn the true name of Jester Spirit.

★ **Strobe**

Location: Jagged Nails. *How Obtained:* Talk to the Club Manager on the left side of Jagged Nails about Strobes and he gives it to you. *Function:* Use the Strobe to paralyze Vladimir so you can get close enough to use the Stake on him.

★ **Tickets**

Location: Morgue. *How Obtained:* Talk to the mortician who isn't busy about Grinder. He unlocks the cabinets with the Tickets inside. *Function:* Used to get past the bouncer in The Cage.

★ **Time Bomb**

Location: Your Inventory (after you collect the Detonator and Explosives). *How Obtained:* When you collect the Detonator and Explosives, they automatically combine to create the Time Bomb. *Function:* Used to blow open the Bremerton safe guarded by four Orcs.

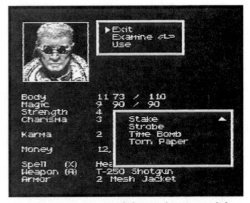

Get the Detonator and the Explosives and they combine to make the Time Bomb.

★ **Torn Paper**

Location: Morgue. *How Obtained:* Examine the Slab. *Function:* The Torn Paper is an obscure clue about the location of Matrix Systems.

★ **Toxic Water**

Location: Bremerton. *How*

Fill up your Potion Bottles at the Water Fountain in the Town Square.

Obtained: Shoot the Poison Ooze until it disintegrates into a puddle of Toxic Water. Use the Potion Bottles on the Toxic Water. *Function:* The Toxic Water is one of two items you need for the Invisibility spell.

★ **Water**

Location: Water Fountain. *How Obtained:* Use the Potion Bottles on the Fountain. *Function:* The Water is one of two items you need to get the Invisibility spell.

Locations

★ **Agent's Office**

Description: The body in here seems familiar to you, but you won't find out why until later in the game. *Items:* Door Key, Memo.

★ **Apartment 6**

Description: This is the first location with a Bed. You use the Bed to use Karma points and save the game. *Items:* Filing Cabinet, Ripped Note, Shades, Video Phone.

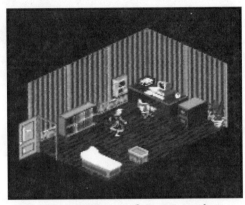

This is Apartment 6. It ain't much, but it's all you got.

Q: Where's the key to Apartment 6? A: Examine the body that "Seems familiar..." in the Agent's Office.

★ **Arena**

Description: This combat arena in the Caryards is a great place to build up nuyen—if you're tough enough to handle the competition.

Q: How do I fight The King to get out of the Caryards? A: Ask the Arena Owner about The King. He offers to set up a match.

Q: The Arena Owner says there aren't any more

The Arena is a festival of carnage! Don't compete until you're powered up, though.

Shadowrun

opponents. What now? A: Nothing. When you defeat the final opponent, you're finished with the Arena and can't make any more money there. Here are the opponents you'll face: Gang Member (300 nuyen); Heavy Dude (700 nuyen); Heavy Dude (1,000 nuyen); Mage (2,000 nuyen); Mage (3,000 nuyen); Samurai Warrior (4,000 nuyen); Ferocious Orc (5,000 nuyen); Gang Leader (6,000 nuyen); Troll Decker (7,000 nuyen); Mage (8,000 nuyen).

★ **Bremerton**

Description: The abandoned ship that the Jester Spirit calls home. Getting to the Spirit is an adventure in itself! *Items:* Broken Bottle, Detonator, Dog Tag, Green Bottle, Safe Key, Toxic Water.

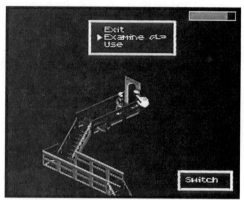

Q: All of the doors are rusted shut. How do I get into the ship? A: Use the Crowbar on one of the doors to pry it open.

Q: How do I get to the safe guarded by four Orcs?

You can't run past the four Orc guards. Kill them with the stair switches.

They shoot me to pieces. A: Use the switches on the stairs leading down to the safe to close the room and flood it, drowning the Orcs.

Q: How do I open the safe being guarded by four Orcs? A: Use the Time Bomb and move away before it blows.

Q: How do I get past the green Toxic Oozes? A: You need to get the Green Bottle out of the safe elsewhere on the ship and use it on the Oozes.

Q: I can't kill the Jester Spirit. Why not? A: Your goal is not to kill the Jester Spirit, but to capture him. Keep shooting until he says "You should not have come..." then talk to him and speak his true name to defeat him.

Q: I speak his true name, but he laughs at me! A:

The Jester Spirit has only one true name, and you'll need to kill Vladimir to find it out.

Shadowrun

Then you don't have his true name. You have to force Vladimir at Dark Blade into telling you the true name by using a certain sharp pointy wooden object.

★ **Business Man's Office**

Description: The Business Man describes Shadowrunners and certain street skills to you. *Items:* Grenades (100 nuyen). Ask the Business Man about Firearms.

★ **Caryards**

Description: After you talk to Glutman in The Cage, he takes you here. Unfortunately, you can't stay, and it costs several thousand nuyen to leave. *Items:* Slap Patches. Ask the Little Boy about Heal.

Q: How do I leave the Caryards? A: There are two ways. You can pay The King 4,000 nuyen (less if you have the Negotiation skill), or you can defeat him in the Arena. Buying your way out is much easier.

★ **Dark Alley**

Description: A dark, dingy alley. The first time you enter here, a crook shoots Decker, then he starts shooting at you. You'll find your first weapon and armor here, and encounter a disciple of Dog for the first time. *Items:* Beretta Pistol, Worn Leather Jacket.

Don't even try fighting The King. Buy your way out of the Caryards.

Q: How do I defeat the crook? A: Quickly pick up the Beretta Pistol next to the Decker's body and use it, then shoot the crook. Examine his body and take the Worn Leather Jacket. Use the jacket as your new armor.

Q: What should I do about the glowing eyes at the end of the alley? A: Walk next to the glowing eyes and a dog will come out and talk to you. Talk to

Vampires and other spooky creatures infest Dark Blade.

Shadowrun

the dog to earn Dog as a topic word.

★ **Dark Blade**

Description: Home of the bloodsucking Vladimir (who knows the location of the Jester Spirit) and about a dozen well-armed thugs (who don't attack until Vladimir gets what he wants from you). *Items:* Bronze Key.

Q: How do I get into Dark Blade? A: You have to call and make an appointment of sorts. Get the phone number from the Shaman in the Talisman Shop.

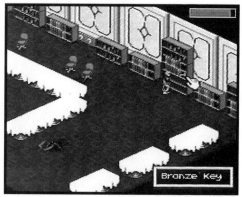

The Bronze Key doesn't appear until you talk to Vladimir.

Q: I call Dark Blade, but they won't open the gate. A: Ask about Magic Fetish to gain their interest and make them open the gate.

Q: I can't unlock the Bronze Gate in the kitchen. A: After your encounter with Vladimir, go into the Dark Blade library and look closely at the bookshelves to find a Bronze Key.

Q: I'm in the underground crypts, but where is Vladimir? A: After you enter the crypts, walk down and left into the next screen, then walk down and right to find stairs. Climb down the stairs into Vladimir's chamber.

Q: I try to use the Stake on Vladimir, but I can't get close enough. A: You need to paralyze Vladimir with the Strobe, then use the Stake.

★ **Docks**

Description: In this area, you'll find Matrix Systems, the Dog Shrine, and the boat to Bremerton. *Items:* Explosives, Mermaid Scales, Pool of Ink.

Q: I can't get to Bremerton because the boat driver won't take me there. A: You need to drive away the mermaids in the harbor. Go talk to the bartender in the Wastelands Club about Ice.

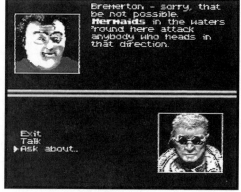

The boat driver isn't budging until you get rid of the mermaids in the harbor.

Shadowrun

★ **Dog Shrine**

Description: The home of the Dog Spirit. Come here with specific objects to earn spells.

★ **Dr. Maplethorpe's Office**

Description: This street doc is as good as Ed (of Ed's Patch & Fix) is bad. He'll fix the cortex bomb in your head and sell you a few goodies. Ask him about Heal to buy Slap Patches. *Items:* Dermal Plating, Skill Software.

★ **Ed's Patch & Fix**

Description: An incompetent street doc.

Q: Should I let Ed give me an exam? A: Not unless you have 2,000 nuyen so that you can pay the other street doc in the game to disable the cortex bomb that Ed activates in your head!

★ **Glutman's Office**

Description: This is the office with the Secretary who says her boss (Glutman) is out. *Items:* Computer, Cyberdeck.

```
ERROR CONDITION!
ERROR ANALYSIS.....
- DATAJACK MALFUNCTION
CONNECTION TERMINATED

NO CONNECTION ESTABLISHED.
```

You can't use Glutman's computer at first, but you don't need to anyway.

Q: I try to use the Cyberdeck on the Computer, but I keep getting an error. Why? A: Your datajack is broken, and you need to get it fixed before you can access the Computer. You can hire a Shadowrunner and have him use his Cyberdeck to break in, but the information in Glutman's computer isn't that important.

★ **Graveyard**

Description: Spooky! The Graveyard has four Crypts inside, along with Scary Ghouls that dig themselves out of the ground to attack you. *Items:* Ghoul Bone, Magic Fetish.

Q: How do I open the Crypts? A: Use the Scalpel on the Crypt Doors.

Q: Is there anything in the Crypts? A: You betcha.

Loot the Coffin Lids in the Crypts for nuyen.

Shadowrun

Search each Coffin Lid in the Crypts several times to find hidden nuyen. One of the Crypts even has an injured Shaman inside.

Q: How do I help the Shaman? A: Use the Slap Patch on him.

Q: Are the Scary Ghouls important, or just a nuisance? A: They're important. Keep shooting the Ghouls in the Graveyard (not inside the Crypts) until one of them leaves behind a Ghoul Bone.

Talk to the people in each club for helpful information.

★ **Grim Reaper Club**

Description: The first bar in the game. Bars are where all of the Shadowrunners (except for one) are found, and the patrons are usually filled with information. *Items:* Iced Tea.

Q: How do I talk to the Club Patron? A: Give him an Iced Tea.

Q: How do I use the Video Phone? A: You can't use it until the Jamaican gets off the phone, and he doesn't get off until you talk to the Heavy Dude in The Cage about Ghouls.

★ **Gun Shop 1 (Next to Talisman Shop)**

Description: This is the first location to buy armor and weapons. The only one really worth buying is the Defiance T-250 Shotgun, but you'll need to scrimp and save for it (or kick a few butts in the Arena).

★ **Gun Shop 2 (Next to Dark Blade)**

Description: This Gun Shop has much more potent armor and weaponry than the first shop. Several items are sold out when you first visit.

Q: Do the sold-out items ever come back in? A: Yes, but only after you finish certain sections of the game. Keep coming back to check.

You can't enter the 10th Street Monorail until you meet Glutman in The Cage.

Shadowrun

★ **Monorail Station (10th Street)**
Description: This station is closed for repairs until you meet Glutman in The Cage. After that, it opens. This station takes you to Oldtown Station, and Oldtown Station takes you to the 10th Street Station and to Daley Station.

★ **Monorail Station (Oldtown)**
Description: This station is next to the Caryards.

★ **Monorail Station (Daley)**
Description: This station is next to Daley Plaza.

★ **Morgue**
Description: This is where you begin the game, and you'll come back at least once to find essential items. *Items:* CredStick, Scalpel, Slap Patch, Tickets, Torn Paper.

Q: How do I unlock the Filing Cabinets? A: You need to talk to a mortician and have him unlock them.

Q: Every time I enter the Morgue, the morticians scream and run away. How can I talk to them? A: Use the Shades on yourself before you enter the Morgue.

Q: How can I get the mortician to let me examine Grinder's file? A: You need to trick him into thinking you're Lone Star. Buy the Lonestar Badge and use it before you talk to the Mortician.

Use the Lonestar Badge to trick the morticians.

★ **Sputnik Club**
Description: This club is just outside the Caryards.

★ **Talisman Shop**
Description: This magic shop has three items for sale. Two of them are needed for spells, and the other one is needed to finish the game. *Items:* Black Bottle, Potion Bottles, Stake.

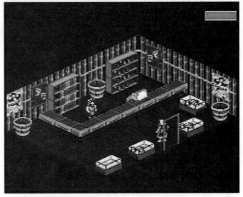
You need every item in the Talisman Shop, but they're expensive.

Shadowrun

★ **The Cage**

Description: The second bar in the game. Maria Mercurial is playing here, and most of the customers have information to share with you.

Q: How do I get past the Heavy Bouncer? A: Give him Tickets.

★ **Town Square**

Description: This is the area with the small park and Water Fountain just outside the Morgue.

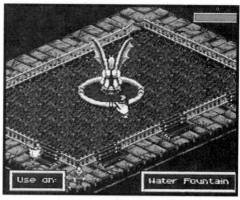

Open the Broken Gate to get to the Water Fountain.

Q: How do I walk to the Water Fountain? I can't get through the fence. A: Look closely at the top of the fence to find a Broken Gate. Open the Broken Gate to reach the Fountain. You'll also let loose the dog, who leaves behind a Dog Collar.

Shadowrunners

★ **Akimi**

Location: Video Phone/ Daley Station (call her and then meet her at Daley Station). *Stats:* Body 7, Magic 20, Strength 1, Charisma 6. *Weapon:* None. *Armor:* None. *Magic:* Powerball lv5, Heal lv4, Invisibility lv5, Armor lv2, Summon Spirit lv4, Freeze lv3. *Skills:* Leadership 4,

Jetboy is one of the weaker Shadowrunners, but he's good to have early in the game.

Negotiation 3. *Note:* To hire Akimi, you have to call her. Ask Anders about Shadowrunners and Akimi to learn her number.

★ **Jetboy**

Location: Wastelands Club. *Stats:* Body 3, Magic 0, Strength 3, Charisma 1. *Weapon:* Beretta Pistol. *Armor:* 1 Mesh Jacket. *Items:* Cyberdeck. *Skills:* Firearms 2, Armed Combat 1, Computer 3. *Note:* If you take Jetboy with you into the Rust Stiletto Hideout, he finds 2,000 nuyen that no other runner does.

Shadowrun

★ **Kitsune**
  Location: Jagged Nails Club. *Stats:* Body 5, Magic 17, Strength 1, Charisma 7. *Weapon:* None. *Armor:* None. *Magic:* Powerball lv4, Heal lv6, Invisibility lv2, Summon Spirit lv5. *Skills:* Leadership 1, Negotiation 3. *Note:* If you defeat the Rat Shaman with Kitsune in your party, she stays with you until she's killed or you win the game.

Spells

★ All six spells are obtained by taking items to the **Dog Shrine**, located in the Docks. The Dog Spirit doesn't appear to you until you have the **Dog Collar, Enchanted Leaves, and Magic Fetish**. Once you have these items and talk to the Dog Spirit, it gives you the Heal spell and sends you to defeat the Rat Shaman.

Bring items to the Dog Shrine to obtain powerful spells.

★ **Heal**: You get this automatically after talking to the Dog Spirit for the first time.
★ **Powerball**: You need the *Ghoul Bone* and *Paperweight.*
★ **Freeze**: You need the *Bottle of Ink* and the *Mermaid Scale.*
★ **Invisibility**: You need the *Potion Bottles*, one filled with *Water* and the other filled with *Toxic Water.*
★ **Summon Spirit**: You need the *Dog Collar* and *Dog Tag.*
★ **Armor**: You need the *Mermaid Scale* and *Serpent Scale.*

Walkthrough

★ **Part 1: The Morgue**
  You start in the Morgue. Examine the Slab. Pickup and Examine the Torn Paper. ("Warehouse 5" is the location of Matrix Systems, which you'll find later on.) Pickup the Scalpel on the middle instrument table. Open the fridge door on the right and Pickup the Slap Patch. Open the door to the office to scare away the morticians. Leave the Morgue. Walk outside to the street.
★ A punk named Decker approaches you and starts a conversation. Select "Talk" from the menu and ask about Firearms and Hitmen. End

Shadowrun

the conversation. Walk to the Town Square with the Water Fountain and Open the Broken Gate. Pickup the Dog Collar. Walk down and left in the direction Decker was running. Go down the steps into the Dark Alley that Decker runs into.

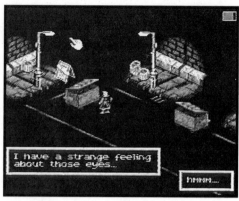

★ In the Dark Alley, walk to Decker's body. Pickup and Use the Beretta Pistol, then shoot the Orc. Examine its body and

Approach the glowing eyes at the end of the alley and talk to the dog.

Pickup and Use the Leather Jacket. Walk left to the end of the Alley and approach the glowing eyes. Select "Talk" from the menu to learn about Dog, then end the conversation. Leave the Alley and walk back to the Town Square.

★ Walk down and right to exit the Town Square area. Now walk right and enter the red building on the left, next to the Monorail Station. Walk into the door directly across from the one you came in (this is the Agent's Office).

★ Examine the body and Pickup the Door Key, then Pickup the Memo from the desk and Examine it. Leave the Office and walk out to the Monorail Station. Walk up and left into the alley next to the Station. Enter the apartment building on the next screen.

★ Examine the doors to find Apartment 6 and use the Door Key to unlock the door. Go inside. Examine the Video Phone. Pickup and Examine the Ripped Note to learn Sassie's phone number. Open the Filing Cabinet and Examine it for a few nuyen. Pickup and Use the Shades. Use the Bed and save the game. Remember to come back here whenever you need to save.

★ Leave your Apartment and walk into the white

Take a rest and save the game whenever you're in Apartment 6.

building across from the Dark Alley. There are two doors. Open the door on the right and take the Paperweight from the desk, then return to the hall and open the door on the left to enter Glutman's Office.

★ Pickup the Cyberdeck. If you try to use the Cyberdeck on the Computer, you get a message telling you that your Datajack is broken. You have to get

Glutman's Office holds the invaluable Cyberdeck.

it fixed (or hire a Runner) before you can jack into the Computer, although the file inside the Computer isn't needed to complete the game. Leave the Office and walk back to the street. Walk up to the Grim Reaper Club and go inside.

★ Talk to the Club Manager (bartender) and ask about Hitmen and Shadowrunners. End the conversation and the Manager pours you an Iced Tea. Pickup the Iced Tea and talk to the Manager again. Ask about Shadowrunners, Decker, and Datajack. End the conversation. Talk to the Busy Man and ask about Heal, Street Docs, and Shadowrunners. End the conversation. Give the Iced Tea to the Club Patron and talk to him. Ask about Tickets, Grinder, and Maria. End the conversation. Now you know that there are some Tickets in the Morgue, but how do you get them?

★ Leave the Grim Reaper and walk into the building on the corner, to the left of the white building. Enter the door at the end of the hall. Talk to the Business Man and ask about Shadowrunners, Hiring, Negotiation, and Lone Star. Say Yes to buy the Lonestar Badge for 150 nuyen. End the conversation and Use the Lonestar Badge to put it on. Walk to the Morgue.

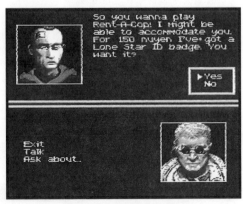

Buy the Lonestar Badge from the Business Man.

Shadowrun

★ The morticians don't recognize you with your Shades on (and don't run away). Talk to the Mortician who isn't busy. Ask about Grinder. Say Yes and the mortician unlocks the Filing Cabinets. Open and Examine both Cabinets to find Tickets and a Credstick. Pickup items and leave the Morgue.

Sweet-talk Sassie to get the number for Glutman's Office.

★ Walk to Apartment 6 and use the Credstick in the Video Phone. Call Sassie and ask about Calls. End the conversation and Use the Credstick in the Phone again. Call Glutman and his secretary answers. Ask about Glutman and The Cage, then end the conversation.

★ Time to head for The Cage, but first you need to take care of some business at the Graveyard. Walk to the entrance of the Grim Reaper bar and walk up and right to the next screen (which is the entrance to the Graveyard). If you like, you can wait on the street and talk to the Loyal Citizen and Heavy Dude when they walk past you. Ask the Citizen about Maria and The Cage, and ask the Heavy Dude about Lone Star.

★ Open the Bronze Gate and enter the Graveyard. Break into the Crypts with the Scalpel and examine each Coffin Lid several times to find hidden nuyen. (Not every lid has nuyen, though.) Open the Crypt on the far left side of the Graveyard last. Inside this Crypt is an Indian Shaman. Use the Slap Patch on him and he starts a conversation. Ask about Magic Fetish, Shaman, and Dog. Search the Coffin Lids for nuyen, and leave the Crypt.

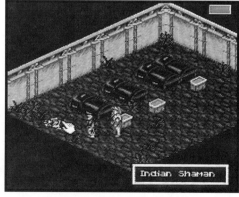

Use the Slap Patch on the Indian Shaman to perk him up.

★ Leave the Graveyard and walk up and right to the entrance of The Cage. Go inside and give the Tickets to the Heavy

Shadowrun

Bouncer. Talk to the Heavy Dude and ask about Ghouls and Hiring. (Now you can hire Jangadance in the Grim Reaper.) Talk to the Shady Character (he's Glutman) and you're taken to the Caryards.

Part 2: The Caryards and Oldtown

★ There are four areas in the Caryards. The first area is the one with your Bed. The second area of the Caryards has several people with useful information. The third area is the bottom-right section of the Caryards where Heavy Dudes and Mages attack you. The fourth area is the Arena in the upper-right section of the Caryards.

★ Save the game on the Bed and walk down and right into the next screen. Talk to the Gang Member about Caryards and King. Talk to the Street Kid about Decker and The Matrix. Talk to the Heavy Dude about Drake. Talk to the Little Boy about the Caryards and Heal. The Boy offers to sell you Slap Patches for 100 nuyen when you ask about Heal. When you're done talking, walk to the Arena.

There are several talkative types in the Caryards.

★ Talk to the Arena Owner. Ask about Negotiation and say Yes to learn the Negotiation skill for 1,000 nuyen. End the conversation and talk to the Owner again. Say Yes to fight in the Arena. Defeat your opponent, leave the Arena and save the game, then return to the Arena and fight again. Keep fighting to earn Karma and nuyen. If you're too weak to survive in the Arena, use the power-up area in the Caryards. Once you make several thousand nuyen, walk to

Battle in the Arena to build up Karma and nuyen.

Shadowrun

The King and talk to him. Say Yes to pay your way out of the Caryards. The higher your Negotiation skill, the less nuyen you need to pay. (You can also get out of the Caryards by asking the Arena Owner about King to fight him, but he is *very* difficult to defeat.)

★ Once you're out of the Caryards, go into the Sputnik Club and talk to the customers. When you're done, go back to the street. Walk down and left to the next street, then walk up and left to the alley (near the female Gang Member). Go into the alley and up the stairs to Ed's Patch & Fix. (Make sure you have at least 2,000 nuyen before you go inside.)

The incompetent street doc activates the Cortex Bomb in your head.

★ Talk to the Street Doc. Ask about Datajack and Examination, then say Yes to pay 500 nuyen for the exam. The doc discovers and accidentally activates a Cortex Bomb. (He gives you a much-deserved refund.) Talk to the Street Doc and ask about Cortex Bomb and Street Doc. End the conversation and leave the Patch & Fix. Walk back to the street and walk up and left to two shops. The left shop is the Talisman Shop and the right shop is the Gun Shop.

★ Talk to the Indian Shaman in the Talisman Shop and ask about Talismans and Shaman. End the conversation. You need all of the items for sale in the Shop eventually, but you don't have to buy them now. Just remember to come back when you have enough money to buy the items. Walk to the Gun Shop. Buy yourself better armor and a better weapon. It might be worth your time building up nuyen to afford the T-250 Shotgun.

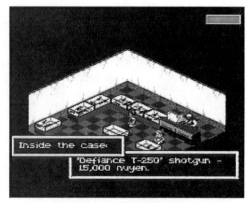

Equip yourself for the battles to come in the Gun Shop.

Shadowrun

Part 3: The Dog Shrine

★ Walk back to the Caryards and enter the Monorail Station. Walk up and left into the next screen and take the monorail to Daley Station. Walk outside and you're ambushed by two Ferocious Orcs. Defeat them both. The second one starts a conversation when you defeat him. Talk to him once and end the conversation. Pick up the nuyen and the Iron Key dropped by the second Orc. Go down the stairs and the dog starts a conversation. Talk and end the conversation. Time to get the bomb in your head shut off! Walk down and right to walk into Daley Plaza, then walk up and right onto the street. Go across the street (watch out for the cars!) and walk down and

Two Orcs are waiting to assassinate you at Daley Station.

right when you reach the other side. Walk into the building on the next screen to enter Dr. Maplethorpe's Office. Talk to the Secretary and ask about Cortex Bomb. Say Yes to pay 2,000 nuyen for the exam. The Secretary opens the door into the exam room, so go inside. Talk to Street Doc and ask about Cortex Bomb, then end the conversation. (Maplethorpe also sells Slap Patches for 100 nuyen; ask about

Heal.) Maplethorpe takes out the Cortex Bomb and starts a conversation with you. Talk and ask about Head Computer, Matrix Systems, and Cyberware. Leave the Office and walk back to Daley Plaza. Walk left into town from here and look for the Wastelands Club. Go inside and you're attacked by a Ferocious Orc guard. Defeat him and walk down the stairs to the floor of the

Dr. Maplethorpe removes the Cortex Bomb and gives you a plug for his Cyberware.

Shadowrun

club. Talk to Anders (one of the Runners) and ask about Shadowrunners, Akimi, and Steelflight. Talk to the Decker and ask about Drake, Matrix Systems, Raitsov, and Rust Stilettos.

★ Hire a Shadowrunner in the Wastelands before you leave. You'll need him to make your run into Rust Stilettos turf. (If you hire Jetboy, he finds 2,000 nuyen during your

Hire a Shadowrunner in the Wastelands for your run into Rust Stilettos turf.

run that no other Runner will find.) Once you leave the Wastelands, walk up and right to Rust Stiletto turf. A Heavy Dude will start a conversation. Ask about the Rust Stilettos and end the conversation, then attack the bad guys. When you defeat them all, use the Iron Key on the door to unlock it and go inside.

★ The first room of the hideout has four Stiletto members. Defeat them all and two Ferocious Orcs come into the room. Defeat them and one of them drops a Crowbar that you need much later on in the game. Pickup the Crowbar and go into the second room. Defeat all of the gangsters in here and one of them starts a conversation when you defeat him. Ask about Drake and end the conversation. When the battle is over, pick up the nuyen and the Password. Examine the Password. Leave Rust Stiletto turf and find the entrance to Jagged Nails.

(It's the door with two guys in suits and a lineup of people.)

★ Talk to the Cruel Man and say Yes to pay your way inside for 50 nuyen. Move the Hand Glove onto Kitsune and press the B button to talk to her. She appears next to you. Talk to her and ask about Dog. Kitsune gives you Enchanted Leaves. Ask about Hiring to hire Kitsune. If you defeat the

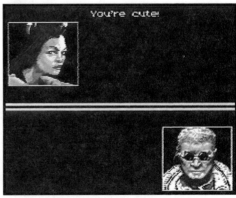

Talk to the "foxy" Kitsune to get the Enchanted Leaves.

Shadowrun

Rat Shaman (you'll find out about him later on) with her following you, she'll stay with you for the rest of the game.

★ Leave Jagged Nails and walk down and right past the Drake building, then walk down and left to find the Docks. Go into the first door to enter Matrix Systems. Defeat the Mage guards and use the Cyberdeck on the Computer. Download the data and jack out to get 2,000 nuyen and a data file. Examine DF_MT-AI in your inventory. Leave Matrix Systems and walk up and left into the next screen. Go into the second door from the right to enter the Dog Shrine.

★ Walk into the circle on the ground and the Dog Spirit appears. If you have the Dog Collar, Enchanted Leaves, and Magic Fetish, the Spirit talks to you and asks you to defeat the Rat Shaman. He also gives you the Heal spell. Leave the Shrine and walk up and left to another door. Go inside.

The Dog Shaman sends you on a quest to kill the Rat Shaman.

★ Walk to the top of the building to find what looks like your gal pal, Sassie, but when you get close enough, "Sassie" turns into an octopus. Defeat the octopus and it leaves behind 2,000 nuyen and a Pool of Ink. If you have the Black Bottle, Pickup the Ink and go back to the Dog Shrine to get the Powerball spell.

★ Walk to Daley Plaza and walk down and right into the narrow alley. Keep going down and right into the graveyard, then walk up and right into the sewers. Walk up and right a few screens, then down and right, to find the Shaman. (You can explore the other rooms in the sewers along the way to build up your Karma by

Sassie turns into a tentacled freak when you get close to her.

Shadowrun

killing the rats.) If you need to leave the sewers, don't worry; the rats you destroy won't regenerate when you come back.

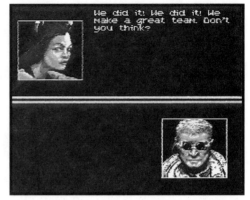

Kitsune stays with you permanently after you beat the Rat Shaman.

★ Defeat the Rat Shaman and the Jester Spirit starts a conversation. Talk to him and ask about Jester Spirit. When you end the conversation, Kitsune talks to you and says what a good team you are. Ask about Jester Spirit and Dark Blade. Now Kitsune stays in your party you until you win the game or she's defeated, in which case she returns to Jagged Nails.

★ Go back to the Jagged Nails bar and talk to the Club Manager on the right. Ask about Vampires and he mentions Strobes. Talk to the Club Manager on the left about Strobes and he gives you the Strobe. Leave Jagged Nails and go to the Dog Spirit. Ask about Dark Blade, Dog, Drake, Jester Spirit, and Raitsov.

★ Return to the Talisman Shop and buy the Stake and the Potion Bottles, then talk to the Indian Shaman and ask about Dark Blade to learn the phone number. Now take the monorail to the 10th Street station and walk to the Town Square next to the Morgue. Use the Potion Bottles on the Water Fountain to fill one bottle up with water.

★ Call Dark Blade from any Video Phone and ask Johan about Magic Fetish. He invites you over to Dark Blade. Go to Daley Station and walk down and right from Daley Plaza to find the gate to Dark Blade. Go inside.

★ Before you go into Dark Blade, walk to the Gun Shop on the right side of the building. Talk to the Shopkeeper and ask about Firearms. There are some excellent items for sale, but several more are

Make a phone call to open the gate of Dark Blade.

Shadowrun

sold out. These sold-out items go on sale later in the game, so keep coming back here to see if they're available. Buy the most powerful armor and weapon available, then leave the shop and go into the main building.

Part 4: Dark Blade

★ Talk to the Mage at the door and ask about Magic Fetish. Walk up and left into the reading room and talk to Vladimir. Ask about Magic Fetish. Give the Fetish to Vladimir and talk to him again. Ask about Jester Spirit to learn the name and location of the Jester Spirit. The name he tells you at this point is false. End the conversation and Vlad walks through the wall! Now use your Cyberdeck to access both Computers. The left Computer has the datafile DF_DB-Jester. The right Computer has an account worth 10,000 nuyen.

Vladimir wants the Magic Fetish before he gives you any information.

★ When you leave the reading room, the Mage attacks you. Walk down and right into a meeting room. Defeat the guards and walk onto the right side of the room. Take the Bronze Key on the third bookshelf from the right. Walk back into the main hall and go up and right into the dining room. Walk up and left into the kitchen and defeat the guards. Walk to the Bronze Gate on the right side of the kitchen and use the Bronze Key to unlock it. Go through the gate to enter the underground crypts.

★ Walk down and left one screen, then walk down and right and go down the stairs into Vladimir's

Search the third bookshelf from the right to find the Bronze Key.

Shadowrun

chamber. Kill the four Ghoul guards; try shooting them from the stairs, since they can't climb up to attack you. Use the Strobe on Vladimir to paralyze him, then use the Stake on him. He screams and begs you not to kill him. (Keep dreaming, Vlad.) Ask about Jester Spirit and he gives you the false name again. Use the Stake again and ask about Jester Spirit again. This time, he gives you Laughlyn, the true name of the Spirit. Use the Stake one more time to kill Vladimir and earn a quick 5,000 nuyen!

Use the Strobe on Vladimir to get the Jester Spirit's true name out of him.

★ Go to the Docks. Walk down and left and defeat the Massive Orc guard. Pick up the Explosives he drops. Talk to the Boat Driver and ask about Bremerton and Mermaids. Walk to the Wastelands and talk to the Club

The Mermaid Scales are needed to get the Freeze Spell at the Dog Shrine.

Manager. Ask about Ice. End the conversation and talk to the Busy Man standing next to the band. Ask about Ice and say Yes, then ask about Docks and he dumps the ice there to drive away the mermaids.

★ Go back to the Docks and walk up and left to the door of the Dog Shrine. Walk down onto the small wooden plank and pick up the Mermaid Scales. Go to the Dog Shrine to get the Freeze spell. Walk to the Boat Driver and talk to him. Ask about Bremerton and say Yes to hire the boat for 1,000 nuyen.

Part 5: Bremerton

★ Walk up and right several screens, defeating the thugs in your way. Climb up the ladder, then walk down and left to the next screen.

Shadowrun

Defeat the thug and the dog. The dog leaves behind a Dog Tag. Pick up the tag and walk to the rusted door on the far left. Use the Crowbar to pry it open and go inside.

★ Shoot the Poison Oozes and use the Switch on the wall to open the door. In the next room, walk up the stairs and follow the tunnel to a flight of stairs. Climb down the stairs to reach a room with an Orc

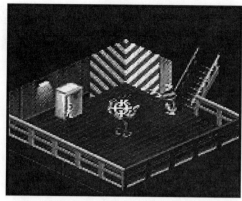

The single Orc guard has the much-needed Safe Key in his grubby hands.

guarding a safe. Defeat the Orc and pick up the Safe Key from his body. Use the Safe Key to unlock the Safe and open it. Pick up the Detonator (which joins with the Explosives to create a Time Bomb in your inventory) and the Broken Bottle. Examine the Broken Bottle for a clue as to what you need.

★ Climb back up the stairs and walk through the room with the Oozes into the next room. Go down the stairs and walk down and right into the next room. Keep going down and right through the next door. There's a Poison Ooze in this room that shoots at you. Defeat the Ooze and it leaves behind a puddle of Toxic Water. Use your Potion Bottles to pick up Water, then go into door that Ooze was guarding.

★ Climb down two flights of stairs and go through the door to the third flight of stairs. Press switch next to door to close airlock door. Now climb back up one flight of stairs and press switch next to the door to flood the chamber with water. When the water reaches maximum pressure, press the switch again. Climb down to second switch and use it to open airlock door, then climb all the way down into the room with the safe. By flooding the room, you eliminated an extremely nasty group of four guards.

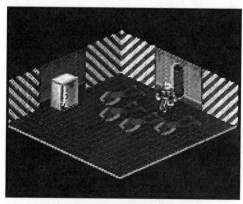

Hit the switches on the stairs to flood the safe room and kill the guards.

Shadowrun

★ Use the Time Bomb on the Safe and stand clear. Open the Safe and take the Green Bottle inside. Examine it. Now climb back up the stairs to the room with the Poison Ooze. Walk up and left into the next room, then walk up and right and go through the door on the right. Walk past the toxic ooze into the next room. Walk down and right into the next room. Walk up and right to the switch. Use the switch and go through the door into the next room. Walk right into the next room.

Use the Time Bomb to blow up the safe.

★ There are two puddles of slimy toxic waste on the ground that block your path to the switches. Use the Green Bottle on the puddles to destroy them. Press both switches, then go through the door. The

Keep shooting the Jester Spirit until he yells at you.

mines on the ground will explode *if* you pushed both switches. Go through the strange door into the spirit world!

★ There's only one path to the Jester Spirit, so keep going through the rooms until you find the Spirit. Aim at the mask and shoot it until the Jester says "You should not have come here. You are no match for the Jester!" Now you can point to the mask and talk to the Jester. Ask about Laughlyn to defeat him, then ask about Bremerton, Dark Blade, Drake, and Jester Spirit. End the conversation and Pickup the Jester Spirit. A door appears in front of you. Walk into it and you're transported back to the Docks.

Part 6: Drake Building

★ Visit the Dog Shrine to get the Summon Spirit and Invisibility spells. Your goal now is to fight through the Drake building and reach the

Shadowrun

helicopter on the 7th Floor, which takes you to the Volcano where Drake is hiding out. Hire a Runner or two if you want, then go into the Drake building. Use your Cyberdeck on the Computer to activate the elevator to the 2nd Floor.

Psychotic guards attack as soon as you leave the elevators in the Drake Building.

★ On each floor of the building, you're ambushed by guards as soon as you exit the elevator. Use one of the fighting methods described in Combat Tips to beat the guards, then use the Computers to activate the elevator and download data files and nuyen.

★ When you reach the 7th Floor, you're attacked by two Security Cannons. Defeat the gunners shooting at you and walk to the helicopter on the right. Talk to the pilot and ask about Volcano to have him fly you there.

Part 7: The Volcano

★ The Volcano has five Sub-levels, numbered from 0 to 4. Sub-level 0 doesn't have any guards, just an elevator door that takes you down to Sub-level 1, the first "real" sub-level.

★ Like in the Drake building, there are plenty of computers and plenty of guards to deal with. The Troll Deckers are armed with machine guns, but if you're wearing the Concealed Jacket or Partial Body Suit, you won't take much damage.

The massive Troll Deckers patrol the halls of the Volcano.

★ Sub-level 4 is the toughest level. The first room is filled with heavy-duty guards. Use an Invisibility spell as soon as you get off the elevator, walk down and right into the room, then walk up and right into a narrow tunnel with a Naga. Use the In-

Shadowrun

visibility spell to stay hidden and shoot the Naga to destroy it. Walk up and right into the next room to fight another Naga. Go up and right once more to defeat a third Naga. This one leaves behind a Serpent Scale. Stand on top of the Scale and pick it up. If you don't stand on it, the Scale slides away from you.

There are three Nagas between you and the Serpent Scale for the Armor spell.

★ Walk down and left back to the room with the guards. Walk down and right and go through the door into a room with several Troll Deckers. Shoot the Deckers (or use Invisibility and run past them) and run down and right into the next room. Go up and right past the grenade-throwing scientists to find Drake. His fire breath is extremely dangerous! Use the Jester Spirit on Drake to cause some damage, then cast Invisibility on yourself and attack Drake's head until he turns to stone. Walk into the door next to Drake and talk to the scientist. Ask about Drake and Head Computer. End the conversation to fly back to the Drake Building.

Part 8: Aneki Building

★ Go to the Dog Shrine to get the Armor spell, then visit the Gun Shop next to Dark Blade. Buy the AS-7 Assault Cannon. Now walk to Dr. Maplethorpe's Office. He has a Dermal Plating device for sale that protects you from damage in The Matrix. Buy it if you want, then leave the office and walk up and left into the next screen. Instead of going across the street to Daley Plaza, walk up and right to the building. The guard asks you for a pass, but there isn't one in the game and you

don't need one anyway. You can shoot the guards or just walk past them into the building. Use your Cyberdeck to tap into the Computer and activate the elevator, then ride up to the 2nd Floor.

★ The Aneki building has

The guard wants a pass. Give him some bullets instead. (Or play it smart and run past him.)

Shadowrun

two rooms on every floor, to the left and right of the elevator. If you wait by the elevator doors for too long, a Troll Decker comes out of an elevator and attacks you. Defeat the guards in both rooms and use all the Computers before you go up to the next floor.

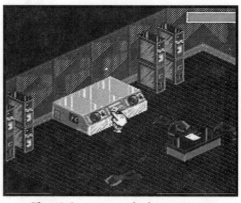

★ The AI Computer is in the left room on the 5th Floor. Defeat the guards and use your Cyberdeck

The AI Computer is the last computer in the game. Beat it and you win!

on the AI Computer. Destroy the main CPU and jack out. That's it! The game takes over from here and shows you shooting your way out of the building and escaping via helicopter. After that, you get programmer credits and several reward screens. A great ending to a great game!

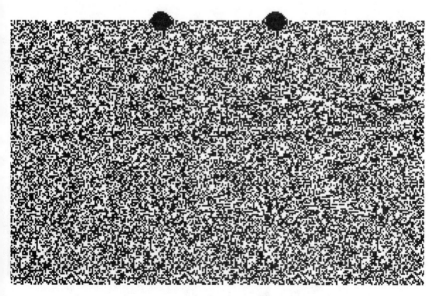

See page 298 for viewing instructions.

SKY BLAZER

BY SONY IMAGESOFT

Introduction

Here's an excellent platform game that was released with very little fanfare. While it doesn't have any Hollywood celebrities in it, you will find an extraordinary amount of gameplay with some of the coolest bosses you've ever seen. The character's move- ment is somewhere between Peter Pan in the game *Hook* and the main character in *Strider*. There are dozens of challenging stages, each with a battle against an awesome boss.

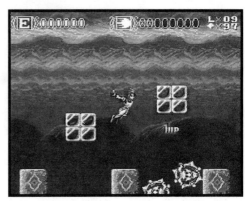

A cross between Hook and Strider, Sky Blazer has great bosses and gameplay.

Awesome Strategies

★ **Controls:** Use B to jump, Y to punch, and X to activate selected magic. The L and R buttons select between the magic potions available.

★ **FIRST LEVEL:** This is an excellent opportunity to master the controls. Practice grabbing onto the sides of the walls, then jump from them to reach higher areas. After hitting most enemies you'll receive a power- up of energy or magic power. Practice using your punching instead of your magic, since on many lev- els you'll run out of magic power and will need punching skills.

★ The **red potion** near the halfway mark seems out of reach. It will refill your magic power completely when you grab it, but if you already have full magic power there's no reason to risk grabbing it.

You must get to the red potion from the right side by using a small jump.

Sky Blazer

The trick to getting to it without falling to your death is to jump to it from the right side, not the left. You must make a short jump (tap the jump button) to reach the block next to it, then climb over and grab it. When you complete this level you'll watch an animation sequence, then you'll meet the Old Man.

★ **FALTINE'S WOODS:** Watch between the leaves for signs of enemies in the trees. When jumping to the next tree, always be ready to punch. Jump rapidly in the leaves of the trees to avoid sinking. Also be careful not to fall off the bottom of the screen, since you'll fall to your death during most of this level. Climb the highest trees about halfway through to find a **1-Up** next to a grey collapsing platform.

★ **THE TEMPLE INFERNUS:** Punch or kick the flames. You'll have to punch the large purple monsters several times to knock them out, or use a Dragon Flash. When you reach flames along the floor, wait for a green moving block to appear, then jump to it.

★ When you enter the second room, be prepared to shoot a Dragon Flash at a **green hovering pod**. It will explode when hit, so keep a distance. When you reach the far right wall, climb up to the ceiling for a **1-Up**, then go left along the second floor.

★ In the fourth room you'll meet the **first boss.** There's a lamp on the floor that moves from side to side. When it stops, a genie rises above it and shoots two fireballs. The fireballs will travel in a straight line to the spot you're standing on when they're launched, so move! The moment you dodge the fireballs, attack the lamp with Dragon Flashes or punches. If you move into it and punch rapidly you can hit it several times, but the moment you stop the genie will reappear and repeat the pattern. You'll gain the **Comet Flash** magic power.

If you keep moving towards the lamp while hitting it you can hit it several times each turn.

★ **CLIFFS OF PERIL:** This level scrolls to the right automatically. Use the jump button to float up, and punch to fire an unlimited fireball. Stay up high to avoid being crushed against the ledges below. When the screen scrolls to the upper-right you can grab a **1-Up** by going under the platform to the right of the second evil plant.

Sky Blazer

★ **TOWER OF THE TARO-LISK:** This level has an awesome tower that you climb up. As you jump to the left or right the tower spins. It's one of the coolest graphic effects we've seen in a Super Nintendo game. Climb up to the first door and enter to collect a **1-Up**. Jump to the upper-left wall, then use your Comet Flash power to reach the top-right ledge. Drop off the

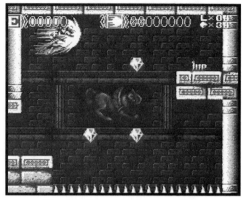

Use the Comet Flash to reach the 1-Up and diamonds in this room.

ledge and use the Comet Flash to the left to collect diamonds and exit.

★ You'll receive an **extra life** for every 100 diamonds you collect. Jump up to the right to the next door and collect the magic power bottle to refill your magic halfway. Exit and enter again to collect enough for full power. You can keep entering and collecting more diamonds to build up lives, or you can drop back down to the last door and collect the 1-Ups twice each time you fill your power energy. Either way, you should try to **build up as many lives** as you have patience for. The average game player will need about 15-25 lives to reach the end of the game, but more never hurts. When you have enough, jump to the spiked blue platform to reach the ledge directly above, and continue climbing up to the next room.

★ The next room is a **zig-zagging climb upward**. Save your Dragon Flash for the pods spitting eyeballs. Save half of your magic power for the next room. Don't rush or you'll end up smashed against spikes.

★ At the **top of the tower** you'll be outside facing winged demons and collapsing platforms. Use your Comet Flash to get across the platforms safely and quickly.

★ As you climb up the second segment of the tower

Use your Dragon Slash to knock the eyeballs out of your way as you climb.

you'll cross a platform with a red dot that turns blue when you jump on it. When the dot is blue, ledges will appear to the left of the next door. Enter the door and collect the **1-Up,** then exit and go back to hit the blue dot. The platforms to the left of the door disappear quickly. You must jump before the first platform appears, but time your jump so you reach it the moment it

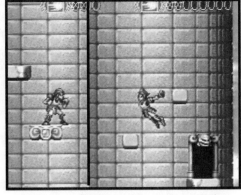

After making the dot blue on the right platform, quickly jump up the left platforms as they appear.

appears. Make short jumps by tapping Jump as you climb up.

★ **The wall on the right will slide to the left** in the next room. You must climb up when the wall is to the right, keeping an eye out for safety spots where you won't be crushed when the wall slides to the left. Save a Comet Flash or Dragon Slash for the pods spitting eyeballs.

★ **The boss** is at the top of the tower. It's an **eyeball** that rolls along the walls of the room in a clockwise direction. As it rolls, it grows larger. The moment the stage begins, run to the left and jump to the wall, then jump right to leap over the eyeball. Go to the left side of the screen, then when the eyeball stops in the bottom-right corner, run and leap to the right to clear a fireball, then punch the eyeball before it begins rolling again. After punching it once, quickly run to the left wall and prepare to leap over it again. Time your leaps carefully, and try to jump as high as you can. Your head should almost hit the ceiling each time. As the eyeball gets larger, the timing of the jump will become crucial. After the fourth hit, run to the left corner and duck to avoid the eyeball. As the eyeball grows, climb up the left wall and jump to the right to leap over the fireball, then throw a Dragon Flash a moment before you land to hit the eyeball. The eye-

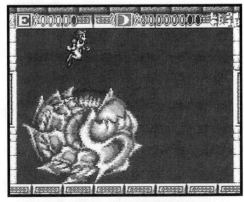

The leap over the eyeball is the most challenging part to beating this boss.

Sky Blazer

ball will grow until it's as tall as the screen, then you'll only need to hit it once more. You'll gain the **Heal** power.

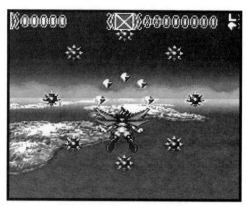

At the end of the bonus round watch out for rings of spikes.

★ **GATEWAY TO THE EAST-ERN PLAINS:** Answer "yes" when the Old Man asks if you're ready. You'll enter a bonus round where you fly through a path of diamonds. You probably won't be able to collect every diamond, but try to collect all you can. Near the end stick to one area of the screen and fly in a small circle to collect the most diamonds. When the diamonds form large rings, be careful! There are rings of spikes in between the rings of diamonds. If you hit the spikes you'll miss out on collecting the last few diamonds.

★ **PETROLITH CASTLE:** No platform game would be complete without a slippery ice level! Ugh! Thanks to excellent game control, this one isn't so bad. In the second room you'll have to drop down through holes to reach the lower floor – grab the walls on your way down to check for spikes before dropping. When you reach the conveyor belts, stick to the platforms or you'll land on spikes.

★ In the next room you'll be attacked by **tiger-like beasts** that jump across high ledges. You want to reach the exit straight across to the right, but before that you should drop down and go to the far right for a **1-Up**. Stand at the edge of each ledge as you climb across the top and prepare to punch if the next beast lunges toward you.

★ The next room has a **ceiling that lowers** and rais-es. Watch for spaces where you can run to, then rush to them as the ceiling rises. In one area you'll have to climb onto

Watch for empty spaces when the ceiling is down, then run to them as it rises.

the side of the ceiling to avoid spikes, then leap to the right above the spikes.

★ **This boss** gets my vote for the coolest boss in this book. The face of a dragon is on a wall made of ice blocks. The entire wall will spin, and on the edge there will be a few blocks missing where you can jump through. When the wall stops, you can make up to three hits each time — one for each eye, and

You can hit the face of the boss three times each time it spins.

one on the face between his eyes. Don't worry if you don't hit him all three times — just concentrate on jumping through the hole in the blocks or you'll be crushed against the wall.

★ **THE SAND RIVERS OF SHIROL:** This level is a large, slow-moving waterfall with blocks. You must climb to the right across the blocks as they drift down the waterfall. At the very beginning of the level, drop off the right side and grab the left wall, then climb down to find a 1-Up. If you grab this **1-Up** at the beginning, you won't have to worry about losing a life on this level.

★ **GATEWAY OF ETERNAL STORMS:** This level is one of the trickiest. There's a **1-Up** near the beginning, and as long as you grab it each time you'll never run out of lives no matter how many you lose on this level. To grab the extra life, drop off the block above it and use the Comet Flash. There's another **1-Up** near the end of the level, but you're better off just hitting the exit a few steps to the right.

★ **STORM FORTRESS OF KH'LAR:** There's safety in a **1-Up** on this level also. From the very beginning, jump to the rising air on the right and take a few steps to the right, then run and leap to the left to grab a diamond and the 1-Up. You must make the leap at the last moment while running, and you must hold the jump button to make a long jump. You'll lose a life if you drop off the bottom of the screen, so always try to stick to the top of this level. As you head to the right, try to knock out each enemy the moment you see them.

★ In the second room, knock out each enemy as you approach them — don't try to go around them. If you find an area difficult to cross, use the Comet Flash.

★ **The boss** has the feet and face of a bird, and the tail and mane of a horse. He splits into three, then they all three attack at once. Stand on

Sky Blazer

the center platform and face left, then punch rapidly to hit all three of the beasts as they come down to get you. If you punch rapidly enough you can destroy them before they have a chance to form a second attack. You'll gain the power of Lightning Strike.

★ **FORTRESS SHIROL:** This is another automatically scrolling area. You'll scroll down, then right, then up

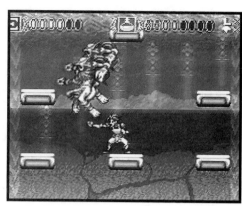

Stand at the center of the screen and punch rapidly to hit all three bosses.

diagonally to the right. At this point, take the higher path to find a 1-Up. Keep your distance from the green pods that explode when you shoot them.

★ **CAVERNS OF SHIROL:** This is a jumping skill test. You must use moving platforms that hang from ropes to reach the exit to the far right. Jump to avoid the lava beasts and their fireballs. The hands on the platforms will only disappear for a moment when you hit them, so run past quickly and move on. The **round gold chompers** that move along the ropes can be punched.

★ The second area isn't much harder as long as you know you can punch those chompers on the ropes.

★ In the third area you'll be attacked by a **wizard** that disappears after each attack. Jump on the first moving block, then jump off to the right and grab the magic power recharge. Climb onto the block above, then jump to the moving block again and ride to the **1-Up.** From here you can use your Comet Flash to reach the exit to the far right. You'll have to use two, then grab another recharge before using another two.

★ **The boss** is a bizarre **winged elephant dragon**. He's *very* attracted to you, so keep away from

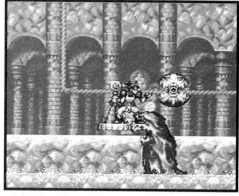

This level is easier once you realize you can punch the gold chompers on the ropes.

him by climbing the walls and platforms. When he stops moving, approach quickly and punch his head when it appears. You can usually hit it a few times. Then dodge him again until a safe opportunity arises for another punch. The center two-block platforms are the safest spot. If he's standing on one, jump and punch him. Avoid letting him trap you in either corner. You'll receive the power of **Warrior Force.**

Wait for the boss to stop, then punch his head when it appears and move away quickly.

★ **THE FALLS OF TORMENT:** There isn't much we can help you with on this level. If you've mastered the basic skills of Sky, you should be able to survive. Try to stay on the logs. If you fall in the water, swim to the nearest stone platform while punching the piranhas that attack.

★ **LAIR OF KHARYON:** We saved this level for last because we hate it! It's not *that* bad, but the current that pulls you while you swim can be very frustrating. Hit each switch you see to change the direction of the currents.

★ In the second room, use your Dragon Flash to shoot the switch.

★ In the third room, enter the door at the center of the water. In the next room, swim up and hit the first switch to swim further up, then shoot a Dragon Flash at the next switch and go left to the exit (there's a power recharge vial above the door). In the next room, go straight down as far as you can go (cannon to left, dragon to right), then go right as far as you can go, hitting the first switch you see. Keep going right all the way, then up all the way. Go left and hit the switch with your Dragon Slash, then go straight down for the door. You'll be in the boss's lair.

Use your Dragon Slash to hit the switches and change the flow of the water.

★ **The boss** is four creatures

Sky Blazer

that open their mouths and release piranhas. The piranhas will become huge very quickly, so try to destroy them quickly. Select your Warrior Force (four arrows), and stay at the center of the screen. When the four eggs appear, let them approach you then use the Warrior Force before they reach you. Grab the items they leave behind, which will hopefully include some magic

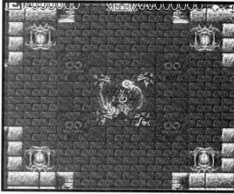

Stay in the middle of the screen and use the Warrior Force a moment before the enemies hit you.

power recharge. Go to the center again and repeat until all four creatures are destroyed. You'll receive the Time Stop power.

★ **SHRINE OF THE WEEPING WILLOW:** In here you'll receive the Mystic Force, and you can get a password.

★ **DRAGONHILL FOREST:** This is similar to the first climb through trees, only the level has more of a maze to get lost in, and there are more enemies. Climb up to the right and enter the first door you see in the tree (about the fourth tree over). Go left and enter the next door in the tree. Go left and enter the door inside the cave you crawl into. Go up and left to find a grey collapsing platform, and a door in a tree to the left. Enter the door and you'll see an arrow of diamonds. Grab them and go right to exit the forest.

★ **THE GREAT TOWER:** More familiar obstacles here. The samurai fight-ers will float towards you and go right through you. Jump over them. When you reach the right wall, climb up and reach the floating grey platform above, then jump up and use a Comet Flash to reach the 1-Up in the upper-right corner. You'll need to use your Comet Flash again near the end to clear some spikes.

★ The next room has a ceiling that lowers to crush

Jump over the samurai fighters – they are very difficult to destroy.

you, then rises again. You've done this before, only now you have to fight a few more creatures. Jump up and shoot the ghosts before approaching them, and remember there's no time limit.

★ In the third room you'll be **chased by huge black marbles**. Stay ahead of them and make leaps of faith to reach the walls to the right each time.

Outrun the huge black marbles and leap to grab the next wall.

★ In the fourth room you'll ride a large **elevator** on a screw. Be ready to jump over the samurai swordsmen when they appear. After a few are on the elevator, use the Warrior Force to knock them all off the elevator.

★ On the outside of the tower you must fall off the left side and guide yourself left or right to avoid the spikes. There are a few platforms to land on for safety near the bottom.

★ Back inside the tower is a **room filled with water.** Swim to the top while fighting the fish and snakes.

★ Back outside the tower you must jump over collapsing platforms while fighting winged beasts. Jump and use your Comet Flash to get across most of the platforms, then quickly hustle across the last few.

★ The next room is not very tall, but reaching the exit is tough. You must climb the walls while avoiding the spiked balls. Take your time.

★ Back outside the tower you'll have to fight a dragon that rises from the bottom to the top. Punch the red crystal ball in his hands while avoiding his flames. Stick to the higher platforms, then when he appears, drop to the lower platform and hit the ball. Quickly jump back to the higher platform and jump to the left to avoid the flames. You'll receive the Fiery Phoenix power.

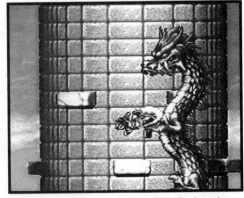

Punch the red crystal ball in the hands of the dragon while avoiding his flames.

Sky Blazer

★ **SHRINE OF DESTINY:**
Tell the Old Man "yes"
you're ready, then pre-
pare for another bonus
round to collect diamonds
(for 1-Ups). The pattern
of diamonds and spikes is
the same as before.

★ **RAGLAN'S CITADEL:**
This is an extremely challenging stage. You must
quickly climb upward
while the screen scrolls. If
the screen scrolls ahead

*Climb up the platforms quickly
before the screen scrolls past you.*

of you, you'll lose a life and have to start over. Keep your Comet
Flash ready in case you need to knock out a pod spitting eyeballs.

★ Inside you'll have to fight the bosses again, beginning with the genie
in the lamp. If you've forgotten how, refer to the earlier part of this
chapter. You now have the Heal power on your side as well. After
each boss you'll enter a safe room with power-ups. Once again you'll
have to battle the rolling eyeball, then the spinning wall of ice blocks,
the underwater piranha hatchers, the flying elephant dragon, and the
Ashura (the final boss).

★ Ashura is one of the most challenging bosses we've met. Begin by
immediately transforming into the Fiery Phoenix and attacking him
three times. Go to the center platform and kneel down facing the
direction of the boss, then punch rapidly as he approaches. After you

hit him, drop down to the
right, then down to the
left to avoid the boss.
Quickly return to the center platform and repeat.

★ That was too easy, but
the fun has just begun.
Here's where the chal-
lenge comes in. **Raglan**
rises from the lava much
larger than before. He
stays to the right side,
punching his arm to the
left. You can safely stand
and climb on the left wall.

*The first encounter with Raglan is easy.
Kneel on the center platform and punch rapidly.*

Sky Blazer

Select your Dragon Flash power. The trick to this boss is timing. When you punch the green gem on his forehead, he'll shoot a laser beam and flames to the left. His pattern is simple — he punches once, retracting his arm, then he punches again but leaves his arm extended. If you hit the gem on his head while his arm is extended, the laser beam and flames

Jump toward Raglan during the first punch and punch the gem between his eyes...

will hit you. Here's the pattern: wait until he retracts his arm, then climb up to the top of the wall. As he punches the first time jump and shoot a Dragon Flash at the gem, then hold left to fall to the bottom floor as his arm retracts between punches. You can do this until you run out of magic power, but you should save half of your magic power for Heal spells. Now you must use punches, which means you have to get closer to his head. As he retracts his arm, climb up to the

top of the wall, then quickly jump to the right. You'll land on his fist as he's punching the first time. Quickly jump and hit the green gem, then jump and fall while holding left to fall to the floor. After eight hits his mouth will open and start to melt. After four more hits his eyes and face will melt. Four more hits and he's a ghost (and you'll be enjoying the fairly decent ending sequence).

...then jump and hold left to fall safely to the floor below.

Awesome Secrets!

★ **PASSWORDS:** The passwords on the following page are for various points in the game. The letters represent the symbols as follows:

Sky Blazer

A=Empty Space (press A button to clear), Y=O (press Y button), X=X (press X button), and B for Triangle (press B button).

Near the end of
the first continent

    A A A B
    X A A A
    X X A A
    A B A A

Beginning of
Eastern Plains

    A B A B
    B A B X
    O O B A
    X O X A

Eastern Plains
With 3 or 4 Powers

    A B B A
    O A A X
    O O A A
    O X B B

Eastern Plains with
Mystic Force/Phoenix

    B B B O
    B A B A
    X B X O
    B X B B

Raglan's Citadel
(Last Area)

    B B B O
    O X B A
    X B X B
    O X B B

See page 298 for viewing instructions.

STREET FIGHTER II: TURBO

BY CAPCOM

Introduction

No doubt you've heard of Street Fighter II by now. It was the first game to take the boring side-scrolling beat-'em-up (where you battle dozens of enemies that look exactly like each other) and turn the main characters against each other. This one-on-one street fighting format has been copied by a multitude of new (and popular) games, but none has matched

SFII Turbo is a new and improved version of the world's most popular SNES game.

the originality of Street Fighter II's characters and moves. This version of SF II contains both the Champion Edition and Turbo versions, and now you can choose to play as any of the four "boss" characters.

Awesome Strategies

★ **Controls:** The buttons can be reconfigured, but if you don't adjust them they will be: A= Medium Kick (Forward), B=Light Kick (Short), C= Hard Kick (Roundhouse); X=Medium Punch (Strong), Y=Light Punch (Jab), Z=Hard Punch (Fierce).

★ Each character has their own unique set of special moves, which requires a combination of control pad and button movements. Mastering all of the moves for one single fighter should be your first step

Ken's Fireball is easy to master. Other character's moves aren't.

Street Fighter 2: Turbo

to mastering Street Fighter II.

★ Several of the special moves in the instruction manual are listed incorrectly (whoops!), and one of them isn't listed at all (double whoops!), so we list the correct versions in this chapter.

★ Some of the combinations in this chapter work with both the Champion Edition and Turbo modes, but others only work in Turbo mode. We'll tell you which ones are Turbo-only.

Combination Moves Are The Key

★ **Combination moves** are the focus of this chapter, since they are the key to Street Fighter II mastery. By using the right combination of moves you can quickly hit your opponent from two to five times, removing some of his energy with each hit.

★ There are three places to hit an enemy fighter: the head, the chest, and the feet. You hit the head with jumping blows, the body with standing blows, and the feet with ducking blows. All combinations alternate hits between these points.

★ Nearly every combination begins with a "late" punch or kick. This means you want to jump at your opponent and deliver a blow at the last possible moment before you land. Your goal is to make the time between your first and second hits minimal, so your opponent won't have time to recover and block.

★ Some combos include "two-in-one" moves where you execute one move while doing the controller motion for another move. For example, Ken can combine the Fierce punch with the Fireball by pressing Fierce halfway through the Fireball motion, then pressing Fierce again to throw the Fireball.

★ If you try a combo and your first blow hits, finish with a combination to dizzy your opponent, then follow up with another combination or a throw. The best time to use combos is when your opponent is already dizzy, since he can't block.

★ Practice combination moves in the two-player mode and use the other player as a punching bag,

Guile tries to recover while Ryu prepares to nail him with a combo.

Street Fighter 2: Turbo

then start fighting against the computer players, increasing the difficulty level as your skills improve. Once you're whipping the computer consistently, go up against an experienced human player for the ultimate challenge.

Ken/Ryu Strategies and Combinations

★ The Hurricane Kick has a "frame" of invincibility. Use the Kick just before a Fireball hits you and you'll spin through it.

★ If you've made a badly timed jump and are about to land on a Fireball or too close to an opponent, use the midair Hurricane Kick to save yourself.

★ If an opponent jumps toward you, jump back and use a Roundhouse kick to hit him, then use a combo while he's getting up.

★ **FIERCE/FIERCE/FIREBALL COMBO:** This one works great against boss characters. Jump at your opponent and throw a late Fierce at the last possible moment, then hit him with another Fierce (standing or ducking), then a Fireball immediately after that.

★ **PUNCH/KICK/DRAGON KICK COMBO:** Get as close to your opponent as possible without getting within sweeping range, then jump at him and use a late Fierce punch, then a low Forward kick, and finally a Dragon Punch to send him to the floor.

★ **ROUNDHOUSE/HURRICANE COMBO:** This one is great against boss characters. Jump at the boss and hit him with a late Roundhouse kick. The moment you land, jump again and hit him with another Roundhouse kick on the way up, followed by a Hurricane Kick while you're still in the air.

★ **FIERCE/FIERCE/HURRICANE KICK COMBO:** Jump at your opponent and hit him with a late Fierce punch. When you land, immediately hit

Strike with a late Fierce punch, then use a standing Fierce...

...and finish with a Hurricane Kick.

Street Fighter 2: Turbo

him with a high Fierce, then floor him with a Hurricane Kick.

★ **EARLY FIERCE FAKE/HURRICANE KICK:** Jump at your opponent with an early Fierce. Your opponent will attempt to counter with his own move, but if you start a Hurricane Kick immediately after the early Fierce you'll send him to the floor.

★ **SHORT/FORWARD/FIREBALL COMBO:** Knock down your opponent, then jump and hit him with a Short, then Throw him when you land, or hit him with a low Forward/Fireball combo.

★ **3-HIT DRAGON PUNCH COMBO:** Jump over your opponent and hit him in the back of the head with a Roundhouse. When you land, throw a Fierce and immediately follow with a Jab Dragon Punch.

Here's a classic Ryu combo. Start with two Fierces...

...and finish with a Fireball. Very nice.

★ **FIERCE/DOUBLE DRAGON PUNCH COMBO:** Get close to your opponent and start with a high Fierce punch, immediately follow with a Fierce dragon punch.

★ **FIERCE/FIERCE/DRAGON PUNCH (KEN ONLY):** Jump toward your opponent and hit with a Fierce punch or Roundhouse kick. Land and

Ken's Dragon Punch hits twice against big guys...

...like Sagat, Balrog, or (in this picture) Zangief.

Street Fighter 2: Turbo

throw a standing Fierce, and execute a Fierce Dragon Punch as you throw the standing Fierce. The Dragon Punch will connect for two hits. This combo only works against larger foes (Zangief, Balrog, Sagat).

★ **DRAGON PUNCH ADVANTAGE (KEN ONLY):** Ken has a wider reach with his Dragon Punch than Ryu (he flies farther to the side on his way up). Use the Dragon Punch to get out of corner traps. For example, if Ryu's using his faster Fireballs to keep you pinned, use the Dragon Punch to fly through the Fireball and nail him.

★ **HURRICANE KICK COMBO (TURBO):** Start with a late Fierce, then a low Forward kick, then immediately start a Hurricane Kick.

★ **KEN/RYU VS. DHALSIM:** Get Dhalsim to either side of the screen, then trap him there with low kicks. He'll get hit every time he tries to hit you. His only other option is to attack with a Yoga Spear. If he tries it, use a Hurricane Kick to send him back to the wall.

★ **KEN/RYU VS. KEN/RYU:** After knocking down your opponent, jump at him with a Short kick and follow with a Jab Dragon Punch as you land. Your opponent will usually be in a blocking position that pushes him away from you unharmed, but as you land from the Dragon Punch he will be in position for a Roundhouse Kick. If he does it, he'll miss you, and you can counter with your own Roundhouse Kick from where you land, or use a Throw.

E. Honda Strategies and Combinations

★ **HIGH AND LOW HIT COMBO:** Jump at your opponent and hit high with a late Fierce, then throw a high Strong, then a low Fierce punch.

★ **HUNDRED-HAND SLAP COMBO:** Jump at your opponent with a late Fierce punch, then press the Strong and Jab punch buttons repeatedly to perform the Hundred-Hand Slap. Even if he blocks you'll drain lots of energy.

Jump at the opponent with a late Fierce, then use...

...the Hundred Hand Slap to suck away his energy.

Street Fighter 2: Turbo

★ **FORWARD/FORWARD/HUNDRED-HAND SLAP COMBO:** If your opponent is down, wait until he stands to perform this combo. Jump over him and use the Forward kick to kick him in the head, then Forward kick as you land and press the Jab and Strong punch buttons rapidly to perform the Hundred-Hand Slap.

★ **SUMO HEAD BUTT:** When getting up from a fall, press the Jab button to Sumo Head Butt your opponent if he is jumping at you.

★ **FORWARD/STRONG/THROW COMBO:** Jump at your opponent to leap over him and hit Forward to execute the Sumo Splash. When you land, press high Strong, then Throw him immediately. To confuse your opponent further, replace the Throw with a Fierce punch occasionally.

★ **FORWARD/FORWARD COMBO:** Jump at your opponent to leap over him and hit Forward to execute the Sumo Splash. Land, turn around, and hit Forward while crouching. You'll score a double hit.

Blanka Strategies and Combinations

★ **CROUCHING FIERCE:** Use the crouching Fierce to trade blows with Fireball-throwers (Guile, Ken, Ryu). It does at least as much damage as the Fireball.

★ **JUMPING FIERCE:** Use a jumping Fierce against an opponent trying a sweep kick or other low move.

★ **ELECTRICITY COMBO:** Jump toward the opponent and throw a Strong punch, then rapidly tap Strong as you fall to activate Electricity. Even if the opponent blocks the Strong punch, you'll take away some energy.

★ **FORWARD/FORWARD/ROLLING ATTACK COMBO:** Jump at your opponent and use a low Forward kick. Immediately hold Back on the control pad to charge for an Attack, then low Forward kick the moment you land and follow with the Attack.

The Electricity combo is easy to do and very effective...

...even if your opponent blocks, he'll lose energy.

Street Fighter 2: Turbo

★ **FIERCE/STRONG/ROUNDHOUSE COMBO:** Jump and hit your opponent with a late Fierce, then without pressing the control pad, press the Strong button. Hit Down on the control pad and finish with a Roundhouse kick.

Fake out your foe with a Jab Rolling Attack...

...then quickly give him a Head Bite before he blocks.

★ **ROLLING ATTACK FAKE:** Fly toward your opponent with a Rolling Attack from the opposite side of the screen to make him block, but use a Jab (short) Rolling Attack so you land before hitting him. Quickly press Toward and Fierce when you land to Head Bite your opponent while he's blocking, or use an Electricity attack. Switch between the Jab and Fierce Rolling Attacks, depending on the distance to your foe.

★ **VERTICAL ROLLING ATTACK FAKE (TURBO):** Do a Vertical Rolling Attack and your opponent should block. You'll land directly next to him, so take a step forward and press Fierce to bite him.

Guile Strategies and Combinations

★ **FIERCE/STRONG/FLASH KICK COMBO:** Jump at your opponent and hold back to charge up for the Flash Kick. Hit your opponent with a late Fierce. Follow with a low Strong punch to the stomach, then finish with a Flash Kick.

★ **FIERCE/FLASH KICK COMBO:** This one is a bit tricky, but very powerful. While standing directly next to your opponent, hold Down for two seconds, then press Up and Fierce, followed immediately by a Roundhouse. You'll punch on the way up and follow it with a Flash Kick too quick to defend against.

★ **FIERCE-FIERCE/SONIC BOOM/BACKHAND COMBO:** Jump at your opponent and hold back immediately to begin charging for a Sonic Boom. As you reach your opponent, hit him with a late Fierce. Press high Fierce, then immediately follow with a Fierce Sonic Boom.

Street Fighter 2: Turbo

*Use a Jab Sonic Boom
to set up the 5-Hit combo...*

*...and finish with a Sonic Boom
and Fierce backhand.*

★ **SHORT JAB/STANDING JAB/FLASH KICK COMBO:** Jump into your opponent with a late Fierce, then hit low Jab, high Jab, then Flash Kick.

★ **FIVE-HIT COMBO:** Throw a Jab Sonic Boom at your opponent and follow it. Jump after the enemy and start pressing Back on the control pad to charge for the Sonic Boom. While you jump, the Boom will hit the enemy. Throw a late Fierce chop as you land, then a standing Fierce uppercut, and begin the controller motion for the Sonic Boom. Complete the Boom and follow up with a Fierce punch for a fifth hit. This combo is blockable, alas.

*Throw a Jab Sonic Boom
at Zangief...*

*...and retaliate when he uses
a Clothesline Spin.*

★ **GUILE VS. BALROG:** Throw a Jab Sonic Boom and follow it. If you see Balrog spin to begin a Turn Punch, hit him with a standing Roundhouse Kick. Sometimes he'll get dizzy from this, which allows you to attack him with any of the above combinations. If he isn't dizzy, back up and repeat the combo. If Balrog jumps at you, kick him with a jumping Roundhouse, high Roundhouse, low Roundhouse, or low Forward.

Street Fighter 2: Turbo

★ **GUILE VS. ZANGIEF:** From far away, throw a Jab Sonic Boom and follow it. If Zangief tries a slow Clothesline Spin, hit him with a low Forward or low Roundhouse Kick. If he tries a fast Clothesline Spin, hit him with a backhand. Sometimes he becomes dizzy and you can attack with any of the above combos. If he jumps over your Sonic Boom, kick him with a low Roundhouse or low Forward kick, or a jumping Fierce.

Chun Li Strategies and Combinations

★ **LIGHTNING KICK COMBO:** This combo works on taller fighters. Jump at your opponent and hit him with a late Fierce, then use a standing Fierce and start tapping Roundhouse immediately to perform the Lightning Kick.

★ **JUMPING FIERCE/FORWARD FIERCE COMBO:** Jump at your opponent with a late Fierce, then hit him with a low Forward kick and high Fierce.

Strike your opponent with up to three Toe Taps...

...then use the Bird Kick to get away before he recovers.

★ **FIERCE/STRONG/FORWARD COMBO:** Jump at your opponent with a late Fierce, then hit him with a Strong punch and a low Forward kick.

★ **LOW FORWARD/HIGH FIERCE COMBO:** This is best used against tall characters. Knock your opponent down, then low Forward kick as he's getting up. Immediately knock him to the ground again with a high Fierce punch.

★ **IMPROVED SPINNING BIRD KICK (TURBO):** Press Down for one second, then press Up and wait a split-second before pressing a Kick button. If you time it right, you'll do a higher Spinning Bird Kick that can pass over Fireballs.

★ **TOE TAP/SPINNING BIRD KICK COMBO (TURBO):** Jump toward your opponent, hold Down, and rapidly press the Forward kick button to knock his head with the Toe Tap. Keep holding Down as you press

Street Fighter 2: Turbo

the Kick button, then press Up and Kick to use a midair Spinning Bird Kick and escape from your opponent. You can score up to three Toe Tap hits.

★ **FIREBALL/FIERCE COMBO (TURBO):** Stand a full screen away from your opponent (who must be trapped against the side of the screen). Throw a slow Jab Fireball and follow it as it hits the enemy. Throw a Fierce punch as the Fireball connects for a double hit.

Zangief Strategies and Combinations

★ **DOUBLE CLOTHESLINE SPIN COMBO:** Jump at your opponent and hold Down while pressing the Fierce button. Quickly use a crouching Short, then press any two punch or kick buttons to start the Clothesline Spin.

★ **FIVE-HIT PILE DRIVER COMBO:** Jump toward your opponent and hold Down while pressing Fierce to do a Body Splash. Land and throw two crouching Jabs, then throw a standing Jab and start the controller motion for a Pile Driver. Complete the motion and press any Punch button to finish the combo. Brutal.

Strike with a Body Splash then a low Short...

...and finish with a Clothesline Spin.

★ **STRONG/ROUNDHOUSE COMBO:** This is best used against tall fighters. Jump over the opponent and press Down with Fierce to hit him behind the head. When you land, high Strong punch then low Roundhouse Kick immediately.

★ **SPINNING CLOTHESLINE FAKE (TURBO):** By hitting any two punch buttons, you send Zangief into a slow Spinning Clothesline, but he's vulnerable from the waist down. By hitting any two kick buttons you activate the faster Spinning Clothesline, and Zangief is invulnerable to attacks below the waist. If your opponent attempts an attack, grab him the moment you stop spinning and use the Spinning Pile Driver. Bam!

Street Fighter 2: Turbo

★ **PILE DRIVER CONTROL:** The direction that Zangief spins during the Pile Driver depends on the direction you roll the control pad. Use clockwise to go to the right, and counter-clockwise to go left. Use this technique to keep your opponent near the far sides of the screen, making him easier to attack.

Dhalsim Strategies and Combinations

★ **TELEPORT CONTROL:** There are four different Teleport locations, depending on the control combination you use. To appear in front of your opponent and far away, press Back, Down, Down-Back, and all three Kick buttons. To appear in front of your opponent and close, press Back, Down, Down-Back, and all three Punch buttons. To appear behind your opponent and far away, press Toward, Down, Down-Toward, and all three Kick buttons. To appear behind your opponent and close, press Toward, Down, Down-Toward, and all three Punch buttons.

★ **AVOID FIREBALLS:** When your opponent throws a Fireball at you, immediately Teleport behind him and use a Throw.

When your opponent throws a Fireball, get behind him...

...and use a Throw or Roundhouse slide.

★ **YOGA SPEAR:** When you use the Yoga Spear, use it rapidly several times to continue hitting the same opponent before he can react.

★ **SHORT SLIDE FAKE/THROW:** Get near an opponent and low Short kick to slide into him. Your opponent will expect a long slide, so he'll stop blocking and prepare to attack. Quickly grab and Throw him the moment you stop sliding.

★ **YOGA FIRE/TELEPORT COMBO:** Stand a full screen away from your opponent and throw a Yoga Fire. If he blocks the Fire, use the Teleport and Throw your opponent while he's blocking.

★ **YOGA FIRE COMBO:** Throw a crouching Short kick, Forward kick, or

Street Fighter 2: Turbo

Jab Punch. Do the motion for a Yoga Fire or Yoga Flame as you make the attack and finish the move.

★ **EVASION COMBO:** When a large opponent jumps at you from a distance, wait until the last second to use the Slide and then Slide under him (press Short once and Forward twice).

Balrog Strategies and Combinations

★ **CROUCHING FORWARD (TURBO):** It was hard for Balrog to stop certain low attacks, especially Guile's crouching Roundhouse and Forward, in the original Champion Edition. Now he can counter with a crouching Forward punch.

★ **DASHING PUNCH COMBO:** Jump at your opponent with a late Fierce while holding Down-Away to charge for a dash. Press low Jab when you land, then high Jab, and finish the combo by moving the control pad Toward your opponent and pressing Short to dash.

Use the Turn Punch to punch through Fireballs...   *...or to knock the bejeezus out of your opponent.*

★ **TURN PUNCH:** Press and hold all three Punch or Kick buttons for one second, then release to perform a Turn Punch. If you release the buttons at the right moment you can punch through projectiles.

★ **FINAL PUNCH:** If you hold all three Punch or Kick buttons you can charge up for a Turn Punch, then use the other three buttons to throw fake punches and kicks to get your opponent off guard. Release the buttons when your opponent isn't blocking. If you hold all three Kick or Punch buttons down for 60 seconds before throwing the Final Punch, you'll connect with a blow that drains half of his energy.

★ **DASHING PUNCH COMBO:** Jump and hold Back on the controller to charge for a dash. Hit your opponent with a late Fierce, then immediately do a Dash the second you land.

★ **SIX-HIT COMBO:** Jump toward your opponent and hold Back on the

Street Fighter 2: Turbo

There are few combos more brutally effective than the six-hit combo...

...as Balrog demonstrates against Zangief.

controller to charge. Hit with a jumping Fierce just before you land. As you land, keep charging and throw three crouching Shorts. As you throw the third Short, press Toward and Short to use a Dashing Punch. Wait for Balrog's arm to come back after he throws the Dashing Punch, then throw a standing Fierce for the sixth hit. Wow!

★ **QUICK MOVE/HEAD BUTT COMBO:** This combo is so fast your opponent won't be able to block both the high and low punches. Start by jumping at your opponent and hitting him with a late Fierce. Then low Jab when you land, Dash Punch into him, and Short kick while simultaneously tapping the Strong or Fierce buttons.

Vega Strategies and Combinations

★ **WALL CLIMB:** The manual got this move wrong, so here's how to do it. Charge Down for two seconds, then press Up-Toward or Up-Back and any Kick button. If you're playing in the Spain background, you'll climb the fence. If you're anywhere else, you'll grab the side of the

The manual doesn't describe the wall climb properly, but we do...

...use the Air Suplex or the Claw Dive as you jump from the wall.

Street Fighter 2: Turbo

screen. If you want to use the Claw Dive, press any button when you're well away from your foe. If you want to use the Air Suplex, push Toward the opponent and any button when you're close to him.

★ **BACKFLIP:** Here's a move not even listed in the manual. In Champion Edition mode, press Back twice to flip away. In Turbo mode, press all three Punch or Kick buttons together. (It was changed in Turbo mode because some players thought the controller tap was inconsistent.)

In Champion Edition mode, press Back twice to Back Flip...

...in Turbo mode, press all three Punch or Kick buttons.

★ **ROLL AND PUNCH COMBO:** This combo works best against dizzy tall characters. Kneel next to them and hold Down-Away on the control pad to charge up. Press Jab, then press Forward on control pad with Strong to roll, then press Strong again when you complete the roll.

★ **HIGH/LOW PUNCH COMBO:** Get in range of your opponent and jump at him with a late Fierce at the last possible moment. Immediately follow with a high or low Strong and low Strong punch.

★ **FIERCE/JAB/ROUNDHOUSE COMBO:** Jump toward the opponent and throw a Fierce or Roundhouse. Land and throw a standing Jab, then finish with a crouching Roundhouse.

Vega's so fast that his combos are very hard to block...

...like the Fierce/Jab/Roundhouse he's using on Ryu.

Street Fighter 2: Turbo

★ **SIX-HIT COMBO (TURBO):** Jump toward your opponent and press Back to charge for a Claw Roll. Throw a Fierce or Roundhouse just before you land. Land and throw a low Short Punch. Begin the motion for the Claw Roll as you throw the Short Punch. Finish the motion and do a Fierce Claw Roll. In Turbo mode, you can score four hits; in Normal mode, you can score three hits.

Sagat Strategies and Combinations

★ **ROUNDHOUSE KICK/TIGER UPPERCUT COMBO:** When you're near your opponent, jump and hit him in the head with a Roundhouse kick, then low Short kick when you land and finish with a Tiger Uppercut.

Sagat's Tiger Punch is even stronger than the Dragon Punch...

...and is a great move to use at the end of a combo.

★ **ROUNDHOUSE KICK/TIGER KNEE COMBO:** Jump at your opponent and kick his head with a Roundhouse, then use a low Short kick and Roundhouse Tiger Knee. Each of these three moves should be done in very quick succession.

Throw your Tiger Shots high and low to keep your opponent off guard...

...you can throw them faster than other opponents can throw their Fireballs.

Street Fighter 2: Turbo

★ **3-HIT ROUNDHOUSE:** Jump at your opponent and hit him with a Roundhouse, then land and use a close standing Roundhouse (if your opponent is Balrog, Sagat, or Zangief) or a close standing Forward (for other opponents). Your blow will hit twice.

★ **STANDING FORWARD LOW/SHORT UPPERCUT COMBO:** When you're close to your opponent, use a high Forward kick, then low Short kick and Tiger Uppercut quickly together.

The 3-hit Roundhouse is simple to do and very effective...

...remember to use Forward instead against shorter opponents.

★ **TIGER KNEE:** Use short jumps to leap over low projectiles (Fireballs, Sonic Booms). Try to land next to your opponent and hit him with a Tiger Uppercut before he recovers from throwing the projectile.

★ **SAGAT VS. BALROG:** Keep Balrog far away by using a low slow Tiger Shot. If he Turn Punches through the Tiger Shot, use a Tiger Uppercut. If he jumps over the Fireball, use a low Roundhouse kick or high Fierce punch.

M. Bison Strategies and Combinations

★ **SCISSOR KICK:** Here's a move that Capcom got wrong in their manual. Charge Back for *three* seconds, not two as the manual says, then press Toward and any kick button. You can use the Kick to jump over Guile's Sonic Booms, but not Ryu or Ken's Fireballs.

★ **JAB/KICK COMBO:** Get your opponent dizzy with one of the other combos, then before he stands up, slide with the low Roundhouse kick to get close to him and push Back to charge up. Throw low Jabs twice, then high Jab. Finish him off by pressing Toward and the Forward kick button.

★ **CORNER TRAP:** 1. Move close to your opponent, crouch, and use a low Forward kick while holding Back on the controller to charge. 2. Stand up and use a standing Forward kick while still charging. 3. Now

Street Fighter 2: Turbo

M. Bison's Corner Trap
isn't foolproof, but it works...

...as demonstrated on E. Honda
in these pictures.

press Toward and any Kick button to use the Scissor Kick. As soon as you start the Scissor, hold Back on the controller to start charging again. 4. After the second Scissor hit, repeat Step 1 by using a low Forward kick. Your opponent will lose energy even if he blocks. To escape the corner trap, Ryu, Ken, and Sagat can use an Uppercut, and Guile can use his Flash Kick. Against these guys, fake the Scissor Kick to make them use a special move, and use the Scissor Kick and a combo to dizzy them.

★ **LANDING:** The direction Bison falls after hitting an opponent in the air depends on which direction you press the control pad (left to right or right to left).

Awesome Secrets!

★ **DISABLE SPECIAL MOVES:** Turn on the game and when the Capcom logo appears, press Down, R Button, Up, L Button, Y, B. You'll hear a chime. Start a new game and you won't be able to use any special moves!

★ **TEN-STAR SPEED IN TURBO MODE:** Turn on the game and wait for the Street Fighter II logo to appear, then press Down, R Button, Up, L Button, Y, B on Controller 2. You need to finish entering

Play the Turbo mode
with up to ten stars of turbo speed.

Street Fighter 2: Turbo

the code before the screen with the giant scrolling Turbo logo. You'll hear a chime if you enter the code. At the title screen, you can crank the Turbo mode up to ten stars of speed.

★ **DISABLE SPECIAL MOVES IN VS. MODE:** Enter the Vs. Mode and choose your fighters. When the Stage Select screen appears, press Down, R Button, Up, L Button, Y, B on Controller 2. Now you can disable special moves for each fighter. Once you've entered the code, press START on Controller 2 to bring up the screen again.

Ending Sequences

★ As in the original Street Fighter II, you get to watch a different ending sequence for each character you finish the game with. The ending also changes depending on a few other factors. Here are the endings:

1. Finish the game at Level 1-3 to view a simple "Congratulations" screen.

2. Finish the game at Level 4 or higher to view the ending for the character you used, including the boss endings from the arcade version. Finish at Level 7 or higher and you also get to see the programmer credits.

3. Finish the game at Level 4 or higher in Turbo mode to view your fighter on a winner's platform with you on the highest platform in the center.

4. Finish the game at Level 8 to see a digitized picture of M. Bison and Ryu. (This is the box art for the Japanese SF II.) Finish at Level 8 in Turbo mode to see the newer SFII Turbo box art for the Japanese version.

5. Finish the game at Level 8 without using any continues to view the deluxe credits with all of the arcade programmers included.

6. Finish the game at Level 8 without using any continues and without losing a single round to view a special ending for experts only.

SUPER BOMBERMAN

BY HUDSON SOFT

Introduction

Bomberman and Bomberman '93 are probably the best multi-player games ever released for the TTI Duo system (AKA the TurboGrafx-16), and now SNES owners can get in on the fun with Super Bomberman and the Super Multitap (a five-player adapter bundled in with the game). Super B has two modes of play. The Normal Mode is a one- or two-player

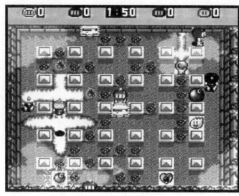

Four players at once make Super Bomberman an incredibly fun game.

simultaneous game where you bomb through 48 stages, fighting monsters and bosses as you search for power-ups. Kind of fun, but it gets boring after a while. The *real* reason to play Super Bomberman is the Battle Mode, where up to *four* players battle it out on one of twelve different Battle Zones. The graphics are kind of cutesy, and the music is annoying, but the game is incredibly fun and the Super Multitap is worth owning so you can play the five-player SNES games coming out in the near future. Check it out!

Attacks

★ All of the strategies in this chapter apply to the **Battle Mode**, which is infinitely more intesting than the Normal Mode. Besides, if you use these strategies to build your skill in the Battle Mode, you'll be able to smoke through the Normal Mode with ease.

★ Your first task as a beginner Bomberman should be to learn how to **incubate a bomb**. How, you ask? Just

Use the code at the end of the chapter to play with tiny Bombermen (can you see them?).

Super Bomberman

drop a bomb and stand on it for a few moments, then kick it at an enemy Bomberman and watch it blow up in his face. A bomb pulses twice, and explodes on the third pulse, so learn just how long you can wait before kicking the bomb. And watch out that the other Bomberman doesn't kick the bomb back at you!

Punch your bombs at enemies to hit and dizzy them.

★ If you have the **Punch power-up**, drop a bomb and incubate it, then punch the bomb to hit another Bomberman. Your enemy will be knocked dizzy and won't be able to recover before the bomb explodes.

★ If there's a Bomberman hiding on the other side of the screen, keep laying bombs and **kicking** them at him. You can drop and kick four bombs before you have to duck around the corner to avoid the explosion.

★ If the Bomberman on the other side of the screen is hiding in an area where he **can't move up or down**—usually between two intersections near the edge of the screen—punch bombs off your side of the screen to trap him. He might punch them back at you, so watch out. If he punches back two bombs, get out of there before they go off.

★ Always **chase the weaker players** if they have power-ups you want or need. (There's no room for mercy in Super Bomberman.) Keep attacking them until they die and the power-ups might appear right next to you. Then again, they might not. That's what you get for being mean to newbies.

★ The best strategy of them all, depending on how good the other players are, is to let the other Bombermen kill each other off while you **hide in the**

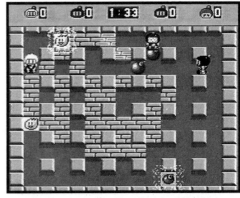

Are you tired of getting bombed? Hide out and let the other players bomb each other.

Super Bomberman

corner and just grab the occasional power-up. If the players you're up against are good, they'll catch on to your wussy tactics and come after you with a vengeance, so be ready to run!

Touch the Diarrhea Skull and spread your disease around to the other players.

★ If the other Bombermen have a bunch of bombs, and you're still stuck with one, keep grabbing the Skulls until you get the **Diarrhea Skull** (uncontrollable bomb dropping). Now touch all the other Bombermen, stand back, and watch them panic and kill themselves.

★ If you're trapped by your own bomb, and you have the **Detonator power-up**, turn psychotic and take another Bomberman down with you. Detonate your bomb just as another Bomberman drops a bomb in line with your own bomb. If you and the other guy are the last two Bombermen, the match is a draw and no one gets credit for a victory.

★ If another Bomberman has Detonators and you don't, get aggressive and follow right behind him, using your **Punch** and **Kick** to knock his bombs away. This is very dangerous, but sometimes the other Bomberman gets confused by your daring technique and blows himself up.

Warp Zone

★ Tired of players who keep using the **Warp Holes**? Bomb the Holes to get rid of them. If you place them just right, and if you have full-length Flame, three bombs will blow up over all the Warp Holes simultaneously.

★ Don't play as the **Blue Bomberman** (Player 2) or you'll be at a serious disadvantage, because you can't see where you are on the screen. (Don't you just *hate* that?)

Tunnel Zone

★ This Zone is very, *very* dangerous. Always be careful when you're walking past a tunnel entrance.

★ Establish control of the **long tunnel** in the middle of the Zone and use it to launch secret attacks on the other Bombermen. Place a bomb at

Super Bomberman

the entrance of the long tunnel, then kick it into the tunnel. The tunnel hides the sliding bomb and the Bombermen on the other side won't know what hit them.

Western Zone

★ **Don't move** at the start of a round and don't drop any bombs unless another Bomberman is trying to kill you. Stay calm.

★ **Players One and Four** can gang up on **Player Two** and kill him at the start of every round. Player One should move right and drop a bomb at the intersection; Player Four should just drop a bomb from where he starts the round. Player Two is now

Player Two can be killed at the start of every round if Players One and Four work together.

trapped. This tactic is extremely cruel—and extremely fun to watch if you're not Player Two.

★ **Escape** from the first available exit and **drop a bomb at the opening**. This traps the other Bombermen in the center while you grab all the power-ups.

Flower Zone

★ The **Tractors** can't hurt you. Try laying a bomb underneath a Tractor just as it passes.

★ There are only two **Detonator icons** in this Zone, so get them both as soon as possible.

Awesome Secrets

★ **Tiny Bombermen:** Select the Password option and enter 5656. The game returns to the title screen. Now choose a Normal or Battle Mode game and the Bombermen will be incredibly small (roughly the size of the characters in Lemmings). The tiny Bombermen turn around corners a bit faster, but otherwise, they're the same as normal Bombermen.

SUPER EMPIRE STRIKES BACK

BY JVC

Introduction

Super Empire Strikes Back is a spectacular sequel to Super Star Wars, with more mega-bits (12), more levels (over 20), a higher level of difficulty (even on the Easy mode), Force Powers that give Luke Skywalker amazing new abilities, and best of all, a password system so you don't have to play through the entire game in one sitting. The graphics and sound are

Did you know that Sculptured Software programmed both this game and Mortal Kombat?

better than ever, with more Mode 7 flying sequences and lots of sound samples taken from the movie. For example, when you run out of lives, Yoda appears on the screen and says "Do or do not. There is no try."

Awesome Strategies

★ **CONTROLS:** Press Y to use your weapon. Press B to jump. Press B again at the top of a jump to execute a "superjump" for more height. If you're using the Lightsaber, you'll also execute a Spinning Attack. Press A to switch between different weapons. Press X to use a special weapon or a Jedi Power. Press L and R to look up and down and scroll the screen slightly. The controls can be reconfigured in the Option Menu.

★ Super Empire is a very challenging game, so go ahead and set the difficulty level to Easy when you first start playing. If you manage to beat the game

Luke's Spinning Attack is the most powerful in the game. Use it constantly.

Super Empire Strikes Back

on Easy, go back and try to beat it on Brave and Jedi. If you finish the game on the Jedi level, you're a truly incredible player (and probably don't need this book, but we're glad you bought it anyway).

★ Of all the different **Force Powers**, the only really useful ones are Elevation and Heal. The other ones are interesting, especially Mind Control, but you don't need to use any of them to finish the game. Fool around with the Powers when you first get them, but try to save your energy for Elevation and Heal.

★ Super Empire is loaded with **hidden items** that are revealed only when you shoot them with your blaster or slice into them when you jump into the air with your Lightsaber. Jump and shoot all over the place as you play through the game to reveal hidden items. We point out some of the best hidden items (especially 1-Ups) in this chapter.

Hoth

★ **STAGE 1:** Climb up the icy mountain slope to reach your **Tauntaun** at the top. Enemies attack you constantly, but you'll get **Hearts** from your enemies as you superjump up the hill, so this stage is very easy. Don't worry, things get much tougher starting with Stage 2!

★ **STAGE 2:** The Tauntaun has a much larger Health Sword than you do, so keep it alive and stay on it. As long as you do this, the Tauntaun will take damage from the attacking creatures instead of you. To dismount the Tauntaun, press Down and B; to mount the Tauntaun, just jump onto its back. Don't shoot the Tauntaun while you're dismounted or you'll hurt it.

★ Switch to the Blaster and use it to shoot the **Hoth Hogs** on the ground as you run to the right. If a creature leaves behind a Health Sword, dismount the Tauntaun to pick it up. Otherwise, you'll extend the Tauntaun's Energy Sword instead of Luke's.

★ Look for tiny **dark piles on the snow**. These piles sprout into **crystals** when you run or jump over them. If you run over them, they'll hurt the Tauntaun, so jump over them and then turn around to shoot them for points.

★ The **bridge of ice** crum-

Use the Blaster when you're on the Tauntaun to shoot the Hoth Hogs.

Super Empire Strikes Back

bles under your weight, so run straight across to the right without stopping or you'll take a fatal fall. Don't jump to the left or you'll be trapped on the wrong side of the screen with nowhere to go but down.

★ You're probably wondering how to take the Heart in the snow to the right of the bridge. Dismount the Tauntaun, stand over the Heart, and press Down and B to jump "into" the snow and take the Heart.

Drop into the pit to the right of the Heart to find three hidden 1-Ups above invisible ledges.

★ There's a pit to the right of the Heart. Instead of jumping over the hole, drop *into* the hole and steer left as you fall to land on an **invisible ledge**. Sneaky! Dismount the Tauntaun and switch to your Lightsaber, then use superjumps to spin around and reveal items. You might have to drop down the invisible platforms (press Down and B) to find everything. You should find **three 1-Ups**, a Health Sword, and a Blaster Power-Up. There doesn't seem to be a way to jump out of here, so jump onto the spikes at the bottom of the pit to kill yourself and start the stage again. Keep dropping into the pit to build up your extra lives, then jump over the pit when you've maxed out your lives.

★ Look for a **spitting plant** inside the ice. Dismount the Tauntaun and destroy the plant to reveal a Blaster Power-Up.

★ Near the end of the stage, the jumps get much trickier. Use the R button to look down and see where the ledges are *before* you jump. Keep going until you find a cave conveniently labeled "Enter Cave." Dismount the Tauntaun and enter the cave.

★ **STAGE 3:** In this stage, there are three **wind tunnels** in the roof of the cave. At the top of each wind tunnel are hidden

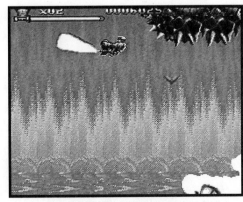

Jump into the air in the cave and you may get sucked into wind tunnels (see next page)...

Super Empire Strikes Back

power-ups. The **first wind tunnel** is close to the beginning of the stage. Go to the right until you reach the first spitting plant, then keep jumping into the air until the wind tunnel sucks you into the air. Jump back and forth at the top of the tunnel to score several small Hearts and a **Blaster Power-Up**. Drop out of the tunnel after you get the Blaster.

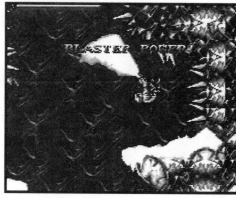

...with hidden items at the top of the tunnel. All of them have Blaster Power-Ups.

★ Stay on the higher ledges as you go to the right to find the **second wind tunnel**. Look for a long ledge with two tiny ledges on the left side. Jump straight up from the left side of the long ledge to enter the wind tunnel. At the top of the tunnel, go left for a large Heart, then go right to find another Heart. Shoot into the air above the Heart to reveal another Heart and a **1-Up.**

★ After you leave the second wind tunnel, start going downward until you reach the bottom of the cave. Continue right to find a pool of icy water. Swim right until you reach the wall, then shoot into the air to find a **Blaster Power-Up** and a Health Sword. Jump up and left onto the ice ledge, then keep going right.

★ The **third wind tunnel** is just before the Wampa Beast (the boss). If you lose a life during your battle against the Wampa Beast, you'll start your next life just below the tunnel. Jump into the tunnel and go left for a Health Sword, then right to find a hidden **Blaster Power-Up** next to the wall. Drop out of the tunnel and walk right into the lair of the Wampa Beast!

★ Switch to your Blaster and stand on the left side of the cave as the **Wampa Beast** comes onto the screen. Blast the Beast in the head as it breathes its **icy breath**. (If you get hit by the breath, you'll be

Shoot the Wampa Beast in the head while it breathes its ice breath (see next page)...

Super Empire Strikes Back

frozen for several seconds.) As soon as the Beast's breath stops, super-jump to the other side of the screen before it punches you with its claw. Keep jumping back and forth after each breath to avoid the claws and keep shooting its head until it blows up.

Then jump to the other side of the screen before it whacks you with its claw.

★ **STAGE 4:** This small stage is somewhat like Stage 2, only the jumps are much trickier. Remember to look down to see where the next ledge is before you jump from one ledge to another, and always shoot the flying creatures (called **Dagles**) before you start a jump. Otherwise, you might get knocked off the ledge and into spikes. Keep going right until you find a cave.

★ **STAGE 5:** There are more wind tunnels in this stage, along with plenty of annoying Wampas. Use your Blaster to get rid of them, and don't get too close.

★ The **first wind tunnel** is above a spike pit with a small ledge in the middle of the pit. The best way to get sucked into the wind tunnel is to jump up and right from the left side of the pit, but be sure to get rid of the Wampa first. If he freezes you with his breath, he'll probably push you into the pit and kill you. There's a **1-Up** and several Hearts at the top of the tunnel.

★ The **second wind tunnel** is above a small ledge with a long ledge on the left. (Look for an **Ice Cat**—the monster that shoots spikes out its back—on the long ledge.) There are four ledges in the tunnel, with a few Hearts and a Health Sword.

★ The **third wind tunnel** is above a group of small ledges. Keep looking upward to see it. There's a Shield at the top.

In Stage 5, kill the Wampa before you jump up into the first wind tunnel.

Super Empire Strikes Back

Look for two 1-Ups on invisible ledges after you leave the cave in Stage 5.

★ The **fourth wind tunnel** is also above a group of small ledges, but this one's better than the last one, because it has a 1-Up at the top! Take the 1-Up and keep going up and right until you see a blinking **red arrow**. Jump into the wind tunnel above the arrow to soar out of the cave and back onto the surface of Hoth. From here, go left until you reach the wall, then jump into the air to land on an **invisible ledge**! There are **two 1-Ups** at the top of the screen. Uncover them with your Blaster or Lightsaber and take them, then go to the right until you walk onto a ledge that collapses beneath your feet. Press the B button to "jump" with the ledge and catch the symbols in the air for big points. The stage ends when the ledge reaches the bottom of the hill.

★ **STAGE 6:** There's no Tauntaun in this stage, so you'll have to go it alone as you run to the right. Use the Lightsaber and keep superjumping to use the Spinning Attack, which works great. When you get to the top of the hill, you'll be attacked by several tiny Imperial droids. Go past the Droids to find the big boss, an **Imperial Probe Droid**.

★ Stick with the Lightsaber and superjump into the Probe Droid with the Lightsaber, or shoot its arms from a distance with your Blaster. When you've destroyed all of the arms, the Probe Droid starts flying around and shooting bullets down at you, but you can destroy it with one or two good Jumping Attacks.

★ When the Probe Droid blows up, continue going to the right. You'll eventually walk onto another small ledge and start sliding down the hill. Get as many of the symbols as you can. When the ledge

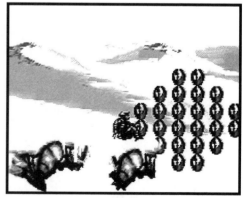

Use your Jump button to leap into the air and collect the symbols.

Super Empire Strikes Back

reaches the bottom of the hill, keep jumping so you don't sink into the water along with the ledge. Once you're off the ledge, jump out of the water and go to the right until a second, and much larger, **Probe Droid** starts attacking.

* If your Blaster isn't powered up, the Droid can be a real pain to destroy. The best plan of attack is to **stay on the middle ledge** and wait for the Droid to

Stay on the middle ledge and jump behind the Imperial Droid when it appears.

appear at the bottom of the screen. If the Droid is on the left or the right, jump to the other side of the screen to jump over its bullets and shoot it from there. If the Droid is in the middle, jump behind the Droid (it can only shoot forward) and attack it. You can also go after the Droid with your Spinning Attack, but this only works in the Easy mode. You take too much damage in the Brave and Jedi modes.

* When you've destroyed the Probe's first form, it attacks with a long **flaming "tail."** Use a Spinning Attack from below to quickly destroy the Droid and finish the stage.

* **STAGE 8:** The major dangers in this stage are the **Imperial Spider Droids**. Use your Lightsaber and Spinning Attack throughout the stage to destroy the Spider Droids.

* Watch the roof closely for **loose beams**. When you see a beam, jump on top of it to make it collapse or slide under it before it falls on you. You can't shoot the loose beams out of the roof; you have to run under them or jump on them to make them fall.

* Slash or shoot open the **crates** on the ground to uncover items.

* Use a low Lightsaber slash or shoot your Blaster diagonally to hit the **flaming traps** in the ground.

Watch the roof and jump over or slide under the loose beams to avoid being hit.

Super Empire Strikes Back

★ Make it through the first part of the stage and you'll come across a **Speeder Bike**. Once you're in control of the Speeder Bike, move to the far left side of the screen and move up and down while holding the Y button to keep shooting rapidly. This technique will destroy most of the enemy Stormtroopers before they even appear on the screen to attack you.

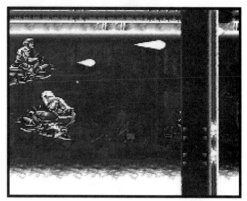

Stay on the left side of the screen and move up and down while shooting.

★ After about a minute of flying, the Snowspeeder blows up and you fall to the ground. Run to the right to get into your Snowspeeder and finish the stage.

★ **STAGE 9:** There are three "missions" to complete in this stage. **Mission 1:** Destroy 10 **Probe Droids** and 10 **Speeder Bikes**. Shoot the Droids and Bikes from as far away as possible, then pick up the Hearts they leave behind when they blow up. You'll have to climb into the air to avoid the large hills constantly in your path. **Mission 2:** Destroy 5 **AT-ST** Walkers. The best technique in this mission is to shoot a Walker from far away, then fly past it and turn around for another pass. As long as you keep moving, the AT-STs can't get a good bead on your Snowspeeder. **Mission 3:** Destroy 5 **AT-AT** Walkers. When you press the L or R Button, a large cable launches from your Snowspeeder to the right side of the screen. You have to use this cable to entangle five AT-ATs and destroy them. Attack an AT-AT slightly to the left, then let fly with the cable just before you pass the AT-AT. Now fly to the right and in circles around the AT-AT to wind the cable around it legs. You'll hear a beep every time you complete a loop around the AT-AT. Do three loops and the AT-AT

Fly past the AT-AT on the left side and use your cable to entangle the Walker's legs.

Super Empire Strikes Back

collapses. Don't fly too far away from the AT-AT or the cable will snap and you'll have to try again. If you run low on energy, fly away from the AT-ATs and shoot a few Speeder Bikes to get some Hearts. After you've destroyed the fifth AT-AT, fly toward the sixth AT-AT to enter the final Hoth stage!

Collect the Health Swords on the legs of the AT-AT before you go through the door.

★ **STAGE 10:** Stay on the far left side of the screen and shoot the attacking Imperial troops. You'll eventually eject from the Snowspeeder and land on the snow. Run to the right until you reach the **front leg** of the AT-AT. Jump up the leg until you reach the top of the screen (you'll get a **Health Sword** on the way up), then go right and eliminate the two Stormtroopers guarding the door. Go through the door. (There's another **Health Sword** on the back leg of the AT-AT that you can get before going through the door.)

★ The most dangerous obstacle **inside the AT-AT** are the **laser cannons**. Use your Lightsaber to block the lasers and they'll destroy themselves as the lasers rebound and hit them. Keep going through the doors to climb up to the top of the AT-AT.

★ You'll emerge on the far right side of the AT-AT. Go to the left until you reach the **head of the AT-AT**, which is the final boss! If

Use a Thermal Grenade to destroy the cannons on the head of the AT-AT.

you have a **Thermal Grenade**, use it now to destroy all of the cannons and quickly win the battle. If you don't have a Grenade, destroy the cannons starting with the one on the left and working your way to the right. If you're lucky, one of the attacking Stormtroopers will drop a Grenade for you to use. Destroy all three cannons to finish the stage.

Super Empire Strikes Back

Rebel Base

★ **STAGE 1:** While Luke is taking out the AT-AT, **Han Solo** is trying to evacuate the Rebel Base and find **Princess Leia**. This is a huge stage, filled with twists and turns and a few dead-ends, but if you just keep going to the right whenever possible, you'll eventually find the exit. Of course, you'll want to **explore the dead-ends**

Stage 1 of the Rebel Base is filled with moving bridges. Use them to explore the entire Base.

along the way to find hidden power-ups and other items. Remember to shoot your Blaster into the air to reveal the items.

★ Watch the roof closely for **loose beams**. When you see a beam, jump on top of it to make it collapse or slide under it before it falls on you. You can't shoot the loose beams out of the roof; you have to run under them or jump on them to make them fall.

★ Slash or shoot open the **crates** on the ground to uncover items.

★ Shoot your Blaster diagonally to hit the **flaming traps** in the ground.

★ You won't be far into the stage before you reach a **bridge** that doesn't seem to lead anywhere. To make the bridge move to the right, press Down and Right on the controller. The bridge will fly across the gap. Some bridges go up and down instead of left and right. Push Up or Down on the controller to make these bridges move.

★ Some of the **Stormtroopers** in this stage hold shields in front of them and lob grenades at you. Sometimes you can jump behind these Shield Troopers and shoot them from the rear. You can also get close to them and duck so that they throw their grenades over your head! The best technique is to throw grenades back at the Troopers.

★ Near the end of the stage,

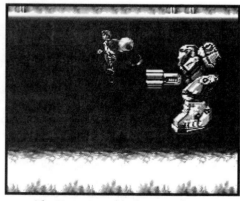

The Hover Droid looks nasty, but it's actually pretty weak. Just don't get shot by it!

Super Empire Strikes Back

you'll encounter a giant flying **Hover Droid**. It looks mean, but it's actually quite weak. Roll away from it when it shoots at you, then blast it while kneeling. It drops a Heart when you destroy it.

★ Get the last few power-ups out of the crates to the right of the Hover Droid (including a Blaster Power-Up), then run right to battle the **Combat Attack Transport** (CAT). This is

Roll under the legs of the CAT when it flies to the right, then jump over it when it flies left.

one of the nastiest bosses in the game, so prepare for a tough battle!

★ Roll under the CAT to the far right side of the screen and shoot the cannon on the end of the CAT. When it flies to the right side of the screen, roll underneath the swinging arms and run to the far left side of the screen. When the CAT starts flying to the left, throw a Grenade and then superjump over it. (If the CAT is high in the air, roll under it instead.) If you timed your throw correctly, the Grenade will hit the arms of the CAT and hopefully blow them up. When you destroy both cannons and both arms of the CAT, it becomes vulnerable and starts trying to crush you. Keep rolling away and shoot it until it explodes.

★ **STAGE 2:** This is a lot like Stage 1, but with a few new obstacles. The first new obstacles are the swinging arms in the ceiling. Get close to them and shoot up and right to hit them.

★ **Princess Leia** is hiding somewhere in this stage. We weren't able to find her, but according to LucasArts, if you manage to track her down, you can skip past the end-of-stage boss. Explore the stage thoroughly—maybe even making a map to keep track of where you've been—and see if you can find her.

★ The end-of-stage boss is an **AT-ST Walker**! Roll

Roll behind the AT-ST Walker and shoot the cannon to weaken it.

Super Empire Strikes Back

underneath the Walker to the right side of the screen and shoot it from behind. There's a Shield hidden in the air, so shoot upward with your weapon to find it. Grab it and then throw Grenades into the AT-ST to destroy the cannon. Once the cannon is gone, the AT-ST is vulnerable, so blast it until it blows and walk to the right to find the Princess.

Shoot into the air on the right side of the AT-ST room to reveal a Shield.

★ **STAGE 3:** You've escaped Hoth in the **Millenium Falcon**, but the Empire is still after you. You'll have to destroy **ten TIE Fighters** while bobbing and weaving through an asteroid field! Fly toward the center of the asteroid field to find the TIEs. If a TIE gets behind you (a **red blip** on your **radar**), move the controller in a circle to shake him. Don't fly straight or he'll lock on and fire. Once the TIE is in front of you (a **green blip** on your **radar**), blast him to pieces. You can shoot or avoid the asteroids, although you're naturally better off avoiding them. When you blow up the tenth TIE Fighter, fly away from the center of the asteroid field to go into hyperspace.

Dagobah

★ **STAGE 1:** Your main objective during the three Dagobah stages is to find all eight of the **Force Powers**. There are several Force Powers hidden in each stage—usually in the trees near the top of the screen. If you don't get all eight Powers during Stages 1 and 2, don't panic, because you can still get all eight in Stage 3. Remember that the only two Force Powers you *really* need are **Elevation** and **Heal**. All the other ones are interesting, but not that useful.

★ At the beginning of Stage 1, jump up to the ledge above you and use the Lightsaber to find the **Health** Force Power. Notice that a Force Sword appears in the upper-right corner, but unfortunately, it's empty! You need to find Force Power-Ups to fill up the Force Sword.

★ Once you have the Health Power, drop down into the slime at the bottom of the screen and go to the far left side of the screen. Jump into the air and use the Lightsaber to find the **Elevation** Force Power and a **Force Power-Up**. You now have the two most useful Force Powers!

Super Empire Strikes Back

★ Use the Elevation Power to climb into the trees and use the Spinning Attack to search around (there's a **Mind Control** Power up there somewhere), or stay near the bottom of the trees to find the **Deflection** Force Power (it's above and to the left of a group of **three giant mushrooms**).

Go into the lower-left corner of Stage 1 to find the critically important Elevation Force.

★ To finish the stage, go to the right and look for the **zigzag path** into the trees. Climb up the path and you'll see (and hear) R2.

★ **STAGE 2:** Now that you've found R2, you need to find **Yoda**. This stage is *much* larger than Stage 1—about three times as long, in fact—so you'll be doing an awful lot of exploration. We've found two Force Powers on this stage.

★ Look for the **Invisible** Power in the area with the giant monsters called **Gundarcs**. Attack the Gundarcs from below, because they're very tough and can kill you easily.

★ Look for the **Anti-Motion** Power above a **giant mushroom** at the bottom of the screen. Jump above all of the giant mushrooms to find a ton of Force Power-Ups.

Use the Spinning Attack to find the Force Power-Ups above the giant mushrooms.

★ There are **two 1-Ups** and a Blaster Power-Up above a small ledge near the top of the screen. Look for it near the beginning of the stage.

★ **Yoda** is on the far right side of the stage at the bottom of the screen. Touch the wise one to move on the next stage.

★ **STAGE 3:** Use Elevation at the beginning of the stage and search along the ledge at the top of the screen to find several Force Powers. Cool! By now, you should have at least **six Force Powers**. If you're missing any, don't worry because you can still get them later on in the stage.

Super Empire Strikes Back

★ After you collect the Force Powers, drop to the bottom of the screen and go to the right. The screen will eventually start scrolling to the right on its own. Activate the **Elevation** Power and use it to fly all the way up the screen. Stay on the ledges at the top of the screen to find all eight Force Powers, one after the other. Take them all, then drop back to the bottom and

If you missed any Force Powers earlier, get them during the final half of Stage 3.

continue going right until the **Swamp Creature Hagobad** appears.

★ **Hagobad** attacks by rising halfway out of the swamp and spitting **poisonous centipedes** at you. Use the Spinning Attack to destroy the centipedes and to hit Hagobad. Aim for Hagobad's eyes first, then go for his nose. There are five vulnerable spots on Hagobad that have to be destroyed. Jump over Hagobad's mouth or you'll take damage. When you've destroyed all five spots, Hagobad becomes vulnerable. Keep using your Spinning Attack and your Heal Force Power until Hagobad is destroyed.

Cloud City

★ **STAGE 1:** Remember the ridiculously long Rebel Base stage? Well, this stage is even worse. Be prepared for a *long* trek through wave after wave of enemies.

★ Since you don't have the Lightsaber, you can't block the **laser cannon**. Instead, run right up to the cannon, then duck and shoot up and right. The lasers will pass harmlessly over your head while you shoot the cannon. (Actually, every once in a while the lasers *will* hit you, in which case

Run directly in front of the laser cannon, then duck and shoot the cannon to destroy it.

Super Empire Strikes Back

you should jump to the other side of the cannon and shoot it from behind.)

4-LOM is the most common enemy in Cloud City. Shoot him before he launches a grenade.

★ When the **Cloud Cars** attack you from above, shoot them in the middle to destroy them. Each Cloud Car drops a Heart when you destroy it.

★ Some of the **platforms** sink under your weight when you jump onto them. Keep doing super-jumps straight up until the platform is as high as possible before you jump across to the next platform.

★ Once you make it inside the city, you'll be attacked by **bounty hunters**. The most common one is **4-LOM**, who shoots a grenade above your head that splits into three grenades. 4-LOM's very weak, so you can usually destroy him before he shoots his first grenade.

★ You'll eventually reach what seems like a dead end, but it's really a **moving platform** like the ones in the Rebel Base. Press Up and Down on the controller to make the platform move. Stop on each level to shoot the enemies and walk into the doors to find hidden items (there's nothing major, though). When you can't go any farther down, go to the right and you'll encounter the next type of bounty hunter: **Bossk**. He takes a lot of hits before he goes down, so duck and shoot him rapidly until he blows up.

★ Keep playing through the stage until you reach a **bug-like creature** that starts spinning into the air. Once you've found this guy, go left and down, then go to the right to fight **IG-88**. Keep shooting IG-88 and he won't have a chance to fire back. You'll find a **Blaster Power-Up** at the end of the corridor. Jump to get it and you'll drop into the tunnel below.

Blast through IG-88 and jump into the air to get the Blaster Power-Up he's guarding.

Super Empire Strikes Back

★ From here, go right until you reach a gap in the ledge. Superjump to the right to land in front of **Dengar**, a bounty hunter who spins his whip in front of him and then uses it to hit you. Destroy Dengar and walk to the right, then drop down to the next tunnel. Go left from here and keep going downward until you reach a **dead end** being guarded by IG-88. Destroy IG-88

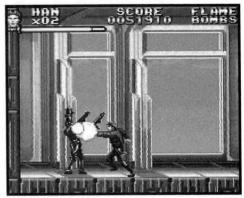

Look for this dead end being guarded by IG-88 and get the hidden Blaster Power-Up.

and then shoot into the air above the wall to reveal a Heart and a Blaster Power-Up. Take them both and climb back up to the tunnel where you first went left. Go right and keep going right and up until you reach the boss.

★ The **boss** is a **giant ship** with plenty of vulnerable spots all over its frame. The problem is that because it's so big, it's very hard to roll under it before it traps you on either side of the screen and crushes you. There's no real pattern to use here. Just keep as far away from the boss as you can and keep shooting it. If you have the Seeker weapon, it'll come in very handy here, since it automatically blasts the boss's weak spots. Destroy the boss and run right to finish the stage.

★ **STAGE 2: Chewbacca** finally makes an appearance! Chewy has two attacks: his Blaster and his **Spin Attack**. Chewy is invincible when he uses the Spin Attack, but it doesn't last for long. The Spin energy regenerates after a while.

★ When you reach the **molten carbon pools**, use superjumps to leap across the ledges in the carbon, and shoot upward to destroy the laser cannons in the ceiling. The ledges slowly sink into the carbon when you stand on them, so don't take too long to get across.

Use superjumps to get across the molten carbon pools and shoot upward at the lasers.

Super Empire Strikes Back

★ If you reach a carbon pool and there aren't any ledges to jump onto, wait for a ledge to appear. Jump onto it and ride across the carbon.

★ There are usually **laser cannons** near the top of a hill. Shoot diagonally upward to destroy the cannons before you try to climb the hills.

★ The boss is an **Ugharra Mining Crusher**. Stand on the middle ledge in the

Stand on the middle ledge and shoot the Mining Crusher when it comes onto the screen.

carbon and shoot the Crusher when it comes down from the top of the screen. The Crusher almost always comes down on the left or right side of the screen, so you're safe staying in the middle. Destroy all the weak spots on the Crusher and then keep shooting it to blow it up.

★ Now the Ugharra pilot attacks you from inside the **cockpit** of the Crusher! He moves fast and shoots a powerful **Ion Cannon**, but he's weak and doesn't take more than a few hits to destroy. Finish him off quickly and jump to the right to finish the stage.

★ **STAGE 3:** It's back to **Han Solo** as he makes his way to the Carbon Freezing Chamber. This isn't a very difficult stage, and there's a ledge with **two 1-Ups** above it, so you can build up your lives by grabbing both 1-Ups, intentionally dying, and getting the lives again and again.

★ Shoot diagonally upward to destroy the **claws** in the ceiling. Don't let them grab you or you'll take serious damage.

★ Shoot the **freezing flame jets** whenever you're riding upward on a floating platform. You won't be hurt if you're hit by a jet, but you *will* be frozen.

★ Check dead ends for **Hearts**. You'll find several of them.

★ Okay, so you *really* want to know where to find the ledge with the **two 1-Ups**. It's near the end of the stage. Look for a grenade-throwing Stormtrooper on the left side of the ledge and a **round laser** (the one that shoots in four directions) on the right side. Shoot into the air above the ledge to reveal the 1-Ups, a Blaster Power-Up, and a Heart. If you die while fighting the boss, you'll start your next life near this ledge. Just backtrack to the left, then go down and right to find it.

★ The **boss** is a huge **Carbon Freezing Unit**. You can jump up the ledges to attack it, but we found the best strategy was to **move into the lower-right corner** of the screen and shoot up and left to hit the

Super Empire Strikes Back

Unit. Duck down as you shoot the Unit to avoid most of the carbon beams. When the Unit blows up, you finish the stage—unfortunately, you finish it frozen in carbonite!

★ **STAGE 4:** Here's another fairly simple stage, with no hidden items and no new enemies—at least until you reach the boss!

★ **Boba Fett** is the galaxy's finest bounty hunter, and he's also the **boss**! He has

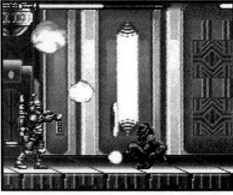

Boba Fett has a variety of powerful attacks. Use your Spin Attack against him.

several attacks. He start out by flying left and right and shooting his **Ion Cannon** at you, then he lands on the floor and shoots a **freezing ray** at you. If the ray hits you, Fett follows up with his Ion Cannon or by launching a **missile** at you.

★ When Fett is in the air, shoot upward diagonally to hit him—he usually doesn't hover above you, but instead he hovers to either side. When Fett lands, charge into him and use your **Spin Attack** to quickly suck away his energy. Get away from Fett before he shoots his freezing ray! Repeat the attack pattern when Fett takes off again. When you defeat him, he leaves behind a trail of Hearts. Take them all and go to the right until Fett returns to the scene with his customized ship, **Slave 1**.

★ Shoot and destroy Slave 1's **cannon** to make the ship vulnerable, then shoot Slave 1 while sliding away from it. If the ship heads straight for you, use the Spin Attack to spin through it. Destroy the ship and walk right to finish the stage.

★ **STAGE 5:** Time for a cool Mode 7 flying sequence! You control the **X-Wing Fighter** in battle against a squadron of **Cloud Cars**. You can fly above and below the cloud cover to pursue the Cloud Cars. The most important strategy here is not to fly *into* the Cloud Cars. Shoot

Fly above and below the cloud cover to attack the Cloud Cars. Dig that Mode 7!

Super Empire Strikes Back

them a few times and then turn away. The Cloud Cars leave behind Hearts, but it takes you a while to reach them. This can be a tricky stage at first, but if you've made it this far into the game, you'll probably get through it in two or three tries.

Use the Elevation Force if (and when) you miss one of the numerous jumps.

★ **STAGE 6:** You're almost at the end! This is a long stage, but it's actually pretty easy since you have the Force Powers at your disposal. Use the **Heal** and **Elevation** Powers whenever you need them. Stay inside the tunnels with the **laser cannons**, because almost all of the cannons have Force Power-Ups inside. Remember to block with your Lightsaber to reflect the lasers at the cannons.

★ You'll encounter **Darth Vader** twice in this level. His pattern is to fly around in the air, land, and then attack with the Lightsaber. Wait for Vader to land, quickly hit him once or twice with the Lightsaber, and then block as he swings at you. When Vader delivers his **finishing blow** (a low Lightsaber swing), he backs up and takes off into the air again. Sometimes he just takes off. Strike him after he backs up and before he flies into the air. Use the **Heal** Power when you're low on energy, and be patient! It takes a long time to defeat Vader. After you defeat Vader for the second time, he uses the Force to destroy the window behind you, and you're sucked out into the next stage!

★ **STAGE 7:** Grab the **symbols** as you fall down the shaft. When you hit the bottom, start going to the right. Use the **Elevation** Power if you miss one of the numerous tricky jumps. You should also use the Elevation to explore this stage a bit to find a few items. There's a door on the far right side

Wait for Vader to deliver his finishing blow, then strike him while his guard is down.

Super Empire Strikes Back

of the stage. Go through it to begin the final battle with **Darth Vader**.

★ **STAGE 8:** Run to the right until Vader starts moving. Use the same fighting strategies you did in Stage 6 to battle Vader, or use another sneaky technique: Run all the way to the right side of the screen and duck down. Slash Vader whenever he gets close, and block him when he attacks you. He should

Hide on the far right side of the screen to sucker Darth Vader into attacking.

find it almost impossible to hit you, and you should get plenty of hits in on him.

★ Every so often, Vader stops fighting and uses the Force to make a bunch of **metallic rubble** fly onto the screen. Use your **Spinning Attack** to destroy the rubble. One or two pieces of rubble usually have

a Force Power-Up inside, so keep using your Heal Power. When the rubble stops appearing, Vader starts attacking again.

★ When you get Vader down to **four dots of energy**, the rubble starts flying onto the screen constantly, and Vader keeps attacking. Use your Spinning Attack to hit Vader and to destroy the rubble. Keep grabbing the Force Power-Ups and use your Heal Power to keep up your energy.

When Vader uses the Force, use your Spinning Attack to destroy the rubble.

Defeat Vader to win the game and get your well-deserved ending sequence. Now you just have to wait for Super Return of the Jedi, scheduled to be released in 1994!

SUPER MARIO ALL-STARS

BY NINTENDO OF AMERICA

Introduction

Wow! This might just be the best cartridge game ever released, because it features *four* all-time classic games for the original NES system: Super Mario Bros., Super Mario Bros. 2, Super Mario Bros. 3, and the never-before-seen Super Mario: The Lost Levels. The Lost Levels is the Japanese version of Super Mario Bros. 2 which was never released in the States.

Super Mario All-Stars brings four classic NES games to the Super NES in style!

(The American version of Super Mario 2 is a reprogrammed version of a Japanese game called Dream Factory.) Each game has brand-new graphics and sound, but the same great playability.

We've squeezed as much information and as many secrets into this chapter as humanly possible, with a particular focus on The Lost Levels, since you've probably played (and maybe even beaten) the other three games before. You're not going to find walkthroughs of every level—we'd need to write an entire book to cover this cart completely—but you'll find all the "most wanted" hints and tips. Read on and enjoy playing the best game(s) of all time!

Awesome Strategies - Super Mario Bros.

★ **World 1-4:** There's a large empty area just before Bowser. Jump around in the air to find six hidden blocks and six coins inside.

★ **World 4-3:** Ride any of the platforms in this level so far down the screen that it breaks off the rope, but jump off in time to save yourself. You'll score 1,000 points.

★ **World 4-4:** Here's how to get through this mazey level. From the start, jump over the lava pools and then jump onto the higher path. Run to the right, over all of the gaps, and keep going until your path reconnects with the lower path. Continue going right and jump up the blocks until you reach the gap in the upper path. Drop into the gap and go left to drop next to lava. From here, run right until you reach Bowser.

Super Mario All-Stars

★ **World 6-4:** Like in World 1-4, there are six hidden coins in the area before Bowser.

★ **World 7-4:** This is a tricky level much like World 4-4. From the start of the level, jump past the lava pool and drop onto the lower path. Run to the right until you reach two ledges. Jump onto the middle ledge and continue to the right, then jump onto the higher path. Keep going

World 6-4: Hit the invisible blocks in the room before Bowser for six coins.

right until your path reconnects with the lower path. Jump up to the ledge next to the spinning fire. Go to the right until you reach two ledges. Drop down to the middle ledge and walk left to drop to the bottom of the screen. Walk right and jump onto the middle ledge; walk right and jump onto the highest ledge. Go right, drop, jump up and right, and run to the right to find Bowser.

★ **World 8-4:** From the start of the level, walk right and go into the third pipe. Walk right and go into the fourth pipe you reach (it's the one in the air). Walk right and go into the third pipe. Swim through the water level and go into the pipe on the far right. Walk right to find Bowser.

Awesome Secrets – Super Mario Bros.

★ **Blow Past Bowser:** If you reach the end of a level as Super Mario or Fireball Mario, try letting yourself by hit by Bowser. You'll be invincible for several seconds, which is plenty of time to run past Bowser, jump on the key, and drop him into the lava.

★ **Flagpole Fireworks:** Watch the timer as you jump onto the flagpole at the end of a level. If the right-hand digit on the

Hit the flagpole when the timer says 1, 3, or 6 to get fireworks and bonus points.

Super Mario All-Stars

timer is 6 when you hit the flagpole, you'll get six fireworks explosions and 3,000 points (500 points for each explosion). If the right-hand digit is 3, you'll get three explosions. If the right-hand digit is 1, you'll get a single explosion.

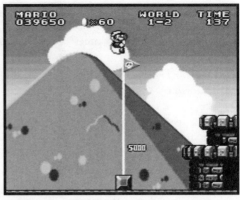

Hit the top of the flagpole to score 5,000 points. Try to get the fireworks, too!

★ **5,000 Points at the Flagpole:** To score 5,000 points at the flagpole, you have to jump from the stairs to the top of the pole. Back up to the left edge of the top step, use the Dash button to speed up, and jump as you reach the right edge of the top step. Make the jump correctly and you'll score 5,000 points.

★ **Unlimited 1-Ups:** You can earn unlimited 1-Ups in World 3-1, on the last stairway before the flagpole. When the Koopa Troopa comes down the stairs, jump on him once to freeze him and keep jumping on him to earn a 1-Up every time you jump. You can use this trick in several other areas, but don't build up *too* many lives or the counter will roll over to zero.

★ **Warp Zones:** There are three warps in the game. **Warp 1 (World 1-2):** Jump onto the blocks above the pipe just before the exit pipe and walk to the right. You'll find a Warp Zone leading to Worlds 2, 3, and 4. **Warp 2 (World 4-2):** Climb the Ivy Vine about a third of the way through the level, then walk to the right to find a Warp Zone leading to Worlds 6, 7, and 8. **Warp 3 (World 4-2):** Jump onto the blocks above the pipe just before the exit pipe and walk to the right. You'll find a Warp Zone leading to World 5.

Awesome Strategies – The Lost Levels

★ Luigi's a better jumper than Mario, so use him for a *slightly* easier time playing through The Lost Levels.

★ **World 1-1:** Here's an easy way to get 127 lives. From the start of the level, walk right to the Koopa walking on the blocks. Hit one of the blocks to make a mushroom appear, then hit the block to make the mushroom bounce to the ground. Take the mushroom *without* going so far to the right that the Koopa and blocks disappear off the screen. Walk under the blocks and wait for the Koopa to move onto the far

Super Mario All-Stars

right block, then smash the other blocks so that the Koopa is stuck. Jump onto the (now-empty) mushroom block and smash the blocks above you, but leave the block above the Koopa. Now jump up and right, into the block above the Koopa, and let yourself fall straight down. You'll bounce off the Koopa shell and bounce it into the wall to score points and eventually 1-Ups. The counter

World 1-1: Build up 128 lives with a simple trick at the beginning of the level.

will stop counting when it reaches 127 lives. And as if you needed it, there's a 1-Up in an invisible block just to the right of the second pipe.

★ **World 1-2:** There are two 1-Ups and two mushrooms in the blocks above the second set of stairs. Smash through one of the blocks to the right of the items, then hit the item blocks one at a time and grab them as they fall through the hole.

★ **World 2-1:** Go down the first pipe after you collect the Star to enter an underground bonus area. The pipe is underneath a ledge, so the best way to get there is to jump from a pipe on the right over to the bonus pipe. After you exit the bonus area, go right to the grass ledge and jump into the air to find two invisible blocks, one of them with a mushroom inside. And there's an Ivy Vine in one of the blocks about halfway through the level that goes to a cloud bonus area.

★ **World 2-2:** There are two invisible blocks on the left side of the pipe in the air. Hit the blocks and jump up to the pipe, which leads to a bonus area.

★ **World 2-4:** There's an invisible block at the top of the stairs past the second lava pool from the start of the level. Jump up and hit the block to get the mushroom inside. if you manage to stay Super Mario until you reach

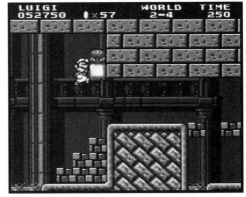

World 2-4: Jump up at the top of the stairs to hit an invisible mushroom block.

Super Mario All-Stars

Bowser, smash into the blocks above you to find a coin block.

★ **World 3-1:** Go down the second pipe in the group of four pipes to enter a bonus area. When you leave the bonus area, walk right against the wall, then jump up to hit an invisible block with a mushroom inside. Now you can smash through the blocks and finish the level.

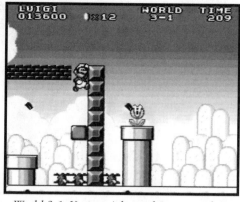

World 3-1: You can't leave this area without getting the mushroom out of the block.

★ **World 3-3:** Hit the flying Koopa out of the air at the start of the level, then jump onto the green or red Koopa and kick the shell to the left. Follow the shell as it bounces to the right and you'll get a 1-Up. There's an invisible block in this level with a mushroom inside. Jump into the air above the ledge to the left of the second group of rope platforms.

★ **World 3-4:** A maze level! Aargh! From the start of the level, go past the first two lava pools, then drop into the tunnel to the right of the third lava pool. Continue right and jump over the pipe, staying on the lower path. Keep going to the right and staying on the lower path until you reach the pipes. Jump to the first pipe, then jump onto the high ledge above the second pipe. Go to the right and drop to the bottom of the screen, then jump into the air to hit four invisible blocks. Use these blocks to jump up and right onto the highest ledge. Continue going right and stay on the highest path until you reach Bowser.

★ **World 4-1:** Get a running start before you hit the spring to jump over the water near the start of the level. If you don't get a running start, you won't bounce far enough to reach the other side. And remember to jump off the spring when it's bouncing *up*, not when it's still bouncing down. Climb up

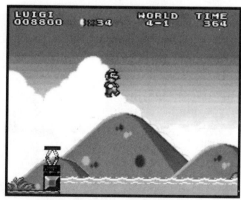

World 4-1: Get a running start and jump on the spring to leap over the water.

Super Mario All-Stars

the stairs past the water, then stand on the right side of the stairs and jump straight up to hit an invisible block with a 1-Up. When you reach the three pipes next to each other, go down the pipe on the left into a coin bonus area.

World 5-1: You'll have to adjust your jumps to counter the gusts of wind.

★ **World 4-4:** There's an invisible block with a mushroom just past the first (and only) pipe in this level. Hit the block and then run to the right to catch the mushroom before it falls into the lava.

★ **World 5-1:** The wind starts blowing in this level right after you reach the top of a set of stairs. Drop onto the right side of the stairs and jump straight up to hit an invisible block against the stairs. Jump straight up from the invisible block to hit another block with a 1-Up inside.

★ **World 6-1:** There's an invisible block with a 1-Up above the second group of blocks from the start of the level. It's probably the easiest hidden 1-Up to get in the entire game!

★ **World 6-4:** It's time for another crazy mazey level. Go to the right and over the lava pool, then jump over the pipe and stay at the bottom of the screen as you go to the right. Keep going right until you reach the Hammer Brother. Jump to the highest ledge and run right until you fall back to the bottom of the screen. Go right and over the pipe, then run under the next pipe. Stay at the bottom of the screen as you go to the right until you reach Bowser.

★ **World 7-3:** This level is a series of jumps from one spring to the next. When you jump, keep going to the right until the next spring is between the left side of the screen and the middle of the screen, because this is usually where you fall back onto the screen.

World 7-3: Don't jump too far. Just move to the next spring and wait to fall onto the screen.

Super Mario All-Stars

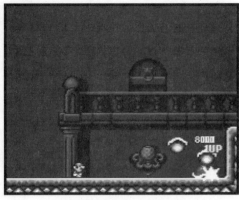

World 7-4: Run behind the Koopa shell to earn a 1-Up.

★ **World 7-4:** There's an invisible block with a mushroom inside next to the wall above the first spinning fireballs. Get it because you'll need it! And a word of advice: *don't* jump onto the blocks at the top of the screen, because once you pass the platforms moving up and down, there's no way to drop back down. You'll just have to wait until the timer runs out and you lose a life. You can score a 1-Up just after the three small lava pools: Hit the red Koopa next to the third pool and kick its shell to the right, then run behind the shell as it hits enemies and scores points.

★ **World 8-3:** The only way to jump across to the rope platform at the end of the level is to jump up and hit two invisible blocks above you. One of them has a poison mushroom inside, so watch out.

★ **World 8-4:** From the start of the level, go to the right and go into the first pipe you reach. (It's the pipe underneath the small ledge.) You'll enter an underwater area, so swim to the right and enter the pipe to return to the castle. You'll appear in an area with two pipes. Go to the far left side of the screen and jump straight up to hit an invisible block with a mushroom inside, then go into the pipe on the right. From here, go to the right until you reach a large lava pool. Jump onto the platform floating in the lava. Wait until the platform drifts to the right, then run to the right and leap over the spinning fireball. Keep going right until you reach Bowser.

★ **Worlds 9-1 and 9-2:** These swimming levels are tough, but also unexciting. *This* is your reward for not warping? Ho-hum.

★ **World 9-3:** Go into the only pipe in this level to enter a coin bonus area.

World 8-4: Run and jump over the spinning fireballs to get to Bowser.

Super Mario All-Stars

When you finish the bonus area and drop back to the pipe, go to the right to face off against Bowser, who's a bit out of his element. Or jump onto the ledge at the top of the screen and run to the right over Bowser's head.

* **World 9-4:** This tiny underwater level spells out a message, although you might not know it, because it's not in English. Each group of blocks

World 9-4: The blocks spell a Japanese word that means "thank you." (No, thank you!)

forms a Japanese text character, called a *kanji*. Translated, the kanji characters spell out the Japanese word "arigato," which means "thank you" in English. Interesting!

* **World A-2:** Jump straight up from the spring to hit a block with a 1-Up inside, then jump to the right to follow it and catch it as it falls off the blocks.

* **World A-3:** There are long and short cloud platforms in this level. There's an invisible block with a mushroom above the right side of the second small cloud platform. It's the one with three coins to the right of it.

* **World B-1:** There's an invisible block with a 1-Up inside between the first two pipes from the start of the level.

* **World D-4:** During the above-ground part of this level, you'll have to make a big jump from a set of stairs to a pipe. Don't jump right away, though. Keep moving to the right until you can see the pipe, and see the Piranha coming out of it. If you jump without being able to see the pipe, you'll jump right into the jaws of the Piranha. You'll encounter Bowser *twice* in the final part of the level. The first time, he'll be under a row of Question

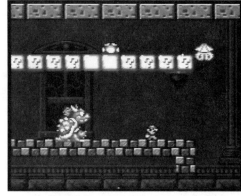

World D-4: Sneak under Bowser and hit the Question Block for a mushroom.

Super Mario All-Stars

Mark blocks. Run underneath him and hit the fifth block from the right to get a mushroom.

Awesome Secrets – The Lost Levels

★ **Flagpole Fireworks:** Watch the timer as you jump onto the flagpole at the end of a level. If the last digit of your coin total matches the last digit of the timer, you'll get fireworks. If the digit is an odd number, you'll get three fireworks (worth 1,500 points). If the digit is an even number, you'll get six fireworks (worth 3,000 points). For example, if you finish a World with 16 coins and 166 on the timer, you get six fireworks.

★ **World 9:** To reach the World 9 levels, you have to finish World 8-4 without warping. You can continue the game, and you can save and continue. You just aren't allowed to use warps, not even reverse warps. If you finish World 8-4 without having warped, you'll go to World 9-1. Otherwise, you'll go to World A-1.

★ **Warp Zones:** The Lost Levels has a multitude of regular warps and *reverse* warps that take you back to earlier levels. Remember that you can't use any Warp Zones if you want to reach World 9.

★ **Warp 1 (World 1-2):** Hit one of the blocks above the second pipe from the start of the level to create an Ivy Vine. Climb up the vine and go right to a Warp Zone leading to World 3.

★ **Warp 2 (World 1-2):** Jump onto the blocks just before the exit pipe and walk to the right. Go down the first pipe you find to enter a secret area and go as far to the right as you can. There are two invisible blocks in the air just to the left of the lava. Jump into the air to hit them, then jump to the top of the screen and run to the right to find a Warp Zone leading to World 4.

★ **Warp 3 (World 1-2):** Jump onto the blocks just before the exit pipe and walk to the right. Keep going to the right and up the stairs to find a Warp Zone leading to World 2.

★ **Warp 4 (World 3-1):** There are two ways to reach this reverse warp that goes back to World 1. The first way is to use the spring to jump over the

World 3-1: Use the spring to bounce over the flagpole and reach the Warp Zone.

Super Mario All-Stars

flagpole at the end of the level and keep going right until you find the Warp Zone. The second way is to go down the first pipe from the start of the level, which takes you into an underground coin area, then takes you to the Warp Zone.

★ **Warp 5 (World 5-1):** Climb the Ivy Vine near the end of the level (it's in the last group of blocks before the flagpole) to find a Warp Zone leading to World 6.

★ **Warp 6 (World 5-2):** Jump onto the blocks just before the exit pipe and walk to the right to find a Warp Zone leading to World 7.

★ **Warp 7 (World 8-1):** Count the number of upside-down pipes from the start of the level. After you reach the fifth upside-down pipe, walk right and go into the next pipe you reach. You'll go to a Warp Zone leading to World 5.

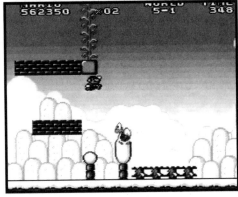

World 5-1: Climb up the Ivy Vine to find a Warp Zone to World 6.

★ **Warp 8 (World A-2):** Jump onto the blocks just before the exit pipe and walk to the right to find a Warp Zone leading to World B.

★ **Warp 9 (World B-4):** Go down the last pipe before Bowser (the fifth pipe from the start of level) to find a Warp Zone leading to World D.

Awesome Strategies – Super Mario Bros. 2

★ **Luigi and the Princess** have the best jumping abilities, so they're the best characters in the game. Of course, you may like Toad or Mario instead, so experiment with each character until you find the one you want.

★ **World 1-1:** There's a shortcut to the Birdo boss. When you reach the underground waterfall area, climb up the vine and then jump to the left across the waterfall. Use bombs to blow through the wall and go through the door. Once you're outside, jump up and left until you're off the screen, then run left to find Birdo.

★ **World 1-3:** It takes three bombs to eliminate Mouser. it's best to throw the bombs onto Mouser's ledge from the right side. If you throw from the left, you have to throw hard enough for the bomb to reach Mouser on the right.

Super Mario All-Stars

★ **World 4-2:** Ride on the Autobomb to get through the spikes near the end of the level. If you grab the Cherry along the way, an extremely helpful Starman appears.

★ **World 4-3:** Don't kill Birdo at the beginning of the level. Jump onto the right side of Birdo and wait for him to spew an egg, then jump onto the egg and ride to the right across the huge expanse

World 4-3: Jump onto Birdo's egg and ride across the water.

of water. It's the only way across! Against the boss, Fryguy, attack with mushroom blocks from the higher ledges. Fryguy splits into four smaller enemies after taking some hits. Hit each of the smaller enemies once to destroy it.

★ **World 5-2:** There's a long drop near the end of the World. Steer left or right to avoid the spikes, then steer to the left or right side of the screen when you're close to the end of the drop. Don't go *all* the way to the left or right or you'll land on spikes.

★ **World 5-3:** Clawglip, the boss, throws rocks at you. Some of his throws are so strong that the rocks fly over your head, and some throws land in front of you and bounce toward you. Watch each throw and catch the rock if the throw is hard enough, then toss it back at Clawglip.

★ **World 6-1:** When you find the huge row of Jars, go into the fifth Jar from the right (for a Key) and the third Jar from the left (for a 1-Up). The other Jars don't have anything interesting to find.

★ **World 6-2:** When you're riding the Albatoss as it flies to the right, you'll need to jump over *three* Albatosses headed the other way. Be ready to make this jump after you

World 6-2: You have to make this big jump over three Albatosses.

Super Mario All-Stars

pass the two small ledges.

★ **World 6-3:** Climb up the ladder at the start of the level, then walk left and jump into the quicksand. Push to the left until you start passing through the wall, then keep tapping the jump button (to keep from drowning in the sand) and holding left until you come out on the other side of the wall. Go through the door to take a shortcut almost all the way to the end of the level.

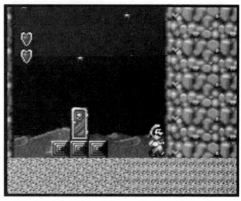

World 6-3: "Swim" through the quicksand to find a shortcut to the end of the level.

★ **World 7-2:** Wart's Castle is very much like a maze, with two different paths to Wart. They're both equally hard, so take either path to the room with the Mask Gate. (Easier written than done!) Take the crystal but watch out, because the Mask Gate attacks you. Hit the Gate with the mushroom blocks three times to make it open. Go into the Gate to face off against Wart.

★ **Wart's attack pattern** is easy to see, but hard to dodge. Stay on the left side of the room and wait for the machine in the middle of the room to spew out a vegetable. Grab the veggie and jump to the left to dodge Wart's bubbles, then jump to the right and feed Wart the veggie while his mouth is open. If you're playing as the Princess, use your floating jump to jump *behind* Wart. Wait for him to spit, then throw the veggie into him, and jump back over him to grab another veggie. Keep whacking Wart with vegetables until he bites the dust and you win the game.

World 7-2: Hit the mighty Wart with veggies as he opens his mouth to spit bubbles.

Super Mario All-Stars

Awesome Secrets – Super Mario Bros. 2

★ **Warp Zones:** There are four warps hidden in Super Mario 2. Here's how to get to every one of them.

★ **Warp 1 (World 1-3 to World 4-1):** Carry a Potion Jar to the right side of the tower. Throw the Potion into the Jar. Enter sub-space and warp by going down into the Jar.

★ **Warp 2 (World 3-1 to World 5-1):** Go past the first waterfall at the beginning of World 3-1, then fall down the second waterfall and land on the narrow hill in the middle of the waterfall. Go through the door on the hill. Inside is a long row of grass. The 10th piece of grass from the left (it's also the sixth one from the right) is a Potion. Take the Potion and use it to enter sub-space next to the Jar just past the grass. Warp to World 5-1 by going down into the Jar.

World 3-1: Jump down the second waterfall and go through the door into a warp area.

★ **Warp 3 (World 4-2 to World 6-1):** Play through World 4-2 to the section of the World with all the whales. Find a Potion and hold onto it until you reach the platform with the Jar on it. Use the Potion to enter sub-space and warp by going down into the Jar.

★ **Warp 4 (World 5-3 to World 7-1):** From the start of World 5-3, go right and climb up the ladder. There's a ledge with a Jar above the top of the ladder. To reach this ledge you'll have to do a Power Squat jump (Luigi is the best character for jumping). Once you've reached the ledge, use a Potion to enter sub-space and warp by going down into the Jar.

World 5-3: Use a Power Squat jump to reach the ledge above the ladder.

Super Mario All-Stars

Awesome Strategies – Super Mario Bros. 3

★ **The Raccoon Suit** is the most important power-up in the game, so learn how to use it. Fly all over the place with the Suit to search for power-ups. Here's a rule of thumb: If you try to fly up to the top edge of a stage and the screen doesn't move, there isn't anything up there. If you don't have a long runway to take off with, you can sometimes build up flight power by running back and forth in a small area.

★ With the **Hammer Bros. Suit**, you can throw hammers and hurt normally invulnerable enemies like Boo Diddly (the ghost), Thwomp, and Stretch. You're also invulnerable to fire when you kneel while wearing the suit.

★ If you see a jump that can't be made, chances are there's an **invisible block** somewhere. Jump around and see if you can't find it.

★ If you hit the left side of a **Mushroom Block**, the Mushroom inside goes to the right, and vice versa. This is important to remember in levels with automatic scrolling in order to collect the power-ups.

Hit the left side of a Mushroom Block to make the Mushroom go right (and vice versa).

★ If you want to eliminate a **Koopa**, stomp on it, pick it up, and let go of it while holding it over a pipe.

★ Hold onto a **Koopa** and use it a shield as you run through an area. You'll lose the shell after a single attack.

★ **World 2-1:** You can fly up above the first closed area and enter the pipe there by bashing through the blocks with the Raccoon tail. Hit the POW and collect the coins.

★ **World 2-3:** Take a flight at the start of the World to find a POW high in the

World 2-1: Bash through the blocks with your Raccoon tail and go into the pipe.

Super Mario All-Stars

air, then use it and drop down to the coin pyramids (which are block pyramids until you use the POW). There's a 1-Up inside one of the pyramids.

★ **World 2-4:** Fly up along the far left edge of the stage and break through the blocks to the top of the World. You'll find a bunch of coins for the taking. Grab them all, including the ones in the

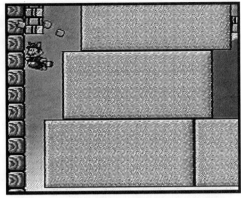

World 2-4: Smash through the blocks on the far left to break through to a coin area.

blocks. Use the Koopa to get up to the next row of coins above the blocks. Find the POW and use it to change the other blocks to coins.

★ **World 2 Pyramid:** Take the upper path and you'll find an upside-down pipe protected by wooden blocks. There's an invisible block close to the wooden blocks. Find it and jump up into the pipe. Get the POW on the bottom block and then collect all the coins. When you're done, the rest of the blocks will turn to coins. Go back down the pipe and head to the left to finish the level.

★ **World 2 Desert:** Pick up a Koopa shell at the start and hold onto it to use as a weapon against the Sun later on. You can either run through or jump over the Tornado about halfway through the stage.

★ **World 3-4:** Walk past the upside-down pipe and keep going until a Cloud Man appears. Run back to the left of the pipe and get a Koopa shell. Drop the shell under the pipe and stand on the middle platform. Now watch the shell bounce back and forth, hitting the Cloud Man's green balls and scoring 1-Ups.

★ **World 3-5:** There's a hidden 1-Up beneath the long upside-down pipe, in an invisible block.

★ **World 3-9:** Get a Koopa shell and drop it between the two cannons under-

World 3-9: Drop a Koopa shell between two cannons and watch the 1-Ups build.

Super Mario All-Stars

neath the row of wooden blocks. The Koopa will bounce back and forth and hit the cannon balls as they are shot out of the cannons.

World 5-3: Put on the Kuribo's Shoe and bounce over the Munchers.

★ **World 4-5:** Find the area with four cannons. Jump up and tap the block that's just at the top of the screen. You can bounce off a cannon ball to get extra height on your jump. After you hit the block, jump onto the highest cannon and make a long jump over to the vine. Climb to the top of the vine to find a Tanooki Suit (in the Question Block) and a POW.

★ **World 5-1:** If you have the Raccoon Suit, fly up at the beginning of the stage to find a pipe that leads to a secret area. Go to the right and fly up the second narrow gap in the secret area, then walk right into a room with a treasure chest. After you leave the secret area, walk to the right and hit the four 1-Up blocks.

★ **World 5-3:** There's a 1-Up in a hidden block above the black flowers (called Munchers). Wear the Kuribo's Shoe and you can jump over the Munchers without getting hurt.

★ **World 5 Mini-Fortress:** Play through the level to find an area with four bricks blocking a hole above you. Break the blocks and fly up into the hole. You'll find a power-up and a pipe. Go down the pipe and collect the coins, then fly straight up where the arrow points up to find a 1-Up.

★ **World 5-5:** Break the blocks over the second pipe and go down it to find a secret room with coins and a Raccoon Suit.

★ **World 6-5:** The only way to finish this level is to use the Raccoon Tail to

World 5-5: Break the blocks over the second pipe and go into a secret room.

Super Mario All-Stars

fly up the second-to-the-last upward gap. Before you fly up there, grab a Koopa shell and fly up the gap with it. Drop the shell on the Piranas to defeat them and break open the walls. Go up the pipe to finish the stage.

★ **World 8 Final Fortress:** You can't defeat Bowser; you have to let him defeat himself. Avoid Bowser's fireballs and stand on the blocks in the middle of

World 6-5: You've got to have the Raccoon Suit to finish this level.

the room. Duck down and let Bowser jump on you. He'll miss you and smash into the blocks you're standing on. Bowser will jump again and break more blocks. Keep standing in the holes that Bowser makes and duck or run away at the last moment before he hits you. When Bowser breaks through the last layer of bricks, he'll fall off the screen and you'll win the game. If you're wearing a Frog Suit, Raccoon Suit, or Hammer Bros. Suit, you'll get an ending different from the normal one.

Awesome Secrets – Super Mario Bros. 3

★ **The Card Game:** This appears on the map screen every time you score 80,000 points. There are eight different patterns to this game, and we've got pictures of every pattern for you. The last three cards in the third row are always the same, so don't choose them at first; choose other cards so you can figure out the pattern you're playing with.

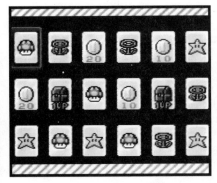

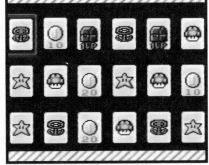

Super Mario All-Stars

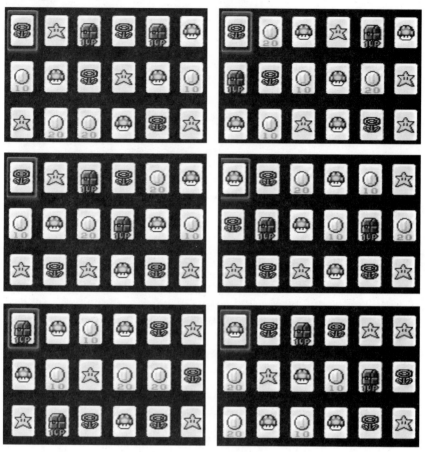

Every time you play the card game you'll be playing one of the eight boards pictured on this or the previous page. Reveal one card and match it to these boards, then try to identify which board you're playing on when you turn over the next card. You can then proceed to make every match on the board perfectly.

★ **White Mushroom House:** If you get a minimum number of coins in certain stages, you'll make the White Mushroom House appear on the map. It's usually incredibly difficult to get the number of coins you need, but the items in the Houses (usually P-Wings) are worth the effort. World 1-4: 44 Coins, P-Wing. World 2-2: 38 Coins, Anchor. World 3-8: 44 Coins, P-Wing. World 4-2: 22 Coins, Anchor. World 5-5: 28 Coins, P-Wing. World 6-7: 78 Coins, Anchor. World 7-2: 46 Coins, P-Wing.

★ **Unlimited 1-Ups:** Early in the game, grab a Mushroom and a Leaf to become Raccoon Mario. When you reach World 1-2, stand at the end

Super Mario All-Stars

of the tall pipe with Goombas coming out of it. Wait until about five Goombas are on the ground, then jump as high as possible and land on a Goomba. Jump again and land on another Goomba. Keep jumping on Goombas without hitting the ground and you'll score lots of points and eventually 1-Ups. You can use this same trick in the World 2 Mini-

Stay in the air and keep jumping off the Goombas to score 1-Ups.

Fortress, with the three Dry Bones in the first screen. Keep stomping on the Dry Bones over and over to earn 1-Ups.

★ **White Treasure Ship:** In Worlds 1, 3, 5, and 6, you can turn the wandering Hammer Brother into a White Treasure Ship loaded with coins if you end a round with a specific score. Collect a number of coins that is a multiple of 11, then score points until the tens digit of your score (the second number from the right) matches the multiple of 11. You *also* have to stop the timer at the end of the stage on an even number. For example, you could get to the Ship by collecting 44 coins, scoring 10,140 (4 X 11 = 44) points, and finishing with the timer at 152 (an even number).

★ **Three Magic Whistles:** There are three Whistles in Super Mario 3 that let you warp ahead to later Worlds. Here's how to find them.

★ **Magic Whistle 1:** Play through World 1-3 until you reach the area with orange, white, and blue platforms in a diagonal pattern, and two green platforms above and below them. Stand on the middle white platform and hold Down on the control pad for several seconds. You'll eventually fall behind the screen. Move to the right without jumping (or you'll return

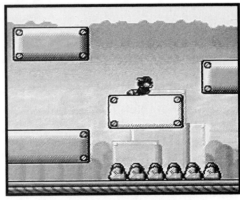

Duck down on this platform to get to the first Magic Whistle.

Super Mario All-Stars

to the front of the screen) to reach a room with a treasure chest. The Magic Whistle is inside the chest. Blow the Whistle to warp to World 2, 3, or 4.

★ **Magic Whistle 2:** You must be Raccoon Mario to get the second Whistle. Play through the World 1 Mini-Fortress until you reach the area where the Dry Bones appear. Fly straight up from where you find the Super Leaf,

The second Magic Whistle is in a secret room of the World 1 Mini-Fortress.

and over the wall to your right. When you can't go right any further, press Up on the control pad to enter a room with a treasure chest that holds the second Magic Whistle. Blow the Whistle to warp to Level 5, 6, or 7.

★ **Magic Whistle 3:** Play to the end of World 2-4. Fight the Hammer Brothers and get the Hammer from one of them. Use the Hammer on the rock in the upper-right corner of the map to reveal a hidden path. Fight the Fire Brothers in the hidden area to earn the third Magic Whistle.

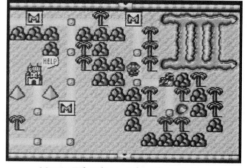

Magic Whistle number three is in a hidden area of the World 2 map.

★ **Warp With Two Whistles:** To warp to World 8 with only two Whistles, grab the first Whistle (World 1-3) and the second Whistle (in the World 1 Mini-Fortress). Once you have the second Whistle, blow it to reach the warp screen. Now blow the *first* Whistle to warp to World 8.

TUFF E NUFF

BY JALECO

Introduction

What? A fighting game? Joy! Actually, this is a pretty decent fighting game. It's no Street Fighter II Turbo, but hey, what is? With a selection of four characters (actually 11 once you enter a secret code) and some cool-looking special moves that get more powerful as you advance through the game, Tuff E Nuff makes a very good third choice when you're burned out on SF II and Mortal Kombat. A Japanese version of Tuff E Nuff was released, titled *Dead Dance*, and it included a little more blood.

Tuff E Nuff stand out from average fighting games with tons of characters and cool special moves.

Awesome Strategies

★ If you want to be a master at Tuff E Nuff, you have to master the **special moves**. Each of the four main characters has his or her own special moves, which are performed with a controller move and button press. Some moves are easy to execute, while others require precise timing. Select the **1P vs. 2P mode** and use the second player as a punching bag while you practice your moves.

★ When you think you have the special moves mastered, start playing the **Story mode**, beginning on the easy level and increasing the difficulty as your skills increase. The ultimate goal is to finish the Story mode at the highest level of difficulty.

★ Offense is important, of course, but **defense** is the key to staying alive. You'll

Go on the defensive, then counter-attack with a special move.

Tuff E Nuff

beat the best when you mix well-timed blocks with rapid punches and special moves.

Boss Code

★ Tuff E Nuff normally only lets you select from four characters (Syoh, Zazi, Kotono, and Vortz). But did you know that you can play as any of the 11 characters in the game? All you have to do is enter a **secret code** (of course).

★ At the title screen, select the START option and the screen with three boxes (1P vs. COM, 1P vs. 2P, and STORY) appears. Now press the controller Left three times, Right three times, and Left seven times. Press START and you'll hear a funky sound. Now you can play the 1P. vs COM mode with any character in the game!

★ If you want to play a **two-player match** with the boss characters, first enter the 1P vs. COM code above, then hit RESET before you choose a character. Use the START option to get to the three-box screen again. Now

Use the boss code for 11 characters instead of four.

press the controller Right three times, Left three times, and Right seven times. Press START and you can play a two-player game with any of the 11 characters.

Special Moves

★ Okay, you've entered the Boss Code, but there's a slight problem—you don't know what the bosses' special moves are! Never fear, because we have a list of the special moves for all **seven boss characters**. *Toward* means to push the controller towards your opponent, and *Away* means to push the controller away from your opponent. Also remember that you have to do these controller motions quickly.

Beans

★ **Rotorfist**: Beans jumps into the air and does an aerial spin punch.

Press Away from your opponent, then push Toward and Big Punch.

★ **Jump Knee Attack**: Beans jumps into the air and does a huge kick, then lands on the ground and kicks again. Press Away from your opponent, then roll the controller to Down and press Big Kick.

★ **Head Slam**: Brutal! Beans grabs the head of his opponent and pounds him face-first into the turf. Get close to your opponent, then press Toward and Big Punch.

Beans uses the Head Slam on anyone who makes fun of his name (which is everyone).

Dolf

★ **Bazooka Shot**: Dolf slowly (too slowly, actually) unleashes a bazooka missile. Press Down and Away from your opponent, then roll the controller to Toward and press Big or Small Punch.

★ **Bazooka Throw**: Dolf trips his opponent, then smashes his chest in with the bazooka. Get close to your opponent, then press Toward and Big Punch.

The Bazooka Shot looks cool, but it's way too slow to be effective.

Rei

★ **Mystic Orb Lightning**: Rei shoots a large black ball. Really weird-looking, but it works. Press Down, then roll the controller Toward your opponent and press Big Punch.

★ **Orange Tremor Flame**: Rei shoots an orange flame across the ground. Press Down, then roll the controller Toward your opponent and press Small Punch.

★ **Dragon Assault**: Rei surrounds himself with a glowing dragon. A very

Tuff E Nuff

short-range attack. Press Down and Toward your opponent, then push Toward and Big Punch.

★ **Snake Lightning Fist**: Rei punches straight up. Press Down and Toward your opponent, then push Away and Big Punch.

★ **Back Throw**: A boring move. Get close to your opponent, then press Away or Toward and Big Punch.

Counter aerial attacks with the Snake Lightning Fist.

Gajet

★ **Back Suplex**: It's, um, a Back Suplex. Press Away from your opponent, then roll the controller Down, then Toward your opponent and press Big Kick.

★ **Climax**: Gajet does a jumping punch. Use it against a jumping opponent. Press Down, then roll the controller Toward your opponent and press Big Punch.

★ **Neck-Hanging Bomber**: Gajet grabs and chokes his opponent, then slams him into the ground. Get close to your opponent, then press Away or Toward and Small Punch.

Gajet chokes the life out of his opponent before slamming him to the turf.

★ **Power Slam**: Gajet shows off his upper-body power with this devastating body slam. Get close to your opponent, then press Away or Toward and Big Punch.

★ **Dagger Attack**: Gajet grabs his opponent and stabs him a few times. Get close to your opponent, then press Away or Toward and Small Kick.

★ **DDT**: Yet another nasty-looking power move. Get close to your opponent, then press Away or Toward and Big Kick.

Sirou

★ **Blue Tremor Flame**: Sirou shoots a blue frame across the ground. Press Down, then roll the controller Toward your opponent and press Big Punch.

★ **Free Arm Throw**: Sneaky Sirou lets go of his sword just long enough to chop his opponent to the ground. Get close to your opponent, then press Away or Toward and Big Punch.

Sneaky Sirou pokes his foe with a Free Arm Throw.

K's

★ **Electromagnetic Storm**: K's lets loose with an electric bolt that stretches all the way up the screen, so there's no way to avoid it. Press Down and Away from your opponent, then roll the controller to Toward and press Big Punch.

You can't avoid the Electromagnetic Storm, only block it.

★ **Thrust Claw Dive**: The name says it all. Press Away from your opponent, then roll the controller to Down and then Toward while pressing Big Punch.

★ **Claw Throw**: K's uses his claw to casually toss his opponent over his back. Get close to your opponent, then press Toward and Big Punch.

K's? What kinda name is that?! At least he's got cool moves like the Claw Throw.

Tuff E Nuff

Jade

★ **Crescent Rainbow Force**: Jade throws a big, *big* fireball. Press Down and Away from your opponent, then push Toward and Big Punch.

★ **Plasma Fists**: Jade thrusts both fists into the air. A perfect counter-move to a jumping attacker. Press Down, then roll the controller to Away and press Big Punch.

The omnipotent Jade zaps his unfortunate opponent after a Lift Slam.

★ **Piston Slam**: Jade grabs his opponent, shakes him like a rag doll, and tosses him all the way across the screen. Get close to your opponent, then press Towards and Small Punch.

★ **Lift Slam**: Jade grabs his opponent, slams him into the ground, and then shoots him just to make sure he's hurting. Get close to your opponent, then press Towards and Big Punch.

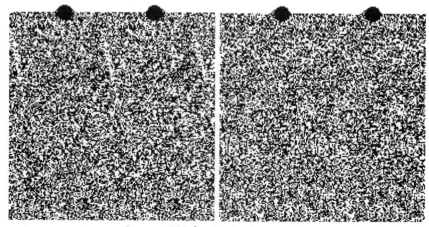

See page 298 for viewing instructions.

See page 298 for viewing instructions.

ZOMBIES ATE MY NEIGHBORS

BY KONAMI

Introduction

Zombies Ate My Neighbors (ZAMN) is a great game that plays like a combination of Gauntlet, Robotron 2084, and ToeJam & Earl. You control one or two heroic kids running around in search of helpless victims awaiting rescue from a variety of monsters: zombies, blobs, werewolves, Martians, and even giant babies! The game starts out easy and gradually be-

Repulse alien invaders, zombies, and other nasty creatures with your trusty Squirt Gun.

comes very difficult in the later levels. There are a whopping 55 levels (48 regular and seven bonus levels), and a two-player simultaneous mode to add to the fun. This is easily one of the best games around.

Awesome Strategies

★ **CONTROLS:** Press Y to fire. Press B to cycle through the different weapons. Press X to use an item. Press A to cycle through items. Press the L or R buttons to toggle the radar on and off. Press Start to Pause the game.

★ **WEAPONS: Squirt Gun:** The weapon you start out with. Works great against Zombies. **Soda Cans:** Hand grenades disguised as carbonated beverages! The perfect weapon against Baby Dolls. **Bazooka:** Extremely powerful. Use it to blow through doors, cracked walls, and hedges. The most important weapon in the game, especially on the later levels. **Fire Extinguisher:** Freezes monsters. The longer you squirt the monster, the longer it stays frozen. This and the Ice Pops are the only weapons that work against the Jelly Blobs. **Weed-Eater:** Cuts through weeds and monsters. One of the best weapons in the game. **Ancient Artifact:** Creates a spinning fire around you that destroys any monsters. Good against Werewolves and against the Giant Spider bosses in Levels 36 and 48. **Silverware:** Perfect against Werewolves. **Plates:**

Zombies Ate My Neighbors

Very weak. Use them only if you have nothing else. **Martian Bubble Gun:** Traps a monster inside a bubble. Best against Ants. **Tomatoes:** The worst weapon in the game. Works decently against Martians, but so does your Squirt Gun. **Ice Pops:** A short-range weapon that destroys Jelly Blobs. **Football:** Throw them to football players to keep them from tackling you.

The Martian Bubble Gun is probably the coolest weapon in the game.

★ **ITEMS: Keys and Skeleton Keys:** The regular Keys open all doors except the skull doors. Skeleton Keys open skull doors only. **Monster Potion (red):** Turns you into an invincible purple beast that can smash through doors and walls. You can't swim when you're a Monster. **Ghost Kid Potion (blue):** Turns you into an invincible ghost. You can't open any doors but you can walk *over* water. **Random Potion (question mark):** This is totally random. It could restore your health bar, give you a speed boost, cause damage, turn you into a Zombie, or turn you into the purple Monster. **Speed Shoes:** Gives you a speed boost. **Decoys:** Inflatable clowns that the monsters attack instead of you. Very useful against the Chainsaw Maniacs. **Pandora's Box:** Unleashes energy blasts that destroy every monster on the screen. Save them up for bosses. **First Aid Kit:** Completely restores your life bar.

Secret Item: It's a box with a question mark on it. Pick it up to enter a top-secret bonus level.

★ **Lives are precious** in ZAMN, because it's so hard to earn extra lives during the game. Always keep an eye on your health bar and use a First Aid Kit when you're down to one or two notches on the bar.

★ You start the game with **ten victims**, but as the game goes on, you lose

Save the Pandora's Box until you reach one of the bosses (the Giant Baby or Giant Spider).

Zombies Ate My Neighbors

victims to the monsters. If you start a level with only one victim left, and that victim gets killed, you automatically lose the game. Always try to save at *least* two or three victims. Playing with only one victim left is too dangerous.

★ If you've got a **Jelly Blob stuck to your face**, shake it off by pressing the control pad Left and Right rapidly. If you don't shake it off fast enough, you'll lose one or two notches of health.

★ Save the **Random Potion** until you're down to three or four notches on your life bar, then chug it. If you drink the Potion when you only have one or two notches, and it's a "bad"

Shake the control pad left and right to shake Jelly Blobs off your face.

potion that causes damage, you'll lose a life.

★ Watch the **self-playing "demos"** that appear if you don't start playing the game right away. You'll see interesting strategies and techniques.

★ **LEVEL 1 (Zombie Panic):** There are only **Zombies** in this level, and it only takes one shot from the Squirt Gun to destroy a Zombie. When you're done saving the victims, don't leave the level immediately. Wander around to find extra items. For example, there are two Keys in the middle and the lower-right areas of the level. You should always explore each level as much as possible to find hidden items.

★ There's a **Secret Item** hidden in the hedge at the top of the level. The problem is that **you need a Bazooka** to blow open the hedge, and there aren't any Bazookas laying around. You just have to hope that a Bazooka appears when you open one of the two dressers in this level. It happens very rarely—it took us about a hundred tries before we got one—so if you don't

Level 1: You can't get to the Secret Item unless you're lucky enough to get a Bazooka.

Zombies Ate My Neighbors

get a Bazooka, reset the game and try again or just finish the level. This is the second-hardest bonus level to find; only Level 12's bonus level is harder.

It ain't easy getting to the tentacle bonus level, and it ain't easy to finish either!

★ **BONUS LEVEL (Day of the Tentacle):** The purple Tentacles running around in this level are from another LucasArts game, *Maniac Mansion*, which you might have played on the 8-bit NES. Explore the entire level to find the victims, plenty of items, and a Skeleton Key that you need to open the door to get into the house. Look on the left side of the pool outside the house to find a **1-Up**.

★ **LEVEL 2 (Evening of the Undead):** There are two Bazookas at the start of the level. Use them to blow open the hedges near the house and grab the items inside. Don't use a Key to go through the front door of the house; walk around the back and you'll find an open door. Open all of the cabinets and doors under the sink to get random items.

★ **LEVEL 3 (Terror in Aisle Five):** The Evil Dolls make their first appearance in this level. Use the Soda Cans to take them out, or better yet, just avoid them! You'll find some Ice Pops in the freezer at the top of the level. At the start of the level, use your Bazooka to blow open the window above the two soldiers and take the First Aid Kit. **Don't use any Keys** in this level; you can get everywhere without using even a single Key. Save up your weapons and items for the later levels!

★ **LEVEL 4 (Chainsaw Hedgemaze Mayhem):** There's a First Aid Kit in the hedge just above you at the start. Blow it open with the Bazooka and walk right to another hedge. Shoot it open for a Monster Potion. Trick the

Level 3: Soda Cans are the best weapon against the Evil Dolls.

Zombies Ate My Neighbors

Chainsaw Maniacs into cutting through the hedges so you can save the rest of your Bazooka shots. Don't shoot the hedge in the upper-right corner, because there's only a Chainsaw Maniac inside. There are two Bazookas (10 shots) in the upper-left corner of the level. One last thing: If the Maniacs (and you!) destroy enough hedges, you get a **Massive Destruction Bonus** at the end of the level.

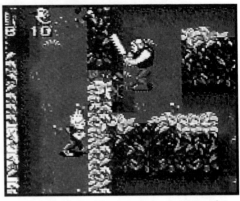

Level 4: Trick the Maniacs into chopping down the hedges and causing Massive Destruction!

★ **LEVEL 5 (Weird Kids On the Block):** In this level, you're chased by "body snatcher" aliens that look just like you. Use the Squirt Gun against them. There are two Bazookas in the upper-right corner, and Silverware in the house in the middle of the level. You'll want the Silver to use against the Werewolves! Chop down the spitting plants with your Weed-Eater to find a few items underneath them.

★ **LEVEL 6 (Pyramid of Fear):** Look for **dark spots on the walls** inside the pyramid. These indicate a secret passage that you can walk through and break through the pile of sand on the other side. (Search the piles of sand, and the jars, to find items.) The **Mummies** are tough to kill; it takes five Squirt Gun shots or one Bazooka shot. Save your Bazooka ammo and use your Squirt Gun, or just avoid the Mummies. Some of the doors in the pyramid close up after you walk through them, so search each area carefully before you walk into the next. Look on the right side of the pyramid for a *long* secret passage with three coin piles inside.

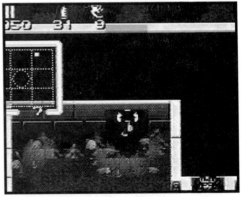

Level 6: Walk into the dark spots on the walls to enter secret passages.

★ **LEVEL 7 (Dr. Tongue's Castle of Terror):** Use the Fire Extinguisher to put out the fireplace and walk through into the north half of the level. (You can also

Zombies Ate My Neighbors

walk through the fire, but you'll take one or two hits.) When you reach the upper-right area of the level with all the doors, use a Monster Potion and smash through the doors instead of wasting all your Keys. Make sure you don't miss the door that leads into the room full of treasure.

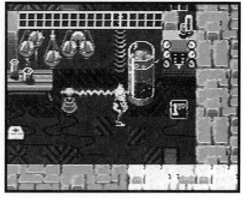

Level 7: Take the secret passage from the upper-right corner to the hidden 1-Up room.

★ There are three doors in the upper-right corner (and a Monster Potion behind the left door). Smash through the right door and walk into the right wall to enter a **secret passage**. Walk through the passage to a grassy area, then walk against the left wall in the grassy area to find *another* secret passage. Walk all the way to the left to find an area with a mad scientist, a **Frankenstein** monster, and several items including a **1-Up**! You can destroy Frankenstein with a few Bazooka shots.

★ **LEVEL 8 (Titanic Toddler):** There's only one enemy in this level, and he's one *big* baby. Use a pair of Speed Shoes and run to the left to grab the victims before the baby squashes them. Walk behind the tree in the lower-left corner to pick up a hidden Pandora's Box. You'll hear a beeping sound when you pick up the Box. Explore the building in the lower-right corner to find a few items, then go back to the baby and use all the Pandora's Boxes you have to attack it. Once you run out of Boxes, drink a Monster Potion and start punching the toddler. Keep attacking until the baby shrinks back to normal size. You need the baby's Skeleton Key to open the skull door and rescue the last two victims.

Level 9: Get the Secret Item out of the hedge at the top of the level.

★ **LEVEL 9 (Toxic Terrors):** This level is filled with **Jelly Blobs**. Use your Fire Extinguisher or Ice Pops to eliminate the Blobs, or just avoid them. Remember

Zombies Ate My Neighbors

that the longer you squirt a Blob, the longer it stays frozen. If you get "slimed" by a Blob, press Left and Right on the pad to shake off the slime. Don't forget to shoot the hedge at the top of the level with your Bazooka to uncover a **Secret Item**.

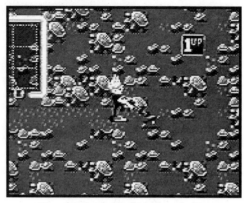

Wander the field of Mushroom Men to find a First Aid Kit and a 1-Up.

★ **BONUS LEVEL (Mushroom Men):** Walk through the secret passages in the hedges on the left side of the level to enter the field of Mushroom Men. Use a Weed-Eater or Potion and walk across the field to find a First Aid Kit, two Pandora's Boxes, and a **1-Up** in the upper-right corner. Use the Weed-Eater to mow down as much fungus as you can to score the **Weed Cutting Bonus** at the end of the level.

★ **LEVEL 10 (No Assembly Required):** You'll need to use a few Bazooka shots here—and maybe even a Monster Potion—to smash through the walls, crates, and doors. Use the Soda Cans on the Evil Dolls. There's a Monster Potion at the top of the level. You'll also find a few First Aid Kits scattered around. Destroy as much stuff as you can and you might get the **Massive Destruction Bonus**.

★ **LEVEL 11 (Weeds Gone Bad):** A pretty simple level. If you don't have a Weed-Eater at the start of the level, walk downward on the long path through the weeds to find one. Once you have one, mow through the weeds to rescue the victims. Also cut down the spitting ferns to find items (for example, there's a **Monster Potion** inside the plant in the lower-right corner). Cut down plenty of weeds to score the Weed Cutting Bonus.

★ **LEVEL 12 (Mars Needs Cheerleaders):** The football players don't hurt you when they tackle you, but they *do* send you flying. The Martians, on the other

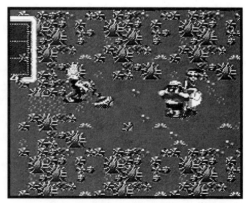

Level 11: Mow down as many weeds as you can to score the Weed Cutting Bonus.

Zombies Ate My Neighbors

hand, hurt you with their Bubble Guns. There are **three Footballs** to be found in this level (one of them in the middle of the football field). Pick them up and throw them at the football players. Complete ten passes to get a big **Pass Completion Bonus** at the end of the level. You can also destroy the pesky UFO. See that hatch on the UFO that keeps opening and closing?

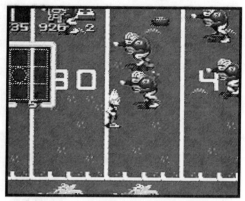

Level 12: Throw Footballs to the players to score big bonus points.

Throw a Soda Can into the hatch when it's open to cause damage. Destroy the UFO to get a big **Alien Invasion Repulsed Bonus**.

★ There's a **Secret Bonus** in this level, but getting it is *very* tough. Firstly, you have to make it to this level with all ten victims. Secondly, you have to *rescue* all ten victims in this level. Miss even one and you won't get the Bonus. If you succeed, you'll get a **Ten Cheerleader Bonus** *and* a Secret Bonus, then you play the bonus level.

★ **BONUS LEVEL (Monsters Vs. The Cheerleaders):** This is the hardest bonus level of them all, with plenty of monsters and plenty of locked doors. Luckily for you there are also plenty of Keys laying around.

★ **LEVEL 13 (Chopping Mall):** A pretty boring level, although there are a few items to find. Go into the upper-left corner of the level to find a Key and a First Aid Kit behind a locked door. There's also a freezer with some Ice Pops inside.

★ **LEVEL 14 (Seven Meals for Seven Zombies):** There's a **secret passage** near the start of the level. Walk into the small alcove and against the right wall to find the passage. Go down the passage to find a room with lots of treasure on the floor.

★ **LEVEL 15 (Dinner on Monster Island):** There's a tiny island in the lower-left corner of the level with

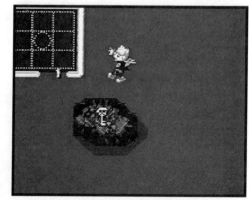

Level 15: Swim to the island in the lower-left corner and take the key.

Zombies Ate My Neighbors

a **Skeleton Key** on it. Swim to the island and take the Key. You'll also find a burning meteor in this level; put it out with the Fire Extinguisher.

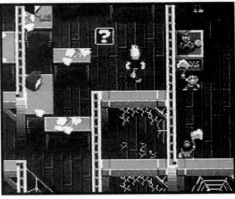

Level 17: Go into the upper-right corner and shoot through the spider web with a Bazooka.

★ **LEVEL 16 (Ants):** You start in the middle of this level, and have to walk outward along the narrow paths. Use the Bazooka to kill the ants, but don't shoot them unless you really have to. There are two **trampolines** near the north side of the level. Jump straight up off the first one, walk right to the second trampoline, and jump up again.

★ **LEVEL 17 (Office of the Doomed):** There's a First Aid Kit near the bottom of the level inside a locked room, so you'll need a Key to get it. Better yet, there's a **Secret Item** and a Monster Potion in the upper-right corner of the level. Both items are behind webs, so you'll have to blast through with the Bazooka or punch through them as the Monster.

★ **BONUS LEVEL (Someplace Very Warm):** Walk into the upper-right corner, then down, to find a **1-Up**. There are items placed all over the lava, so use a Potion to become invincible while you gather them up.

★ **LEVEL 18 (Squidmen of the Deep):** There's a **baby on an island** in this level that's hard to get because the Squidmen keep jumping out and slashing him before you can jump out of the water to save him. Here's the trick: When the baby first shows up on your radar, swim to the left and jump onto the island, *then* run upward and grab the baby before the Squidmen attack him.

Level 18: Run up the island and grab the baby before the Squidmen get him!

★ **LEVEL 19 (Nightmare on Terror Street):** As the sun goes down and the screen starts getting darker, the victims start turning into **Werewolves** (!) and attacking the other victims. Rescue the victims as soon

Zombies Ate My Neighbors

as possible, then search the level to find items. There are Keys all over the place, especially along the top and the bottom.

Lure the Snakeoid into attacking you, then shoot its mouth. Watch out for its tongue!

★ **LEVEL 20 (Invasion of the Snakeoids):** You need at least two Skeleton Keys to get through this level, and three if you want to open all the skull doors. To get the Skeleton Keys, you have to destroy the **Snakeoids** digging through the ground. Here's the best technique to use against a Snakeoid: Lure the Snakeoid into attacking you, then run downward, aim upward, and shoot it in the mouth. When the Snakeoid slides back into the ground, run upward and lure it into attacking you again, then repeat the pattern. Don't get too close or the Snakeoid's **tongue** will hit you. You can also try dropping a Decoy and tricking the Snakeoid into attacking it. Use the Squirt Gun against the Snakeoids; *don't* waste your Bazooka.

★ **LEVEL 21 (The Day the Earth Ran Away):** Explore the left and right sides of the level to find several buildings and several helpful items. There's a **Martian Bubble Gun** on the right side of the level next to the lake, and two First Aid Kits on the left side of the level. There's a UFO in the air, so destroy it with your Soda Cans for big bonus points. The best place to attack the UFO is in a building on the right side of

the level, so that the Martians don't attack you while you're attacking the UFO. Once you're in the building, walk left to trick the UFO into opening the hatch, then hit it with a Soda before it closes.

★ **LEVEL 22 (Revenge of Dr. Tongue):** There's a **Secret Item** behind a skull door, but there don't seem to be any Skeleton Keys on this level. Use your Weed-Eater to chop down

Level 22: Use the Weed-Eater to mow down the spitting fern and find a Skeleton Key.

Zombies Ate My Neighbors

the **spitting ferns** and you'll find a Skeleton Key under one of them. If you're lucky, you'll have a spare Skeleton Key from Level 15 or Level 20. Now, to *find* the Secret Item, find the room with Frankenstein walking around. Go into the secret passage at the bottom of the room and follow it to the skull door.

Grab the Son of Dr. Tongue to score an impressive 10,000 points.

★ **BONUS LEVEL (The Son of Dr. Tongue):** Remember the giant baby from Level 8? He's b-a-a-a-ck! But this time, you've got a great place to attack him. Run into the hallway above the baby and shoot him from there. He won't be able to run over you, and he won't be able to squirt you with his milk bottle (ick). When you defeat the baby, pick up the Skeleton Key and open the skull door. Keep going north until you find a room full of Frankensteins. Run into the upper-right corner of the room and touch the Son of Dr. Tongue to score 10,000 points! Now run downward and open the doors into the treasure room. Too bad there's not a 1-Up on this level. Oh, well.

★ **LEVEL 23 (The Caves of Mystery):** There's not much to find on this level other than a few Bazookas. There's a track running through the center of the level with a few items nearby.

★ **LEVEL 24 (Warehouse of the Evil Dolls):** There's a First Aid Kit in the lower-left corner and a **Secret Item** in the lower-right corner. You need a Skeleton Key to get to the Secret Item, carried over from a previous level. The Secret Item gives you a **Bonus Password** that starts you on Level 25 with all ten victims, but it's not all that useful.

★ **LEVEL 25 (Look Who's Shopping):** *Another* baby! Geez! The best way to attack it is to blow open

Level 25: Attack the giant baby from inside a shattered window to stay away from the ants.

Zombies Ate My Neighbors

one of the windows with a Bazooka and then shoot the baby while you hide inside the window. This way, the ants won't see you and won't attack you. You need to defeat the baby to get the **1-Up** at the bottom of the level, because it's behind a skull door, and the baby has the Skeleton Key. Be sure to grab the First Aid Kits at the top and the lower-right corners of the level.

Level 27: Get the precious 1-Up out of the hedge. You'll need it!

★ **LEVEL 26 (Where the Red Fern Growls):** This level's pretty easy. Use the Weed-Eater to chop down every spitting fern you see and explore the entire level to find a few Potions and Squirt Guns. You can get a **Weed Cutting Bonus** if you chop down enough of the weeds.

★ **LEVEL 27 (Dances With Werewolves):** Use the Artifacts or Weed-Eater to destroy the attacking Werewolves. There's a valuable **1-Up** hidden inside the hedge at the top of the level. Also walk **behind the trees** to find a few more items.

★ **LEVEL 28 (Mark of the Vampire):** There are four Skeleton Keys in this level. One of them is in the upper-right corner, a second Key is in the middle of the level, and the third Key is on the left side of the level, next to a chest. You need these three Keys to get through the skull doors on the left side of the level and go into a room with the fourth Skeleton Key (and a big pile of treasure!).

★ **LEVEL 29 (Zombie House Party):** This level is one *big* house with a lot of doors, so you'll be using a lot of Keys. Keep exploring and opening the cabinet to collect plenty of items. There's a small room near the middle of the level that you'll have to blast into with a Bazooka. (There's a **Ghost Kid Potion** inside the room.)

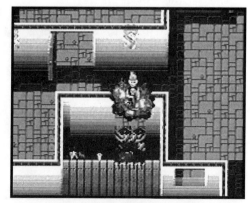

Level 29: Crash the house party with your Bazooka. Don't miss the Ghost Kid Potion.

Zombies Ate My Neighbors

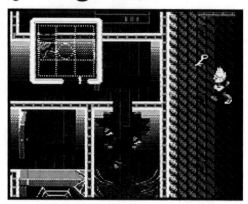

★ **LEVEL 30 (The Horror of Floor Thirteen):** Walk up and right from the start of the level to find **three Keys**. Take them and open the doors on the right to find rooms with a few more Keys on the floor. See the items out on the roof? To get to them, you have to blast through the windows with a Bazooka and then walk onto the roof. You'll find a few Keys on the right side

Level 30: Blow up the window with the Bazooka and walk out onto the roof to get keys.

of the level, and a First Aid Kit inside a room that you can only enter from the roof. (You'll have to blast through a window to get into the room.) There's another First Aid Kit in the lower-left corner of the level. Keep exploring around to find as many Keys as possible.

★ **LEVEL 31 (Look Who's Coming To Dinner):** There are plenty of hedges in this level, and all of them have items inside. Shoot open the hedge in the upper-right corner for a First Aid Kit; at the top of the level for a Random Potion; and the left side of the level for a Bazooka.

★ **LEVEL 32 (Giant Ant Farm):** From the start of the level, go up and open the door to find a Key and a Random Potion. Now you've got to search the level to find **three Skeleton Keys**. The first Key is in the lower-right corner, stashed behind the cactuses. (You can walk along the crevice on the right side of the screen to get around the cactuses.)

The second key is in the upper-right corner, inside a building with a locked door (you'll need a Key). The third key is in the upper-left corner. Look for a long tunnel leading to the left. Walk down the tunnel and then go upward to find the Key.

★ **LEVEL 33 (Fish And Crypts):** This level's a lot like **Level 7** (Pyramid Of Fear), so you shouldn't have any problems.

Level 32: This Skeleton Key is the hardest to find. Look near a long tunnel.

Zombies Ate My Neighbors

Remember to search all of the sand piles and to look for secret tunnels in the walls. There's a **Secret Item** in the upper-left corner. Walk all the way into the upper-left, then walk right and jump into the water. Swim to the right and take the Item, then swim left and jump out of the water. (By the way, this is the last Secret Item in the game.)

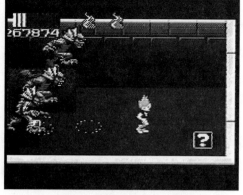

Level 33: Look for the Secret Item in the water in the upper-left corner.

★ **BONUS LEVEL (Curse of the Pharaohs):** You need a Bazooka or a Monster Potion to get the **1-Up** and the Monster Potion in this level—they're both behind **spider webs**. Pick up everything on the ground and finish the level!

★ **LEVEL 34 (I Was A Chainsaw Maniac):** Two victims are behind **skull doors**, so of course you need two skeleton Keys to open the doors. The first Key is in a room near the middle of the level. (If you have at least three victims, you'll see the Key in the room right next to one of the victims.) The second Key is in the lower-right corner of the level behind a crate. Use a Bazooka to blow through the crate and get to the Key. You'll also find a few Bazookas nearby.

★ **LEVEL 35 (Boardwalk of Terrors):** From the start of the level, go downward to find a room with a **First Aid Kit**, then go upward to find a regular Key. Now go to the right and rescue the victims along the boardwalks. Look for the island at the top of the island and take the Key.

★ **LEVEL 36 (Monster Phobia):** This was originally the last level of the game, but LucasArts went back later and added another 12 (very hard) levels after this one. The folks at LucasArts say this is the level they get more questions about than any other, so they supplied us with an **extremely cool map** of the entire level which we've printed on the following two pages. Use it to find the victims and the First Aid Kit, then head for the Giant Spider boss.

★ When you reach the **Giant Spider**, use all of your Pandora's Boxes, then switch to the **Artifact** weapon. Walk right into the Spider. **Hold down the fire button** to keep using the Artifacts. You won't be hurt by the Spider, but you'll hurt it. When the Spider moves away from you, wiggle the control pad toward the Spider to get through the sticky spider webs on the floor. When your Artifacts run out, switch to the

Zombies Ate My Neighbors

LEVEL 36 MAP

1. Cheerleader
2. Soldier
3. Tourists
4. Dog
5. Teacher
6. Baby
7. Cheerleader
8. Baby
9. Explorer
0. Baby
A. Giant Spider
Z. First Aid Kit

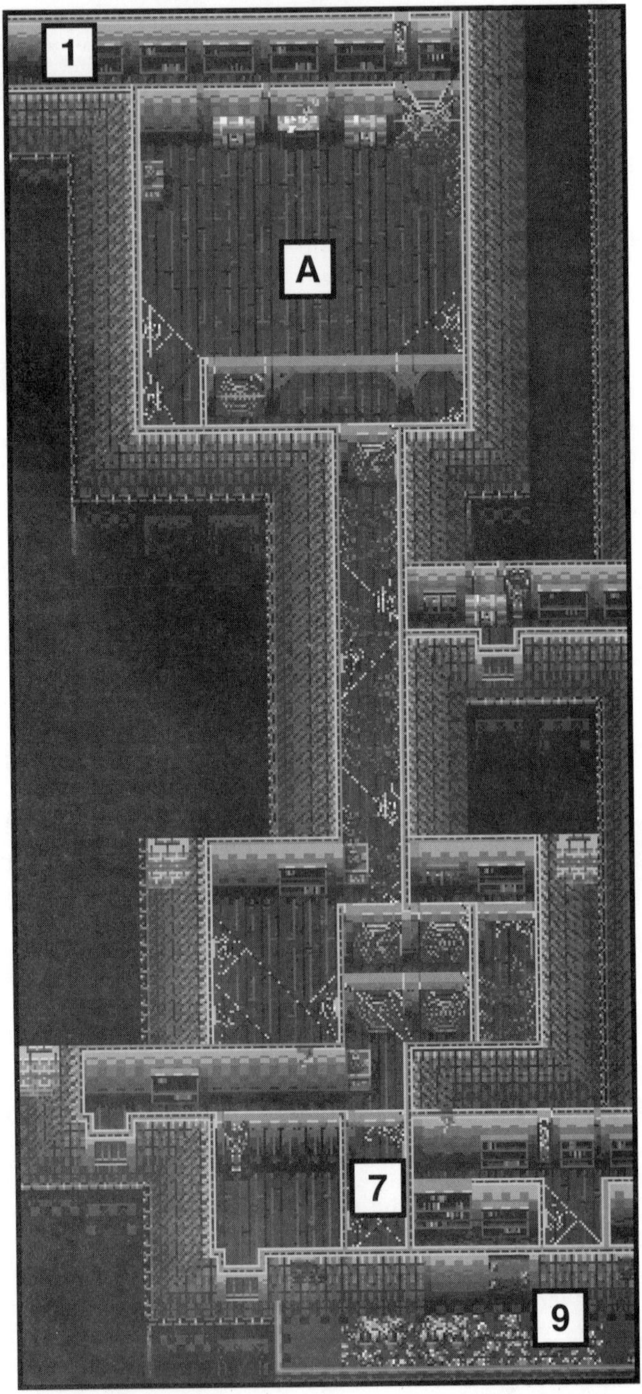

Zombies Ate My Neighbors

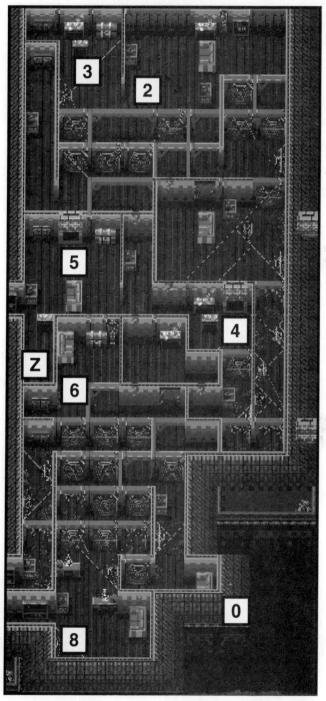

Zombies Ate My Neighbors

Weed-Eater. Kill the Spider and rescue the last victim to finish the level.

★ **LEVEL 37 (Labyrinth of Horrors):** The best items in this level—a First Aid Kit and a Random Potion —are on the far right side of the level, near the Frankenstein room.

★ **LEVEL 38 (Monsters of the Blue Lagoon):** There's a room on the left side of the level with a **1-Up** and Monster Potion inside, but

Level 38: If you don't have a spare Skeleton Key, you can't get into this room.

you need a Skeleton Key to open the skull door, and there are no Skeleton Keys on this level. If you have one from an earlier level, cool. If you don't, tough luck. Search the building in the middle of the level for a First Aid Kit. Don't use a Key to get into the building; go through the hole in the north wall. You can score a **Fish Fry Bonus** if you defeat enough of the Squidmen.

★ **LEVEL 39 (Destroy All Vampires):** You need two Skeleton Keys to open the skull doors and get to the last victim in this level. The first Key is in the upper-right corner, guarded by Frankenstein. The second Key is harder to find; it's inside the **spitting fern** in the lower-left corner. Use the Weed-Eater to chop it down and take the Key.

★ **LEVEL 40 (Pyramid of Fear 2):** You need to beat the Snakeoid at the start of the level and get a Skeleton Key to open the skull door into the

Pyramid. Use the same strategy to beat the Snakeoid that you did in Level 20. To rescue the victims at the north end of the Pyramid, you'll need another Skeleton Key. Look for it on the far right side of the Pyramid.

★ **LEVEL 41 (Martians Go Home!):** There's a **1-Up** on the far right side of the level. Walk into the building in the lower-right corner. Go into the bathroom

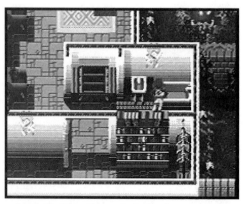

Level 41: Blow through the bathroom wall to get the 1-Up on the far right side of the level.

Zombies Ate My Neighbors

and use the Bazooka to blow through the crack in the wall. Now walk upward to find the 1-Up. Search along the top of the level to find several First Aid Kits and a Monster Potion. You'll need to use a Bazooka to get to the Potion.

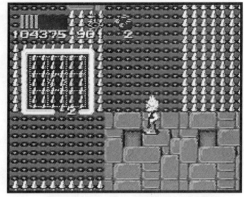

Level 42: Drink a Potion and get through this level as quickly as possible.

★ **LEVEL 42 (Spikes):** If you have a **Ghost Kid Potion** or a **Monster Potion**, use it and finish this level as quickly as possible. There's nothing hidden to find at all, so grab the victims and finish it! If you don't have a Potion, you're in trouble. Run over the spikes when they recede into the floor and take your time. If you rush, you'll die.

★ **LEVEL 43 (Super Fund Cleanup Site):** Search along the top of the level to find two **Ghost Kid Potions** behind a wooden fence. Smash through the fence with a Bazooka. Go into the building in the lower-left corner for a Squirt Gun and Decoys. Now finish the level!

★ **LEVEL 44 (The Curse of Dr. Tongue):** There's only one **Skeleton Key** to be found, in a small room at the top of the level. You need to go through a secret passage to get there; try looking for the passage in the room with the Frankenstein. Don't waste time exploring, just get the Key and finish the level.

★ **LEVEL 45 (Danger in Picnic Park):** There are loads of items hidden **behind the trees**, so search behind them all. There's a hedge near the middle of the level with a **1-Up** inside; it's the hedge with a wall on the right side. Look for the group of three hedges near the top of the level; there's a Bazooka inside one of them.

★ **LEVEL 46 (Day of the**

Level 45: Look for the hedge against the wall and blow it open for a 1-Up.

Zombies Ate My Neighbors

Chainsaw): Blast open the hedge in the upper-right corner for a Bazooka, then use a Monster Potion and punch through the hedges to get to the victims. When you run out of Monster Potions, use your Bazooka to shoot through the hedges. There's a victim behind two skull doors in the lower-right corner. Get the Skeleton Keys on the left side of the level

Level 46: There's a Skeleton Key stashed inside the hedge at the top of the level.

(next to the building) and at the top of the level, **inside the hedge**. There's a Maniac guarding the Key inside the hedge, so watch out.

★ **LEVEL 47 (Grid Iron Terror):** The football field's been overrun with **Snakeoids**, but you don't have to destroy any of them to finish the level. Run across the field once or twice to pick up all of the items, then explore the buildings on the right side of the level to find the victims. Ignore the Snakeoids and save your weapons for the final level!

★ **LEVEL 48 (Curse of the Monster):** Look for a Skeleton Key in the upper-right corner near the Frankenstein. There's a hidden **1-Up** in the lower-left corner of the Frankenstein room. The second Skeleton Key is near the first. After you get the first Key (and the 1-Up), go downward until you find the stairs. Go up the stairs and keep going up until you find the Key.

★ The **Giant Spider** boss is at the top of the level. You need three Skeleton Keys to open the three skull doors. If you run out of Keys before opening the third door, walk into the **secret passage** below the third door to find another one. (It's inside the white blocks in the wall.)

★ Use the same strategy you did in Level 36 to fight the Giant Spider. There's

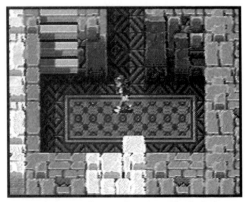

Level 48: Walk into the white blocks below the Giant Spider's room to find a key.

Zombies Ate My Neighbors

Hide in the upper-right corner of the room and shoot the floating head with your Squirt Gun.

a **safe spot** in the upper-right corner of the room where you can stand and attack the Spider. When the Spider blows up, it turns into a mad scientist who turns into a **giant floating head**! Stay in the upper-right corner and shoot the floating head with the Squirt Gun or other weapon when it floats up to attack you. The head shoots its eyeballs at you every once in a while, but you can dodge or shoot the eyeballs. As you damage the head, it gradually loses more and more flesh (yech). Keep hitting it until it finally blows up!

★ Rescue the last victim and go through the exit door to win the game. You get a **fireworks display** and a tally of how many of each monster you killed while playing the game. Then you get to play the Credit Level and take a tour of the LucasArts offices! (The guy who says "Welcome to LucasArts Games—now get back to work" is **George Lucas**.)

Awesome Secrets!

★ **BONUS LEVELS:** The hidden levels are in Level 1, 9, 12, 17, 22, and 33. See the Awesome Strategies for more info. The seventh bonus level is the Credit Level, which you get to play after finishing the game. (You can also use the password below.)

★ **PASSWORDS:** Those nasty guys at LucasArts put in a password system that's almost useless, because it doesn't keep track of the weapons you have, just what level you're on and how many victims there are. When you enter a password, you start with 150 (or 250) rounds of ammo in your Squirt Gun and one First Aid Kit. Try starting on Level 45 with nothing but a Squirt Gun and seeing how long you last! Conclusion: If you really want to beat this game, start at Level 1 and play all the way through. Anyway, here are the passwords: Level 5: XHRS; Level 9: NBGW; Level 13: BFCB; Level 17: FKYQ; Level 21: DXBR; Level 25: PYLQ; Level 25 Bonus Password (10 victims): GYLM; Level 29: YLZD; Level 33: LJQJ; Level 37: FZVM; Level 41: FRPJ; Level 45: BLHR; Credit Level: XWJR.

AWESOME SECRETS!

A Collection Of The Best Tricks And Passwords

AEROBIZ

SOUND TEST: At the title screen, hold down SELECT and press START. The Sound Test screen appears. Press A to listen to each sound.

BATMAN RETURNS

9 CONTINUES: Go to the Option screen and use Controller 2 to press Up, X, Left, Y, Down, B, Right, A, Up, X. You'll hear a series of musical tones. When you run out of lives, you'll have 9 continues.

9 LIVES: Go to the Option screen and press Up twice, Down twice, Left, Right, Left, Right, B, A. You'll hear a series of musical tones. Now use the Rest option to boost your lives up to 9.

BATTLECLASH

DIFFICULTY SELECT: Make sure you have Controller 1 plugged in. At the title screen, press L Button and SELECT simultaneously. Set your options with the Super Scope and the difficulty selection screen appears.

BEST OF THE BEST

KUMATE MODE: Enter the password RHT255457K and your character's stats will be maxed out. Go to the Main Menu and select Ivanov as your opponent. Defeat Ivanov and you can enter the Kumate mode. In the Kumate, select the PAD vs. SNES box until both fighters look the same. Defeat the mirror image and all the opponents from the regular tournament appear in the Kumate.

BRAWL BROTHERS

JAPANESE VERSION: When the Jaleco logo appears, press the following buttons in order as fast as possible: B, A, X, Y. You'll hear a slashing sound and the screen will turn black and gray. Press START and another garbled screen appears. Now press Down three times and START to make the Option screen appear. Set your options and exit the screen. The Japanese title screen appears.

CAL RIPKEN JR. BASEBALL

ALL RIPKEN TEAM: Select an Exhibition Game and press START. On the team selection screen, hold down the L and R Buttons and press START. Now you can choose the AlCal's team.

THE COMBATRIBES

30 CREDITS: Turn on the SNES and hold down SELECT, L Button, and R Button on Controller 2. Press RESET on the SNES and wait for the title screen to appear. Start a new game and let go of the buttons. You'll have 30 credits.

1 ROUND IN VS. MODE: Turn on the SNES and hold down A and B on Controller 2. Press RESET on the SNES and wait for the title screen to appear. Start a Vs. Mode game and you'll fight a tournament of one round instead of three.

Awesome Secrets

5 ROUNDS IN VS. MODE: Turn on the SNES and hold down X and Y on Controller 2. Press RESET on the SNES and wait for the title screen to appear. Start a Vs. Mode game and you'll fight a tournament of five rounds instead of three.

EXTRA LIFE: Turn on the SNES and hold down the L Button, R Button, and Up on the control pad of Controller 2. Press RESET on the Super NES and wait for the title screen to appear. Start a new game and you'll have twice as much energy in your life bar. You can't use this trick with the 30 Credits or 5 Rounds tricks.

PASSWORD: Use this password to play as every fighter in the game: 9207.

SUPER DIFFICULTY: Turn on the SNES and hold down A, B, L Button, and R Button on Controller 2. Press RESET on the SNES and wait for the title screen to appear. Go to the Option screen and the Difficulty will be set to Super.

COOL WORLD

ENDING SEQUENCE: At the title screen, press L Button, Left, R Button, Right, Up, X, Down, B. The ending sequence appears on the screen. Press the A button to switch between different pictures.

CYBERNATOR

6 CREDITS: When the Konami logo fades out and before the title screen appears, press and hold L Button, R Button, and Up, then press START. Keep holding the buttons and when the title screen appears, press START again. Press START a third time when the Game Start option appears. Let go of the buttons and you'll have six credits.

NAPALM WEAPON: Play through Stage 1 (Colony Attack) without shooting *anything*. Destroy the energy unit at the end of the stage without destroying either of the cannons on the side of the unit. You must finish the stage with 2800 points. When you start Stage 2, you'll have the Napalm weapon at your disposal, but if you die during this stage, you lose the Napalm. Once you complete Stage 2, you'll have the Napalm weapon until you run out of credits.

DEATH VALLEY RALLY

75 LIVES: At the title screen, press and hold Left, SELECT, R Button, Y, and START. Keep holding the buttons and when the Zippity Splat screen appears, press and hold X also. When the game starts, you have 75 lives instead of two.

F-1 ROC 2 (aka F-1 Exhaust Heat 2)

SUB-GAMES: Press Y four times and X two times, or X four times and Y two times, to enter a sub-game.

FINAL FIGHT 2

SAME CHARACTER CODE: At the title screen, press Down, Down, Up, Up, Right, Left, Right, Left, and then the L and R Buttons at the same time. The screen turns blue to show that the code worked. Start a two-player game and go to the character selection screen. Have Player 2 choose his character first, then have Player 1 choose the same character. The players will be different colors during the game.

Awesome Secrets

FIREPOWER 2000
LEVEL SKIP: Press the following sequences with the L and R Buttons on each level to skip to the next level with upgraded weaponry. Level 1: R, L, R, R, L, L, R, L, R, R, L, L; Level 2: R, L, R, R, L, L, R, R, R, L, R, R; Level 3: L, R, L, L, R, R, L, L, L, L, R, R, R, L; Level 4: R, R, R, L, L, L, R, R, L, L, R, L, R, L; Level 5: R, L, R, L, L, L, R, R, L, L, R, L, R, L, L.

GODS
PASSWORDS: Level 2: SD1; Level 3: BMH; Level 4: MGB.

THE LOST VIKINGS
LEVEL SELECT: Press and hold X, Y, A, and B simultaneously.

MARIO IS MISSING
FINAL BOSS PASSWORD: Enter the password ZPF*M86 to battle the final boss.

MECHWARRIOR
INVINCIBILITY: Select a contract and a Mech, then begin a battle. When you land on the planet, pause the game, then press A, L Button twice, Y, A, L Button twice, Y, A, L Button twice, Y. The word INVINCIBLE appears on the screen and your Mech is untouchable for the rest of the battle.

NIGEL MANSELL'S WORLD CHAMPIONSHIP RACING
PASSWORDS: Mexico: LZ9ZN40LJ2541STCVL; Brazil: 6CL732YLZ3H07VNBR9; Spain: PZPP693R91Q7NHQ..2; San Marino: R49RGKFH.JBDSV0T79; Monaco: L0XJ.XVCH3L7GDCF0R; Canada: B7JPR46QRB.RG08HNL; France: LV0ZB206FG0K62K2D7; Britain: TKX.B7G3VTJFS1QSKX; Germany: TQP-CLTBTB7X21.JQGT; Hungary: HLL2FWG1Y20FL.1NG5; Belgium: YMGW4BXM3BV61JR565; Italy: 4QX4JKWXT50ZQ..K35; Portugal: 4F3M0TZ507064KGC5D; Japan: R48RR9GT7JB.BZVR4D; Australia: 33DV4B0F1ZZG538GW3; Ending Sequence: PV2JTFBK4Y696H4DXY.

POCKY AND ROCKY
BONUS 1-UP: When you beat the boss at the end of Stage 1, he drops his bowl, which starts bouncing around the screen. Hit the bowl with your swinging attack (press the B button) and a pink cat appears and drops a 1-Up to the ground.
STAGE SELECT: Press and hold X and Y on Controller 1, then press A four times, B four times, A, B, A, B, A, B, A, B. You'll hear a sound to indicate that the code worked. Choose a player and press START. The Stage Select screen appears.

ROBOCOP 3
LIFE BAR RECHARGE: Press START to pause the game and then press SELECT three times to refill your life bar. You can use this cheat as much as you want.

SIMEARTH
SCENARIO SELECT: Highlight the First Scenario command but don't press START. Hold down the L Button, R Button, and Y, then press A to call up the stage select screen.

Awesome Secrets

SOUND TEST AND OTHER CHEATS: At the title screen, hold down the L Button and R Button, then press START to make the Test Menu appear. You can watch the ending sequence, use the Sound Test, or view the Gaia List.

SONIC BLAST MAN
STAGE SELECT: Go to the Option Mode and highlight Music Test. Use the control pad to set the number of the stage you want to play. Press and hold SELECT, then press L Button, R Button, R Button, L Button, START.
VERY HARD DIFFICULTY: At the title screen, press and hold the L Button and R Button and press START. You'll hear a woman scream. Go to the Option Mode and you can set Game Level to Very Hard.

SPINDIZZY WORLDS
LEVEL SELECT: Enter the password MIMICHAN for a level select.

STAR FOX
OBJECT PAINT PROGRAM: Earn at least one continue and then lose all of your ships. When the Continue screen appears, press SELECT on Controller 2 and then press B to toggle through the different objects in the game. Use the control pad and button combinations to scale, rotate, and "paint" the objects.

STREET COMBAT
OPTION SCREEN: At the title screen, move the cursor to 2Players and hold down the L Button and R Button. Press START and an option screen appears. There are two extra characters for you to choose from.

SUPER CONFLICT
CHANGE COMPUTER WEAPON: During a battle against the computer, keep pressing B on Controller 2 to switch the weapon it's using.

SUPER STRIKE EAGLE
PASSWORDS: Libya Day Mission: 066F87FH; Libya Night Mission: 062H869D; Gulf War Day Mission: CGGG4724; Gulf War Night Mission: 90B68G8C; Korea Day Mission: 057F4902; Korea Night Mission: HF3H09H8; Bonus Mission: G6CH4228.

SUPER TURRICAN
LEVEL SKIP: Press START to pause the game, then press Right, Left, Down, Right, A, START. Music will play and you'll skip ahead to the next level. You can skip all the way to the final level.
MUSIC MENU: Go to the Game Options screen. Highlight the Sound Mode option and hold down L Button, R Button, X, A, and the center of the control pad. Press SELECT while holding these buttons down to make the Music Menu appear.

SUPER VALIS IV
EASY DIFFICULTY: At the title screen, highlight Option Mode and press Left twice, Right twice, B twice, and Y twice. Enter the Option Mode and you can set the Game Level to Easy.

Awesome Secrets

LEVEL SKIP: You can use the following trick once you've reached Act 3. Press Up and SELECT simultaneously to skip ahead one level.

TECMO SUPER NBA BASKETBALL
DIFFICULTY SELECT: Select a Pre-Season game, then move the arrow to Control and press A to call up a Difficulty menu.

TINY TOON ADVENTURES
BONUS GAME SELECT: At the title screen, choose the PASSWORD option. Place Elmyra's face in the first box, Shirley the Loon in the second box, and Calamity Coyote in the third box. Press START and a menu screen appears that allows you to choose any of the bonus games. To pick a bonus game at random, choose the ROULETTE option or press the B button.
UNLIMITED CONTINUES: Enter this password for unlimited continues (you'll also skip past the boss at the end of each stage): Plucky Duck, Babs Bunny, Bookworm.

WAYNE'S WORLD
LEVEL SELECT: At the title screen, press START. When Wayne and Garth start singing, press X, L Button, and R Button at the same time, then press Up, Y, and B at the same time. Press SELECT to cycle through the level numbers at the bottom of the screen.

WING COMMANDER
STAGE SELECT AND OTHER CHEATS: At the title screen with START and CONTINUE options, press B, A, B, Y, B, Y, L Button, A, R Button, A, START. An option screen appears that allows you to choose your mission, toggle invincibility on and off, and listen to the sound and music.

WWF ROYAL RUMBLE
BACKGROUND TRICKS: On the wrestler selection screen, press the L Button, then press: L Button twice to stop the background, R Button once to speed up the background, or R Button twice to *really* speed up the background.

YOSHI'S COOKIE
EXTRA ROUNDS: Select the Action option. Set the Round number to 10, Speed to High, and Music Type to Off. Press and hold L Button, R Button, SELECT, and START on Controller 2. The game will say "Yoshi!" Now you can select any Round number up to 99.
NEW VS. MODE CHARACTERS: Select the Vs. Mode. Set the mode to COM, and then press and hold the buttons in this order: L Button, R Button, X, and START. You'll hear the game say "Yoshi!" Press START to get to the character selection screen. Choose your character, then your opponent, and start the game. Notice that your opponent is a different color and that he's much tougher to beat than usual. When you're trapped by an Event, it'll last twice as long as a normal Event.

Awesome Secrets

SEND US YOUR HINTS, TIPS, AND AWESOME SECRETS!

Have you discovered a great tip for your favorite game
that isn't mentioned in this book? Send it to:

SANDWICH ISLANDS PUBLISHING
Awesome Super Nintendo Secrets
292 Puapihi Place
Lahaina, HI 96761

If your tip is good enough, we'll publish your name and your
Awesome Secret in a future edition of Awesome Super Nintendo Secrets!

SIRDS VIEWING INSTRUCTIONS

This book is filled with awesome pictures called SIRDS (Single Image Random Dot Stereograms). SIRDS may look like a random jumble of dots, but by refocusing your vision, you'll see three-dimensional images literally jump out of the page. You don't need 3D glasses to view SIRDS. All you have to do is learn how to view them. Some people can see SIRDS right away, but it takes others several days, so keep trying until you get it. We guarantee you'll be blown away.

Technique #1: Hold the book one to two feet away from your face. Relax your eyes and focus about a foot or two beyond the book. Don't cross your eyes! Focus into the distance. Once your focus is right, it will take a few seconds or a few minutes for your brain to pick out the 3D image on the page. If you focus too far into the distance, try moving the book farther away from your face.

Technique #2: Look directly at the two fusion dots at the top of the SIRDS. Relax your eyes and look through the page so that the two dots separate into four dots. Now adjust your focus so that the center two dots overlap and create a dark third dot. You're now focused on the SIRDS.

Technique #3: Hold the book extremely close to your face and look into the distance. Hold your look long enough for your eyes to focus. Now slowly move the book away from your face, holding the book steady. Look at the fusion dots with your peripheral vision. They will fuse and form a third dot when the book is a foot or two from your face. You're now focused on the SIRDS. If you lose your focus, keep practicing until you can hold it.

Technique #4: We learned of this technique recently, and it seems to work great for several people that had problems with the other techniques. When you view a SIRDS, you must focus your eyes exactly twice the distance that the paper is from your eyes. An easy way to do this is to stand in front of a mirror, hold the SIRDS against the mirror, then look at your eyes. Try to hold the focus of your eyes looking at your eyes in the mirror as you slide the book up slowly into view.

The SIRDS throughout this book are simple drawings, and are not actual clues to a game. If you can't view them, for whatever reason, don't feel like you're missing a crucial clue. They are just totally awesome 3-D drawings.

See page 298 for viewing instructions.

AWESOME BUYER'S GUIDE

Introduction

The question we get asked the most is: "What are the best games to buy". It's a very subjective question, since suggesting a role-playing game to someone that's into sports is bad advice. The following list should have enough detail to help you decide if the games listed are right for you. The list has changed quite a bit since our last books; we've added some hot new games, and we've removed some older games that haven't withstood the test of time.

The Must Buy List

The games on this list are the major stand-outs. Chances are you will enjoy them even if they aren't exactly what you're looking for. Each includes excellent gameplay, which is always our first priority. (*see Awesome Super Nintendo Secrets 1 for full chapter; **see Awesome Super Nintendo Secrets 2 for full chapter; ***see full chapter in this book.)

EQUINOX by Sony Imagesoft **
A total must for RPG (role-playing games) and puzzle fans. Equinox mixes great graphics and totally unique music with addictive gameplay. Find your way through eight increasingly difficult levels.
THE LEGEND OF ZELDA: A LINK TO THE PAST by Nintendo *
An obvious Must Buy for role-playing game fans, but Zelda tends to appeal to everyone. Regardless of your age or playing ability, Zelda will provide many days (possibly months) of enjoyment.
SHADOWRUN by Data East ***
Easily one of the best role-playing games available for the SNES. It's the future. You wake up in a morgue with amnesia. You must avoid being killed by strangers while trying to discovering who you are.
STAR FOX by Nintendo **
The first game to use the powerful Super FX chip is an incredible flight simulator/shoot-'em-up with quick-moving polygon graphics and the best sound and music you'll ever hear from your SNES. There are three different paths through the game and two top-secret stages.
STREET FIGHTER 2 TURBO by Capcom ***
After breaking all previous records in the arcades, Street Fighter 2 was released for the Super Nintendo, and broke several more records for sales and awards won. It's hand-to-hand combat with some of the most interesting characters to ever appear in a video game. Two-player simultaneous gameplay is what made it a huge hit.

Awesome Buyer's Guide

SUPER EMPIRE STRIKES BACK by JVC ***
This spectacular sequel to Super Star Wars has better graphics, better music, more secret areas, and passwords so you don't need to play through the early levels over and over. Platform games don't get any better than this.

SUPER MARIO ALL STARS by Nintendo ***
All of the 8-bit Nintendo Entertaiment System classics are back, only now they have incredible 16-bit graphics and sounds. Along with Super Mario Bros. 1, 2, and 3, you'll also get the all-new Super Mario Bros.–The Lost Levels. There's also a battery back-up so you don't have to start over on World 1-1 every time!

SUPER MARIO KART by Nintendo **
An excellent one- or two-player simultaneous driving game. All of the famous Mario characters are here, ready to challenge you on 15 different tracks and three skill levels. The Battle Mode adds even more value to an already perfect game.

SUPER MARIO WORLD by Nintendo *
Chances are you received this game with your system, but recent sales have been high on systems without the game packed in. If you don't have it, check your local newspaper or "free ads paper" for excellent prices (often $15-20).

SUPER STAR WARS by LucasArts **
Based on one of the most popular films ever made, and totally worthy of its title. Super Star Wars has excellent gameplay, stunning graphics and music, and enough challenge to keep even the best gameplayers busy for weeks.

The Worth Buying List

*The following games aren't totally perfect, but come extremely close. If you can't afford to buy them, or aren't sure you'll like them, try renting them from your local video store first. (*see Awesome Super Nintendo Secrets 1 for full chapter; **see full chapter in this book.)*

THE ADDAMS FAMILY by Ocean *
Very similar to the Mario games, with lots of levels and hidden stuff.

AERO THE ACROBAT by Sunsoft ***
For all you game players that loved Sonic but found it too easy, this is the game for you! Some of the best Genesis graphics and sounds.

ALIEN 3 by Acclaim ***
This is a great platform game with tons of playability and levels.

AXELAY by Konami **
A must for shoot-em-up fans. Totally amazing graphics!

Awesome Buyer's Guide

BATMAN RETURNS by Konami **
Great fighting action and a fun driving stage.

DUNGEON MASTER by JVC **
A great RPG slightly spoiled with only one game save position.

JURASSIC PARK by Ocean ***
A huge map and first-person perspective interiors make a great game.

LEMMINGS by Sunsoft *
Extremely interesting puzzle game. Very cute.

THE LOST VIKINGS by Interplay **
Great puzzle game using three vikings with various skills.

MAGICAL QUEST (starring Mickey Mouse) by Capcom **
It's too easy for experts with unlimited continues, but kids will love it!

MORTAL KOMBAT by Acclaim ***
A censored arcade hit, but the gameplay is more challenging that
what you'll find on that "other" game system.

OUT OF THIS WORLD by Interplay *
Adventure game with cool graphics and great gamplay.

PILOTWINGS by Nintendo *
One of the first and still one of the best. Kids are likely to hate it
when they see it, but will love it when they play it.

PRINCE OF PERSIA by Konami **
Many challenging levels (20!) and fascinating character animation.

ROCK N ROLL RACING by Interplay ***
Best as a two-player game. The music in amazingly real.

SKY BLAZER by Sony Imagesoft ***
A cool platform game similar to the gameplay of *Hook*, only better!
A password system prevents annoying restarts on level 1.

SUPER BOMBERMAN PARTY PAK by Hudson Soft ***
The best party game to date. Up to four players with adapter. Run
in a maze while dropping bombs and throwing them at other players.

SUPER CASTLEVANIA IV by Konami *
Heavy action/platform game that fans of the series will love.

TINY TOONS ADVENTURE by Konami **
Beautiful graphics and plenty of platform gameplay.

ZOMBIES ATE MY NEIGHBORS by Konami ***
It's Robotron meets ToeJam and Earl. Grab the neighbors before the
zombies do.

ALSO AVAILABLE
FROM SANDWICH ISLANDS PUBLISHING

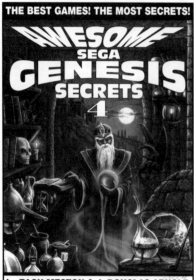

ORDER FORM

The Hottest Secrets and Strategies!
Satisfaction Guaranteed!

Qty.	Title	Price Each	Total
_____	Awesome Sega Genesis Secrets 1	$9.95	$_____
_____	Awesome Sega Genesis Secrets 2	$9.95	$_____
_____	Awesome Sega Genesis Secrets 3	$11.95	$_____
_____	Awesome Sega Genesis Secrets 4	$11.95	$_____
_____	Awesome Super Nintendo Secrets 1	$11.95	$_____
_____	Awesome Super Nintendo Secrets 2	$11.95	$_____
_____	Awesome Super Nintendo Secrets 3	$11.95	$_____
_____	Lunar (Sega-CD) Hint Book	$9.95	$_____
_____	Winter '94 CES Home Video	$24.95	$_____

**All U.S. orders sent by
U.S. Two-Day Priority Mail!**

Subtotal $_____

Shipping $ 3.00

Total (Check/Credit Card) $_____

Name _____

Address _____

City _____ State _____ Zip _____

- -

Visa/Mastercard#_____

Exp.Date _____ Signature _____

SEND TO: Sandwich Islands Publishing,
P.O. Box 10669, Lahaina, HI 96761
OR FAX TO: (808) 661-2715

Video available after January 15th, 1994. NTSC format only.
All foreign orders add $15 for air shipping, $5 for surface mail.

ORDER FORM

The Hottest Secrets and Strategies!
Satisfaction Guaranteed!

Qty.	Title	Price Each	Total
_____	Awesome Sega Genesis Secrets 1	$9.95	$_____
_____	Awesome Sega Genesis Secrets 2	$9.95	$_____
_____	Awesome Sega Genesis Secrets 3	$11.95	$_____
_____	Awesome Sega Genesis Secrets 4	$11.95	$_____
_____	Awesome Super Nintendo Secrets 1	$11.95	$_____
_____	Awesome Super Nintendo Secrets 2	$11.95	$_____
_____	Awesome Super Nintendo Secrets 3	$11.95	$_____
_____	Lunar (Sega-CD) Hint Book	$9.95	$_____
_____	Winter '94 CES Home Video	$24.95	$_____

All U.S. orders sent by U.S. Two-Day Priority Mail!

Subtotal	$_____
Shipping	$ 3.00
Total (Check/Credit Card)	$_____

Name _____

Address _____

City _____ State _____ Zip _____

- -

Visa/Mastercard#_____

Exp.Date _____   Signature _____

SEND TO: Sandwich Islands Publishing,
P.O. Box 10669, Lahaina, HI 96761
OR FAX TO: (808) 661-2715

Video available after January 15th, 1994. NTSC format only.
All foreign orders add $15 for air shipping, $5 for surface mail.

AWESOME GAME GIVEAWAY!

We're giving away three sets of three hot games for your favorite system! Write down your answers for the questions below and send them in to enter the drawing.

WIN THESE HOT GAMES!

SUPER EMPIRE STRIKES BACK *courtesy of JVC*
SUPER STAR WARS *courtesy of JVC*
THE INCREDIBLE CRASH TEST DUMMIES *courtesy of ACCLAIM*

Name _____ Phone _____

Address _____ Age _____

City _____ State _____ Zip _____

Where did you buy this book? _____

Which game systems do you own?_____

_____

How many video games do you own? _____

Which gaming magazines do you read?_____

_____

SEND YOUR ANSWERS TO:
Sandwich Islands Publishing
P.O. Box 10669, Lahaina, HI 96761

Drawings will be held on 2/1/94, 2/15/94, and 3/1/94.
Only one entry per person. Winners will be notified by mail.
All entries will be placed on our mailing list for
information on upcoming video game strategy guide books.